Time, Uncertainty, and Disequilibrium

Time, Uncertainty, and Disequilibrium

Exploration of Austrian Themes

Edited by
Mario J. Rizzo
New York University

LexingtonBooks
D.C. Heath and Company
Lexington, Massachusetts
Toronto

Library of Congress Cataloging in Publication Data
Main entry under title:

Time, uncertainty, and disequilibrium.

  Mostly papers presented at a conference sponsored by the Center for
Applied Economics at New York University in cooperation with the Institute
for Humane Studies held at New York University, Jan. 7–8, 1978.
  Bibliography: p.
  1. Austrian school of economists—Addresses, essays, lectures. I. Rizzo,
Mario J. II. New York University. Center for Applied Economics.
III. Institute for Humane Studies.
HB98.T55   330.15   78–13872
ISBN 0–699–02698–0

Published simultaneously in Canada

Printed in the United States of America

International Standard Book Number: 0–669–02698–0

Library of Congress Catalog Card Number: 78–13872

Contents

List of Figures and Tables

Figures

Table

Preface

The majority of the papers making up this collection were originally presented at the Conference on Issues in Economic Theory: An Evaluation of Current Austrian Perspectives, held at New York University on January 7 and 8, 1978. The conference was sponsored by the Center for Applied Economics at New York University in cooperation with the Institute for Humane Studies (Menlo Park, California). Two papers (in addition to the introductory chapter) were not presented at the conference, however. They are "Imagination, Formalism and Choice" by G.L.S. Shackle and "Radical Subjectivism or Radical Subversion?" by S.C. Littlechild. The former was included (and reprinted with permission from the Spanish journal *Teorema*) because Professor Shackle was unable, for personal reasons, to attend the conference. No conference on Austrian economics would be complete without his participation in some form. Professor Littlechild's paper was included because it clearly presents one important Austrian perspective on Shackle's work.

Any volume deriving out of a conference is clearly a joint product and so I am indebted by many individuals. Most especially, I would like to thank Professors I.M. Kirzner, L.M. Lachmann, M.I. Nadiri of New York University, Mr. G.H. Pearson, and Dr. L.M. Spadaro of the Institute for Humane Studies.

Time, Uncertainty,
and Disequilibrium

1 Disequilibrium and All That: An Introductory Essay

Mario J. Rizzo

Thought is what we directly know. This knowledge in its directness lasts only as long as the particular thought that is present. A thought takes place and in doing so yields place . . . It is a transient. This transcience is time in the sense of a direct experience . . . —G.L.S. Shackle[1]

The notion of time is so primitive and basic an element in man's experience that its neglect by much economic theory constitutes an incredible puzzle.[2] This puzzle is attributable, perhaps, to the almost irresistable lure of formalism—particularly one that cannot adequately handle time. The twin goals of manageability and formalism, then, have transformed the crucial questions that economists ask. So, if we are not careful, the question of time is not one which can even be asked. To consider the role of time in economic life, therefore, often requires that we step outside of the conventional models and begin the job of reconstruction. Although time is frequently relegated to a quite unimportant place in the theoretical corpus of economics, it cannot be totally banished. Time, as we shall see, is so intimately connected with every aspect of economic theory that it is only a heroic artificiality that has kept it from occupying center stage.

The conceptualization of man as engaging in purposeful activity is inconceivable apart from the categories of cause and effect.[3] Unless the means chosen can affect the ends desired in some way, there is no point at all to human action. The categories of cause and effect, in turn, imply the notions before and after. At this point, time has already entered the picture. Time, as we experience it, is inextricably linked to the possibilities of disappointment and surprise. Perfect predictability has nothing to do with phenomenological time, although it is perfectly consistent with time as extension.[4]

Time manifests itself at least four different ways in the structure of economics. A world of disappointment and surprise is one of *disequilibrium* and *discoordination*. The plans of market participants are continually being discoordinated by the imperfect fulfillment of expectations. Disequilibrium

Apologies to Sir Dennis Robertson. I am indebted to Professor Israel M. Kirzner of New York University for helpful discussion and to the Scaife Foundation for financial support of my research. Responsibility for errors remains mine alone.

1

implies that opportunities for mutually advantageous exchange exist, and that those who possess superior information will reap a kind of arbitrage *profit* by seizing these opportunities. Yet to seize opportunities requires that the entrepeneur have *expectations* that turn out to be correct. The nature of expectations and their formation is then, obviously, an important element in the examination of economic process through time. Without disequilibrium, profit, and expectations, the notion of time survives, yet in a skeletal fashion. It is time thus shorn of these attributes that provides the basis for the theory of interest or *intertemporal exchange*. Even in its pure extension sense, time has important implications.

The purpose of this introductory chapter is to examine the notion of time as (1) disequilibrium, (2) the opportunity to earn pure profits, (3) the development of expectations, and (4) the basis for pure intertemporal exchange. This will be done primarily *not* through a summary of the contributions to this volume but, rather, by an attempt to put them in a larger context and to illuminate their essential unity.

Equilibrium and Disequilibrium

Economists really do not have a choice as to whether they will use equilibrium concepts. The notion of equilibrium is as indispensible a tool of analysis as it is a pervasive one. Indeed, "there is no means of studying the complex phenomena of action other than first to abstract from change altogether"[5] The usefulness of equilibrium as a mental tool is not, however, tied up with the question (important though it may be in its own right) of whether equilibrium is exactly or even approximately attained in real world economies. When F.H. Hahn argues that, for example, the Arrow–Debreu construction "contains no presumption that a sequence of *actual* economic states will terminate in an equilibrium state,"[6] he does not thereby conceed its uselessness. The lack of "realism" of a concept is not a sufficient argument against its use. In fact, the abstraction involved in all thinking is quite incompatible with a high degree of "realism." What matters, though, is whether the conceptual apparatus is adequate for its assigned task. To see this more clearly, consider the analysis proposed by Sir John Hicks in chapter 3 of this volume.[7] Let us assert that A was the only cause of B. We are then *really* asserting four things, two of which are counterfactual. The first two are straightforward enough: A existed and B existed. However, to assert a causal and not merely temporal relation we must implicitly make two additional claims: first, the nonexistence of A, ceteris paribus, is perfectly conceivable and second, should that have been the case, B would not have existed. Since, however, by assumption both A and B existed, the previous two claims are necessarily "unrealistic." This argument, clearly, is of fundamental importance for economics since the "category *means and ends* presupposes the category *cause and effect*".[8] The economizing of means to attain ends is only possible because we can perceive causal relations in our everyday life. Hence we are always and everywhere implicitly using "unrealistic" theoretical constructs. In this regard, the economist can neither aspire nor succeed in operating differently from the economizing agents he studies.

Equilibrium theorizing permits us to vary one factor in isolation (say, *A* in the above example) and then to trace out the full effects (*B*) of that change in the model being used.[9] The predictability of the effects *within that model* is an essential ingredient of all equilibrium theorizing. Yet it is important to understand that model predictability need not be translatable into real-world predictability. The contrary assumption merely demonstrates the fallacy of misplaced concreteness and, if pursued to its logical conclusion, would rob economic theory of all but the most crude operational "concepts." The absolute indispensibility of *some* notion of equilibrium implies that in a very real but nevertheless limited sense we are (virtually) all equilibrists.

In 1935, F.A. Hayek elucidated what he thought to be the concept of equilibrium that had generally been in use.[10] For Hayek, equilibrium was anything but a timeless concept for it involved the consistency of individual plans in the context of a near or remote future. The activity of planning thus necessarily implies a temporal framework or horizon. Plan equilibrium can be in turn subdivided into the familiar general and partial categories. In general equilibrium the plans of all economic agents across all markets are consistent; in a partial equilibrium we focus on the consistency of plans for some subset of agents (for example, the equating of buying and selling plans on a single small market.)

Hayek's discussion clarifies a tension that has existed (and continues to exist) between equilibrium viewed as a state of rest and equilibrium viewed as a set of consistent plans. As long as there has been no change in a model's parameters and exogenous variables, the consistency of plans will not be disturbed and in a certain sense a state of rest or balance of forces has been achieved. It need not follow, however, that a state of rest will automatically imply an equilibrium of plans. To be sure, "if individuals react to disappointed expectations in a given constant way, we would have invariant behavior without requiring the fulfillment of expectations."[11] Given the proper constellation of costs and expected benefits, the optimal amount of plan consistency it will pay agents to achieve (especially under stochastic conditions) may be less than full consistency. Equilibrium as a state of invariant behavior involves optimal—not complete—plan consistency.

The state-of-rest notion of equilibrium has undergone considerable expansion in scope since Hayek first wrote. The Hicksian elaboration of

Lindahl's temporary equilibrium method and the more recent work on stochastic equilibrium are just two examples.[12] Ultimately, the equilibrium concept has been so stretched as to include any determinate "state" in which "norms are unchanging."[13] A tentative definition of equilibrium very broadly conceived might be as follows: An equilibrium situation is one that exhibits no tendency to change and that can be derived logically from a model that incorporates the operation of opposing forces. Stationary, dynamic, stochastic, and fluctuating (and so forth), equilibria are merely special cases of the more general concept. Although economists have shown a preference for unique equilibria, this definition does not rule out multiple equilibria so long as the latter are produced (in the sense of logically implied) by a model. On a slightly lower level of generalization, we may say that "an economy is in equilibrium when it generates messages which do not cause agents to change the theories which they held or the policies which they pursue."[14] As a consequence, the equilibrium behavior of an economic agent can be described by "structurally stable equations."[15]

With this idea of equilibrium in mind, we can begin to understand Sir John's virtual equation of equilibrium theorizing with explanation itself.[16] Let us take the case of the price of a certain commodity. We say that agents are in equilibrium if their expectation functions are invariant. The following table represents the price of a commodity i at time $t(Pi_t)$ and the price of i expected at time t to prevail at $t + 1(E_t[Pi_{t+1}])$:

t	Pi_t	$E_t[Pi_{t+1}]$
1	4	4
2	4	4
3	6	6
4	6	6

As long as we are in periods like 1 and 2, expectations can be explained as being in accordance with the function of $E_t[Pi_{t+1}] = k = 4$. However, as between periods 2 and 3 expectations prove incorrect and the function itself changes. This change in the expectation function is a disequilibrium phenomenon. However, it is by no means necessary that this be interpreted as a rupture of the previous equilibrium. This is because there is another function that can consistently explain the behavior in all four periods without recourse to any hypothesized change in the agent's method of forecasting. We can now say that expectations are formed in accordance with $E_t[Pi_{t+1}] = Pi_t$. If we call the first expectation function the true function for the first two periods—the one people "really" had in their minds—then we have "doctored" reality by this little exercise. As Hicks tells us:

> Now we know that the actual experience was not an equilibrium experience; there were surprises, and unforseen changes of course. But it is

hardly possible that the hypothetical experience should not be an equilibrium experience, for it is under *our* control, so there can be no surprises in it. If we then compare the actual experience which is *not* an equilibrium experience with a hypothetical experience which is, we are cheating; so to make the comparison fair we are bound to doctor the actual, supressing the surprises, even though we admit that they are important.[17]

The suppression of the changes in the method by which agents make their forecasts enables the economist to explain real experience *as if* it were equilibrium experience. Although mistakes are thereby included (expectations in period 2 are plainly incorrect,) any fundamental novelty or surprise is excluded: the structure of the system remains invariant. This doctoring of reality is, of course, easier ex post than ex ante. Equilibrium theorizing in the context of explanation is more likely to succeed than in the context of prediction. The epistemological symmetry of these two operations is largely lost in the (asymmetrical) practice of economists. In explanation the selection and arrangement of the relevant facts is much simpler because more is known.[18] The functional relations that are "hypothesized" to explain the formation of expectations can be altered until the correct ones are produced. This arrangement and rearrangement of facts is clearly not possible when the goal is prediction. Suppression of surprise is possible only ex post. In an ex ante sense, the economist is himself in the position of the economic agents, and surprise becomes an ineradicable feature of *his* world as well as theirs.

The suppression of surprise is for Hicks a necessary element in economic explanation. Indeed, he warns us that if the analyst does not suppress surprise "he must confine himself to description. He cannot proceed to the further step, of finding explanations, even of searching for explanations."[19] Hahn states the same conclusion somewhat differently: " . . . one of the reasons why an equilibrium notion is useful is that it serves to make precise the *limits* of economic analysis."[20] For both Hicks and Hahn, then, economic explanation must have the attribute of deriving determinate implications from theoretical constructs: the model predicts what must necessarily happen with regard to, say, expectations. Novelty, on the other hand, seems—in effect—to be a confession of ignorance. Why, for example, did agents change the method by which their expectations were formed in the above illustration? Can this ever be explained without recourse to some "equilibrium" model (in the very broad sense in which the term is here being used)?

It is easy to claim too much with an argument such as that being advanced by Hicks and Hahn. There are, after all, *degrees* of explanation.[21] The analyst need not deduce the actual response of agents to a change; he is still engaging in explanation if he can deduce (from a theoretical construct) the general *pattern* of response. In the above example, even so general a statement that in period 3 expectations will change (without specifying the direction) *because* actual prices have changed constitutes an explanation. Of course, one is free to call even this an equilibrium hypothesis because a general norm of sorts is here being postulated. Nevertheless, we are entitled to ask whether this is a helpful way of looking at the notion of equilibrium. If it is, then there is clearly no room for *dis*equilibrium as an economic concept. We have defined it out of existence. As with all attempts to be overly clever about defining crucial terms, another word would have to be found to express the idea.

If we define equilibrium less broadly we can make room for the idea of disequilibrium. In one sense, the term disequilibrium is merely a prediction of change in the next period even though the model's parameters and exogenous variables are unchanged. This is because the effects of a previous change in, say, an exogenous variable have not been fully worked out. Whether this ends up, ceteris paribus, in Hayekian equilibrium depends on the precise kind of mental experiment that is being performed.

It is the task of disequilibrium economics to trace the path of response to given disturbances. However, each period or step along the path *could* be viewed as an equilibrium relative to the data of that (shorter) period. Clearly, individual plans are not consistent during each of these periods but, nevertheless, there is equilibrium in the sense of no tendency to change during the period. The economist can logically derive each step along the adjustment path from a theoretical construct. Hence the equilibrium path is determinate given the model. Again, we must emphasize that determinateness within a model ought not to be equated with perfect predictability in the real world. The applicability of the model is not thereby necessary or determinate.[22]

Whether we view equilibrium in the extremely broad terms outlined above or take a more conservative position is purely a matter of heuristic and analytic convenience. Indeed, the notion of equilibrium, as both Machlup and Mises have stressed, is "only" a mental tool without any *direct* operational significance.[23] Depending on the purpose at hand we may use either the broad or narrow conception.

The great and crucial virtue of the Hayekian view of equilibrium is that it lays emphasis on the teleology of the adjustment process rather than viewing each step on the adjustment path as a lagged response to what happened in the previous period. Disequilibrium adjustments are, in a very important sense, forward- and not backward-looking activities. Lack of coordination implies hitherto unexploited opportunities for mutually advantageous exchange, while the coordinating *process* implies an attempt to take advantage of these opportunities.

The broad Hicks–Hahn idea of equilibrium, on the other hand, is quite useful in exposing some time-honored fallacies in welfare economics. It reveals once and for all the enormous difficulties involved in the claim that some states of the world are "inefficient" even though the economic agents are engaging in maximizing behavior.[24] If it were economically feasible to do things differently (including changing the political framework) maximizers would do so and at the optimal rate. Inefficiency is thus really the failure of the analyst to see all of the relevant costs and benefits. To say that every economic "state" of affairs is an equilibrium relative to its constraints (as those who wish to conceive of the concept broadly must) is equivalent to asserting the optimality of every state of affairs relative to the same set of constraints. This is because any state of rest is one in which agents do not seek to improve their position by a change in behavior. The optimality claim does *not*, however, imply that we can *measure* the true social opportunity cost of resources by their existing market prices (the question of externalities aside.) As has been emphasized in this volume, outside of what amounts to a Hayekian equilibrium or any traditional form of general equilibrium, market prices do not measure true social opportunity costs.[25]

Application of Equilibrium Theorizing

In recent years, the economics of law and property rights has become one of the most important new fields to which the equilibrium mode of theorizing has been applied. It is perhaps more notable than a number of other such fields only because of the exceptional lack of clarity with which its equilibrium concepts are used. Much of this literature has been concerned with the question of whether legal precedents and institutions are efficient. To the extent, then, that this literature has adopted the broad "we-are-always-in-equilibrium" view of the world, the answer to its central question becomes a tautological "yes."[26] This, of course, will not do, and a somewhat different approach is necessary. Instead, we can ask the question: do certain legal doctrines and institutions minimize social opportunity costs? If this becomes the major focal point then, obviously, the relationship of the real-world economy to the fictitious one of general equilibrium is of paramount importance. How accurately can the economist know the social opportunity costs of different courses of action resulting from different legal frameworks? What is the method by which he can *test* the assertion that a given set of legal precedents even approximately minimizes social costs?[27] These questions have been given precious little attention, but they are clearly crucial.

In his contribution to this volume, H. Demsetz recognizes from perhaps a somewhat different standpoint the difficulties involved in knowing "what the underlying efficiency considerations are." An implication of this is that efficiency arguments "should not be misinterpreted to endorse frequent

involuntary reassignment" of property rights.[28] The *stability* of a given
rights structure is perhaps the single most important factor in promoting
long–run minimization of social costs. In this regard, we might go beyond
Demsetz's remarks and defend a somewhat more radical position. In a
world characterized by substantial ignorance of true social opportunity
costs, case–by–case analysis of the "efficiency" argument can amount to
little more than the fairly reasonable claim that ensuring the long–run certainty of expectations may produce the "best" outcome without directly
aiming at it. In fact, quite recently F.A. Hayek has argued that our need for
rules of all kinds arises precisely out of "ignorance of the particular
facts."[29] The rules of just conduct as embodied in common law are
"emphatically not a balancing of particular interests at stake in a concrete
case, or even of the interests of determinable *classes* of persons."[30] Paradoxically, the balancing of social costs and benefits is only possible in a
world of general equilibrium where it is not needed, and impossible in our
world of disequilibrium where many cry out for it.

The absense of complete plan coordination (Hayekian disequilibrium)
makes the very notion of social cost quite problematic. What is this
"social" and how can it have costs or benefits? How can we sum costs or
benefits across individuals in a *consistent* manner? "For efficiency only
makes sense in regard to people's ends," M.N. Rothbard reminds us, "and
individuals' ends differ, clash, and conflict . . . whose ends shall rule?"[31] In
general equilibrium the plans of all individuals will dovetail and the market
prices of resources will reflect this consistency. Unfortunately, in our world
"there is no single, unambiguous social cost: not everyone perceives the
alternatives sacrificed in the same way."[32]

Profit and X–Inefficiency

Although equilibrium is our hypothetical norm, disequilibrium, ironically,
is the real–world or factual norm. The persistence of discoordination
despite the attempts of economic agents to eliminate it demands explanation. Perhaps one way of framing an explanation is to say that the speed of
the coordination (adjustment) process is slow relative to changes in the
underlying data. However, this is merely a restatement in different language
of the same phenomenon. The lag in the adjustment process is precisely
what cannot be taken as given. Why aren't opportunities for mutually
advantageous trade seized immediately?

One answer is that information is costly, and hence we do not expect
optimizing agents to be aware of all potentially advantageous opportunities.
To be sure, some optimizers will have more information than others
because, say, the marginal product schedules of the former's search time are

greater. The existence of true entrepreneurial profit is crucially dependent on the possession of superior information. For example, most market participants may believe (after optimal search) that one unit of a certain factor of production is worth $5. The possessor of superior information, on the other hand, realizes that its "true" value is $7. This means either that it can be sold elsewhere at $7 or that it has an implicit price in the output market of $7. In both cases, we have two prices for the same thing.[33] Yet can we say necessarily that the individual who buys the factor at $5 and sells it implicitly or explicitly at $7 makes a profit of $2? We cannot. If the individual had spent $2 in time and other resources to acquire this information there would be no economic profit. The additional return would correctly be imputed to these costly information–producing resources.

The crucial issue, then, is to discover why the prices of the information–producing resources do not always fully absorb or wipe out any potential profits. To find the reason we must investigate a fundamental paradox in the market for information.[34] Those who sell or buy information–producing resources are not fully aware of the value of the knowledge that will be produced with these resources. If they were to be fully aware, it would be necessary for the knowledge to have been produced beforehand and then, of course, there would be no demand for the resources. When, therefore, the owners of the information–producing resources sell them they have an inadequate idea of their value. The inadequacy of the sellers' "knowledge about knowledge" is not merely a probabilistic uncertainty where, at least, all of the possible outcomes are known. The more innovative (and hence important) the knowledge that will be produced with the resources, the more doubtful it will be that the sellers will know all of the possible outcomes. They are then "threatened" with novelty or surprise. When, as a consequence, sellers underestimate the value of these resources, opportunities for pure profit will emerge.

In this analysis there is an obvious asymmetry. The entrepreneur-purchasers of information–producing resources are implicitly assumed to have a better notion of the value of the resources than the sellers. If the contrary were assumed to be the case, then the entrepreneurs would incur losses. The existence of entrepreneurial profit requires the postulation of some superior knowledge. This must, however, be knowledge of a special kind: although it must be superior (and hence scarce) it must be absolutely without opportunity cost in its "production."

I.M. Kirzner has examined in depth the nature of this superior knowledge or "entrepreneurial alertness."[35] For the *pure* case of "alertness" we needn't bring into our analysis the purchase of information–producing resources as we did above. Suppose, then, an entrepreneur has knowledge of buyers who are willing to pay $7 (instead of $5) for a certain item. The key question from a long–run perspective is: how did he acquire this information? If it was acquired *undeliberately* then, perforce, the process had no opportunity cost. If its acquisition was deliberate (via optimal search) then it had an opportunity cost and does not constitute a pure case of "alertness." Since alertness is not an optimizing process, the knowledge so acquired cannot be anticipated in even a probabilistic sense. It should be clear, therefore, that the concepts of entrepreneurial alertness and those of novelty or surprise are intimately related. As a consequence, it is impossible to discuss questions of enterpreneurship and profit while maintaining even the broad we-are-always-in-equilibrium framework. It is only by *contrast* to that framework that the entrepreneur can be understood.

In chapter 6 of this volume, H. Leibenstein gives an apparently different answer to the question: why do some opportunities go unseized or why does disequilibrium persist? His answer is that individuals do not always maximize and hence are X-inefficient. Specifically, "nonmaximization and the operation of inertia suggest that not all entrepreneurial opportunities would be undertaken."[36] Many have had problems with this view since any reasons for nonmaximization are translatable into maximizing terminology.[37] This criticism, although valid to a great extent, misses one crucial point. The universality of maximizing requires the postulation of a logically prior maximizing *framework*. To the extent that it does not seem propitious to do this, maximization will not handle every situation. Neither the sellers nor the buyers of information-producing resources can maximize with respect to the full knowledge of what will be produced. Maximization under probabilistic uncertainty can take place with respect to the *possibilities* that are known but not, obviously, with respect to those that remain hidden.[38] Furthermore, the absence of maximization is even more obvious in the context of Kirzner's "alert" entrepreneur. Since the latter acquires knowledge undeliberately he is ex definitione not engaging in maximizing activity: no means-ends deliberation is thereby involved. "It ain't the analysis of what a man don't know as makes an economist Austrian," S.C. Littlechild wittily reminds us, "it's the analysis of what a man don't know he don't know, but nonetheless might discover."[39]

Expectations

Profits exist only in a world of uncertainty and disequilibrium. To talk of persistent and perfectly systematic pure profit opportunities contradicts the economist's basic assumption of rationality. All such opportunities would have already been exploited. Therefore, to discuss the behavior of the entrepreneur in seeking and exploiting these opportunities requires us to examine the general problem of the formation of expectations. In such a world, expectations are important because they determine the nature of adjustments to disequilibria.

In recent years, the most important work that has been done in developing a theory of expectations has gone under the name of "rational expectations." "Expectations," R.F. Muth tells us, "since they are informed predictions of future events, are essentially the same as the predictions of the *relevant* economic theory."[40] This is frequently, although not always, taken to mean that the subjective probability distributions of states of the world are the same for all rational expecters and, most importantly, equal to the underlying stochastic structure of the system. Therefore, the relevant economic theory in Muth's early formation is precisely this underlying structure. Yet can we say that an underlying stochastic structure "really" exists? Do events in the economic world take on the form of repeatable or seriable experiments? For example, the assumption of a monetary policy that results in increments to M that "are statistically independent over time with zero mean"[41] requires a long sequence of similar trials to determine the *objective* character of the distribution. In the absence of such a sequence of trials, what can be meant by an objective or underlying stochastic structure? It can only be the *mental* structure or picture policymakers have of their policy actions. The structure turns out to be little more than their own subjective probability distributions, that is, their expectations of what they themselves would do under many hypothetical repetitions of the same decision. However, it is not clear that such an experiment is even logically conceivable when the outcomes of the alternative policies are considered. Each (hypothetical) outcome changes the state of knowledge on the part of the policymaker and hence the conditions at the start of each "subsequent" trial are *importantly* different. This difference means that we are not engaging in many trials of the same experiment but in many experiments. This is, in essence, what Shackle has called a "self-destructive experiment."[42] Nevertheless, the foregoing interpretation of the stochastic structure as subjective and expectational has important implications. It means that agents will have to form expectations about the expectations of the policymakers.[43] The essence of this process, as G.P. O'Driscoll emphasizes in chapter 7 of this volume, must be the transmission of information rather than the specification of an objective structure.

An alternative formulation of the underlying stochastic structure of the system reveals its essentially long–run character.[44] Consider, for example, a regime of changes in the money stock that has been in effect over a sufficient number of trials to exhibit its stochastic independence over time and zero mean. The nature of the experiment is such that agents could only come to recognize this structure gradually (because it comes into existence only gradually.) There is no prior stochastic structure unless we are already in a long–run equilibrium. In the shorter–run, the key element is again the transmission of information.

From the perspective of what we have already said, the word "relevant" in Muth's formulation of the rational expectations hypothesis covers a multitude of sins. The relevant economic theory, it is true, will generate predictions but the difficulty is precisely in determining *which* relevant theory to use. With respect to *whose* behavior is the relevance of the theory to be determined? It is only in the long run that such a question is unimportant, because in equilibrium all agents hold the same correct theory. Along the path to coordination, however, different agents will necessarily hold different theories. Which theory will, in this context, be *the* relevant one? The answer ought not to be assumed away.

The rational expectations framework, as we have been considering it, has little to say about entrepreneurship and profits. When "the subjective probability distributions used in decision–making by private agents are the same as the probability distributions for the relevant variables implied by the model,"[45] profits take on a purely random character. This is because in such a world there is really no superior information: all agents have the same perfect knowledge of probability distributions. In any given period, some individuals will be the recipients of random profits or losses but, over the long run, no individual will earn profits. In this sense, profits disappear in the long run of the stationary stochastic equilibrium.

Despite the formal equilibrium character of much of the rational expectations literature, that character can be interpreted as quite plausibly asserting a *tendency* that exists even in disequilibrium situations. Changes in policy—to the extent they are perceived by private agents—will alter the utility-maximizing decision of these agents.[46] Whether these decisions will be altered in a predictable fashion is not at issue here; the fact that they will be altered is sufficient. It is then possible to conclude that "econometric models estimated from past data may not be relevant for policy evaluation, since the parameters of such models can be expected to change along with policy."[47]

R.J. Barro and S. Fischer have developed a "bare–bones" rational expectations model that demonstrates this dependence of reduced–form parameters on actual policy pursued.[48] In this model, output increase if the current price level (of which wages are one price) increases more rapidly than the expected price level. Agents are viewed as earning money in this period and spending it in the next. Therefore, they deflate nominal wages by an amount related to the expected rise in the next period's prices. Output moves positively with the quantity of labor supplied which, in turn, is positively related to changes in expected real wages. Assume now the stochastic structure of both the monetary (M) and real (u) variables: M is generated by a random walk and movements in u are negatively correlated over time. Changes in M would therefore cause "permanent" changes in the price level (P),[49] while changes in u would cause self–reversing or "transitory" changes in P. To the extent that the latter is the case, however, the current (unexpected) rise in P will exceed the expected rise in P next period, and expected real wages will rise. As a consequence, the level of output will rise and a Phillips-type relationship is established.

The larger the fraction of unanticipated price movements that are attributed to changes in M rather than u, the *smaller* will be this Phillips-type relationship. This will be more likely the greater is the variance of monetary shocks relative to real shocks. For any given actual monetary shock, the greater the relative *variance* of M, the steeper will be the Phillips curve. Furthermore, since the variance of M is a policy variable, it follows that the reduced-form relationship between changes in M and changes in output is itself dependent on that policy. The simple simulation of policy consequences based on an extrapolation of reduced-form parameters is thus revealed to be bankrupt.

Intertemporal Exchange

The importance of disequilibrium, profits, and expectations can be traced, as we have seen, to the introduction of the time element in economic models. Time, in this sense, is the name we give to *possibility*—in particular, the possibility that something unexpected might happen. Time, however, can be viewed in another, yet far more stylized way. It can be viewed as a pure coordinate axis, a dimension similar to that of space.[50] As a coordinate axis it is the time of most conventional economic models, but preeminently that which provides raw material for the theory of interest. This is the offspring of real time and static expectations.

Since all action takes place in time, both interpersonal exchange and autistic production can be viewed as intertemporal exchange.[51] In the former case, if A exchanges with B, A is giving up something now and receiving something else a (short or long) period of time later. In the second case, production can be usefully viewed as an exchange with nature: Robinson Crusoe gives up, say, leisure now and gets fish at some (near or distant) future moment. In both situations, the phenomenon of waiting is an essential ingredient—waiting permeates every pure interpersonal exchange agreement as well as every process of production.

Waiting can be seen from two perspectives: ex ante and ex post.[52] Ex ante waiting is the time the economic agent expects it *will* take before a desired result will materialize. As with all expectations, he can be quite wrong. Ex post waiting it the time it *has* taken for some result to come about; it is, for example, the historical embodiment of waiting in some current object. From this perspective, capital can be viewed as "congealed time." In a stationary equilibrium there is no reason to distinguish between these views: ex ante and ex post are the same, the past is prologue. However, to the extent that we are concerned about disequilibria and transitional mechanisms, a slurring of the distinction is not helpful.

In chapter 8 of this volume, L.B. Yeager writes in the tradition that wishes to see waiting as productive: more roundabout or time–consuming methods of production are undertaken because they yield a higher return.[53] In Yeager's sense, however, waiting is not merely clock–time, it has both a clock and value dimension.[54] A dollar's worth of labor, for example, may be tied up for three years; in this period of time (compound) interest charges will accrue and this accrual constitutes the price or value of the waiting. The *amount* of waiting is measured in value terms, and hence the quantity of waiting in a production process is not independent of its price. This is because for any given time–shape of flow inputs the weights that must be assigned to the inputs at different periods is determined by the rate of interest.[55]

To consider waiting a factor of production is clearly to push the analysis in the direction of the ex post (objective) view. Normally, arguments in a production function (that is, the factors of production) are defined in objective physical terms—labor as man–hours and capital as machine–hours, and so forth. The production function is preeminently a *physically* specified relationship. The amount of Yeagerian waiting cannot, however, be measured independently of its value dimension. The only way to reconcile this at least partially with the conventional production function is to assume static conditions.[56] In this case, an increase in Yeagerian waiting is also an increase in physically specified waiting and thus results in an expansion of physical output. To view waiting as something that is embodied in output, as Yeager's examples seem to imply, is perfectly permissible under these static conditions (but not under dynamic conditions.)

In Sir John Hicks' contribution to this volume, he discusses ITSO (Intertemporal Switch in Output) as a factor of production of which interest is the price. Although he claims that in other lives it has been called "waiting" ("Marshall and Cassel called it Waiting"),[57] the relationship is not all that clear. Consider first the context in which ITSO makes its appearance. If we fix the initial stock input, terminal stock output and the time–shape of the labor input, we can still vary the time–shape of output in a production process. This "involves first the transference of some elements in the labor flow and of the initial stock, from the production of current flow output to the production of instruments; and secondly the use of the instruments to produce additional flow output, all to be accomplished *within the period*."[58] The sacrifice of some earlier output in order to produce the instruments yields its reward in the form of higher output later—but we must *wait*. In the simple case where the instruments are produced early in the period, the intertemporal switch is unambiguously an example of greater clock-waiting.[59] In cases where the time-shape of output is changed such that the middle of the period loses and both of the ends gain, the matter is not so simple. An unambiguous measure of the relative amounts of waiting involved in each process requires a scheme to weight the outputs that are produced at different instants within the period. This weighting scheme must depend on the rate of interest.

It is better, then, to view ITSO as sui generis. All wisely chose intertemporal switches (whether or not they can be seen as involving more waiting) have a positive marginal product. This is the rise in the undiscounted value of output that emerges as a result of the switch. So ITSO is a factor of production. Yet it is an unusual factor indeed. What, for example, would constitute a zero amount of it? There can be zero clock-waiting but since a marginal increment in waiting is not precisely equal to ITSO, can there be zero ITSO?

Whether we shall view waiting as a factor of production is, as Yeager admits, purely a matter of analytic and heuristic convenience.[60] To the extent that the production function is considered a set of alternative *plans* instead of an entirely technological relationship, waiting can be examined "by having due regard to the effect of time preference upon the present desirability of the prospective future outputs."[61] The function of waiting is to direct the traditional factors toward the production of future goods rather than present goods. Waiting, in its time preference aspect, is like any other kind of preference: it (re)directs production from one line of activity to another as, for example, from cheese to chicken. The same physical commodity at different points in time is then seen as a different commodity. Waiting can thereby be analyzed as an attribute affecting the marginal utility of a good on the individual's present value scale. "Present goods are future goods coupled with avoidance of waiting for them;" Yeager remarks, therefore, "future goods bear a lower explicit price than present goods because part of their total price takes the nonpecuniary form of the waiting that must also be performed to obtain them."[62]

Although the question of how best to perceive waiting is merely one of analytic convenience, it does not therefore follow that it is reducible solely to arbitrary taste. Its analytic convenience is determined by the task we set for it and the ease with which our concept of waiting fits in with other economic categories. In this regard, it is worth noting that our ex ante view of waiting obviates the necessity "to postulate that more waiting (always) means more product."[63] We only need recognize that, at the margin, a unit of waiting will be engaged in only if it is balanced by extra product. As for the general issue, the superiority of the precise view of waiting one adopts must be judged by its fruitfulness in analyzing specific theoretical or empirical economic questions. Yet, in a very real sense, this issue is dwarfed by the common realization of both views that time is indeed important in the productive process.

Notes

1. Chapter 2, G.L.S. Shackle, "Imagination, Formalism and Choice."
2. John R. Hicks, "Some Questions of Time in Economics," in (eds.,) *Evolution, Welfare and Time in Economics,* ed. A.M. Tang, F.M. Westfield, J.S. Worley (Lexington, Mass.: Lexington Books, D.C. Heath and Co., 1976).
3. Ludwig von Mises, *Human Action,* 3rd ed. (Chicago: Henry Regnery and Co., 1966), p. 22.
4. Chapter 2, pp. 19–20.
5. Mises, *Human Action,* p. 248.
6. Frank H. Hahn, *On the Notion of Equilibrium in Economics* (Cambridge: Cambridge University Press, 1973,) p. 7. Emphasis added.
7. Chapter 3, John R. Hicks, "Is Interest the Price of a Factor of Production?" pp. 54–55.
8. Mises, *Human Action,* p. 22.
9. Fritz Machlup, "Equilibrium and Disequilibrium: Misplaced Concreteness and Disguised Politics," *Essays in Economic Semantics* (New York: W.W. Norton and Company, 1967 (1963), pp. 46–49.
10. F.A. Hayek, "Economics and Knowledge," *Individualism and Economic Order* (Chicago: University of Chicago Press, 1948), pp. 33–59.
11. Frank H. Hahn, "Expectations and Equilibrium," *Economic Journal* 62, no. 248 (December 1952): 304.
12. Mario J. Rizzo, "Equilibrium and Optimality: Do We Live in the Best of All Possible Worlds?" (Unpublished paper, New York University, 1977), p. 9–15.
13. Chapter 3, p. 53.
14. Hahn, *On the Notion of Equilibrium,* p. 25.
15. Ibid., p. 20.
16. Chapter 3, p. 56.
17. Ibid.
18. G.L.S. Shackle, *Epistemics and Economics* (Cambridge: Cambridge University Press, 1972), p. 349.
19. Chapter 3, p. 56.
20. Hahn, *On the Notion of Equilibrium,* p. 21. Emphasis added.
21. F.A. Hayek, "Degrees of Explanation," *Studies in Philosophy, Politics and Economics* (Chicago: University of Chicago Press, 1967), pp. 3–21.
22. Fritz Machlup, "Situational Determination in Economics," *British Journal for the Philosophy of Science* (1974): 280.

23. For some discussion see chapter 4, Mario J. Rizzo, "Uncertainty, Subjectivity and the Economic Aspects of Law."

24. Rizzo, "Equilibrium and Optimality," esp. pp. 15–18.

25. Chapter 4, pp. 78–81, and relevant notes.

26. Ibid., pp. 71–73.

27. Ibid., pp. 84–86.

28. Chapter 5, Harold Demsetz, "Ethics and Efficiency in Property Rights Systems," p. 106.

29. F.A. Hayek, *Law, Legislation and Liberty,* vol. 2, (Chicago: University of Chicago Press, 1976), p. 8.

30. Ibid., p. 39. Emphasis added.

31. Chapter 4, Comment, Murray N. Rothbard, "The Myth of Efficiency," p. 91.

32. Chapter 4, p. 81.

33. For this formulation I am indebted to Israel Kirzner.

34. This quite similar to the paradox in the demand for information discussed in Kenneth J. Arrow, "Economic Welfare and the Allocation of Resources for Invention," in *Economics of Information and Knowledge,* ed. D.M. Lamberton (Middlesex, England: Penguin Books, 1971), p. 148.

35. Israel M. Kirzner, *Competition and Entrepreneurship* (Chicago: University of Chicago Press, 1973); "Economics and Error," in Louis M. Spadaro (ed.,) *Austrian Economics: New Directions and Unresolved Questions,* (Kansas City: Sheed, Andrews, McMeel, 1978); "Knowing About Knowledge: A Subjectivist View of the Role of Information," Unpublished paper, New York University, (1977).

36. Chapter 6, Harvey Leibenstein, "The General X-Efficiency Paradigm and the Role of the Entrepreneur," p. 134.

37. George J. Stigler, "The Xistence of X-Efficiency," *American Economic Review.* 66, no. 1 (March 1976): 213–16.

38. Brian J. Loasby, *Choice, Complexity and Ignorance* (Cambridge: Cambridge University Press, 1976), pp. 7–10.

39. S.C. Littlechild, *Change Rules, O.K.?,* (Birmingham, England: University of Birmingham, 1977,) p. 9.

40. Richard F. Muth, "Rational Expectations and the Theory of Price Movements," *Econometrica* 29 (July 1961): 316. Emphasis added.

41. Robert J. Barro and Stanley Fischer, "Recent Developments in Monetary Theory," *Journal of Monetary Economics* 2 (1976): 158.

42. G.L.S. Shackle, *Decision, Order and Time,* (Cambridge: Cambridge University Press, 1961), p. 56.

43. A similar conclusion is reached in another context in chapter 7, Gerald P. O'Driscoll, Jr., "Rational Expectations, Politics and Stagflation," p. 162.

44. Ibid., p. 158.

45. Barro and Fischer, "Recent Developments," p. 156.

46. Robert E. Lucas, Jr., "Econometric Policy Evaluation: A Cri-

tique," *Journal of Monetary Economics* 2 (January 1976, Supplement): 25.

47. Barro and Fischer, "Recent Developments," p. 160.

48. Ibid., p. 155–160.

49. This is because after every unanticipated change in M the expected change in M during the next period is zero.

50. Shackle, *Epistemics and Economics,* p. 278. *See also* chapter 2.

51. Mises, *Human Action,* pp. 194–95.

52. Israel M. Kirzner, *An Essay on Capital* (New York: Augustus M. Kelley, 1966), pp. 73–102.

53. Eugen Von Bohm-Bawerk, *Capital and Interest,* trans. G.D. Huncke and H.F. Sennholz, 3 vols. (South Holland, Ill: Libertarian Press, 1959).

54. Chapter 8, Leland B. Yeager, "Capital Paradoxes and the Concept of Waiting," pp. 209–210.

55. Ibid., p. 189.

56. Yeager is aware of the difficulty. *See* chapter 8, p. 195. *See also* the need to hold the interest rate constant when increasing waiting so as to ensure a positive marginal product of waiting in Leland B. Yeager, "Toward Understanding Some Paradoxes in Capital Theory," *Economic Inquiry* 14, no. 3 (September 1976): 339.

57. Chapter 3, p. 61.

58. Ibid.

59. Ibid.

60. Chapter 8, p. 195.

61. Kirzner, *An Essay on Capital,* p. 101.

62. Chapter 8, p. 196.

63. Kirzner, *An Essay on Capital,* p. 102.

2

Imagination, Formalism, and Choice

G.L.S. Shackle

In the extreme of its possible meanings, the word *origin* brings thought to a stop. For this extreme meaning suggests, beyond the originated thing, a void. *Origin,* in this ultimate sense, tells us not to search for explanation, for circumstances which, if they had been discerned, would have suggested the character of what has been originated, for circumstances which, if they had been different, would have made impossible this particular origination. Origin, in the last resort, means *uncause.* If what has taken form acknowledges no continuity, no inheritance, no necessity, then what has taken form, again in the extremest meaning, is a *beginning.* In using these words, *origin, uncause, beginning,* we implicitly invoke the notion of temporal succession. For we imply two states of affairs, one in which the originated thing is not present, and one in which it is present, and we take the second of these to be the successor in time of the first. *Successor* is taken in mathematics to be a primitive and indefinable notion. But it is difficult to separate the notion of successor, even in its most general and abstract sense, from that of succession in time. A successor is something at which thought arrives after noticing something else. Origin thus impels us to the question of time.

What is in the utmost degree immediate and present to me is thought. It is invoked by Descartes as the conclusive evidence of his being. Thought is what we directly know. This knowledge in its directness lasts only as long as the particular thought that is present. A thought takes place and in doing so yields place, its arrival and departure are one, an indivisible unity. It is a *transient.* This transience is time in the sense of a direct experience, something directly known. Transience is a unity of arrival and departure. Departure leaves a place for a fresh arrival, a successor. Will not this successor depart and require its own successor? How do we conceive of the endless succession? We imagine it as a spatial succession, a line, the calendar axis. This is a constructed meaning of time, a meaning thought out, inferred, not directly experienced. Time as extension is an artifact. Time as a transient thought directly known, and time as a constructed receptacle for succession, are not merely different as it were in quantity. Transient presence is not merely an infinitesimal particle of time–extension, it is thought–in–being in contrast with a content of thought. If this theme is accepted there is an intimate and essential fusing of the ideas of thought, transience, presence,

Reprinted with permission from the Spanish journal *Teorema* (vol. 7, no. 3–4) 1978.

time-in-being. These notions in their essential unity are epitomized in the notion of *the present,* the moment of which, alone, we have direct knowledge, the moment-in-being, the moment of actuality embracing all that *is.* All that *is,* is the present.

Descartes distinguished the thinking being from that something which his thoughts are about. Let us use this tool. The field of his thoughts provides impressions. The thoughts thus suggested, the thoughts that interpret the impressions, are for him reports of *what is,* they are "the news," they are "the present." From these reports, however, he can abstract formal typical elements, the building blocks out of which the picture of *what is* can be supposed to be constructed and into which it can be resolved. Such building blocks are not confined to the arrangements reported from the field. They are in some sense free, permanent, manipulable elements. Their arrangement can be original, the work of imagination, not an account of *what is* in the reported present but of what *might be* in some other present. Can *original* here mean an origin in our extreme sense? Can imagination be a beginning in our extreme sense? To suppose that *origin* and *beginning* in our extreme senses have references in the work of mind is to suppose that history can be nondeterminate, and it is to suppose that this nondeterminacy has its seat in men's power of imagination. Origin and beginning, however, suggest more than their own freedom from antecedents, their own uncause. They imply for themselves a sequel. Being themselves uncaused, they claim to be a cause, to make a difference to what comes after them in time. Can we accept the asymmetry implicit in these words?

If we elect to suppose that each present is rigidly necessitated in every detail by its antecedent present; if, that is, we suppose the course of history from eternity to eternity to be a picture completely painted at some unique and once-and-for-all creation of the world; then choice is the empty name of a delusion of human consciousness. If so, choice repudiates in every aspect and character what we ascribe to it in the intuitive and unselfconscious discourse of life. Each "choice," is so, could not be other than it is; choices, if so, are not made and themselves essentially make nothing. Is choice, in that case, worthy of our interest and inquiry? Let us consider the extreme opposite supposition. If each present leaves its successor wholly unconstrained, so that any state of the world can be followed by any other state; then "choice" is evidently powerless. Choices, in that case, can make no difference. Despite any choice, in that case, the sequel can be anything. Can choice, in this case, engage our interest and attention? The anarchy of Nature is as fatal as the determinacy of Nature to the notion of choice as a source of history. Must we not say that the asymmetry of choice, its character of origin and beginning, yet its setting in motion of a sequel, its uncaused power of causation, is essential to its filling the role that the human craving, instinct, or intuition for dignity, responsibility, and free spontaneous pursuit of imagined glory ascribe to it?

If choice is a beginning in our extreme sense, choices to be made in time-to-come cannot be foreknown. Yet the sequels of such choices will help to compose the circumstances in which the sequel of any present choice will take shape. If so, the sequel of a present choice cannot be foreknown as an unique course of relevant history. Yet if this unknowledge allowed untramelled freedom to imagine the sequel in any form whatever, choice would be powerless and pointless. What, then, can choice do? What difference can choice make? Choice means commitment. In this resolve, which is a private thought and interior moral act, the chooser stakes his self-esteem upon his own making of some public move. A choice that did not commit the chooser in some respect would be no choice. The chooser commits himself to actions specified in some sense and degree, which seem to him to be within his power. Any such action will preclude, at least in some part, some otherwise envisageable courses of history, or it will allow some courses that would, at least in some part, have been precluded. The difference which choice can make is to the seeming *possibility* of this or that imagined course of history. Choice, commitment to acts within the chooser's power, can shift the bounds of the skein of rival imagined histories-to-come to each of which the chooser can find in his knowledge no fatal obstacle. Choice is an interposing or a removing of obstacles, a withholding or allowing of *epistemic possibility*.

If choice in its essential nature is a beginning in our sense, the maker of such a choice has no ground to assign to it a unique, exactly specified sequel. For the course of history-to-come will include the unforeknowable choices-to-come and their effects of allowing or precluding sequels of their own. The present chooser must envisage history-to-come as a skein of endlessly many rival possible courses. Does this imply that his present choice is helpless? It does not, for the skein of imagined sequels, to each of which he cannot find any fatal obstacle, and to which in other words he assigns epistemic possibility, is nonetheless bounded. Whatever commitments his present choice consists of, any sequel of the present must start from the state of things in the present, including those commitments. Any imagined course of affairs that supposes a different starting-point is outside the bounds. The posture of things in the present thus constrains the possible sequels. But besides the posture of things in the particular present, there is the nature of things. The state of things that can be attained from any given present state, within a given stretch of time, will seem limited by the speeds of the processes of Nature, of human responses, of the dissemination of ideas. Posture and Nature, present circumstance and general principle, will set bounds to the skein of imaginable possible sequels of any present choice. Choice, if so, is choice amongst differently bounded skeins of rival imagined sequels. Within such bounds the number of rivals can be proliferated without limit.

From sentences concerning the human experience of time, from an election of a meaning for *beginning,* from the identification of this meaning with the nature of choice, we have reached a conception of the nature of the rival choosables among which any choice must be made. In order that my argument might be apprehended as a whole, I have offered it so far in an extremely condensed form. I wish now to enter into this theme more extensively as the answer to a series of questions:

1. By what means do rival choosable entities present themselves to the chooser?
2. What is the essential nature of such choosables?
3. What is the motive to undertake the business of choice?
4. What is the link between choice and its effect?
5. In the envisageing of sequels to choice, what test is applied?
6. How can choosables each itself consisting of rival imagined sequels be mutually compared?
7. What mode of engenderment of history would be implied by this conception of choice?

Theories of choice seem to be unconcerned with the question of the source of the choosable entities. Are these presented ready-made by the field? Reports from the field are taken to reflect an unique self–consistent whole. Any parts into which the picture of the field, the picture of what *is* in the present in its nature and posture, can be resolved, all elements that can be discerned in it, are compatible co–existents. They are not the rivals, the plural entities in some sense mutually exclusive, whose co–presence in thought is nonetheless an essential condition of the possibility of choosing. The matter can be expressed differently but equivalently. The calendar–axis that is inferred or invented to provide a receptacle for the time–succession, is not only an extensive range of variation but also has its distinct locations labelled with proper names: Thursday, April 1976, and so on. Each present moment is unique and also uniquely named. We are not here saying merely that the present is solitary, unparalled in its presence and sole existence. It is also given an identity. The need for an identity arises in recognition of the present as a transient implying a successor. Reports from the field are labeled with the name of the present in which they are received. In that identified present, *what is* is not open to choice. It has already chosen itself. Choice must concern itself with time–to–come. The entities that are rivals for election by the chooser and are mutual exclusives for his choice, must, before his choice is made, be coexistent in his thought. They are not *reports of what is* but imaginations of what might be.

The field cannot supply the choosables direct. It can suggest the formal, abstract elements for the origination of imagined histories–to–come. Can these be untramelled fantasies composed without constraint? Pure fictions can give pleasure, but they have no direct practical bearing on the conduct of the individual who contemplates them, they require from him no commitment, they do not demand his performance of the business of choice, they are not potential ingredients of history. What tests must be passed by those thoughts of the chooser which will seem to him able to enter into the composition of his rival choosables?

Their form must be that of descriptions of the course of history to come. Evidently such history need be concerned only with what matters to the chooser, it must be the supposed history of affairs in which his interests or his interest are involved. Any such imagined course of history-to-come must, if it is to concern him in his business of choice, be exempt in his thought from fatal obstacles. It must, in the special sense that is relevant to our theme, be *possible*. Any such conceived path of events, if it is to concern him in this business of choice, must be one whose *possibility depends on his choice*. Throughout these sentences, in speaking of possibility we are referring to something in the chooser's thought, to a judgment, to his own appeal to his own knowledge. Possibility, for the chooser, is what is ordinarily called subjective.

Let us say then that the rival choosables are distinct from each other in the respective schemes of personal action to which, in electing one or other of them, the chooser would commit himself; they are distinct from each other in the respective skeins of imagined courses of history-to-come, bearing on his interests, which are made epistemically possible by that election, the histories-to-come composing any one such skein, and rendered envisageable by the appropriate commitment to action, being rivals of each other; let us say that the formal, abstract, typical, persistent, and detached elements with which the chooser's imagination works are found by him in the suggestions from the field, and are composable by him within constraints also arising from the field in reports of its nature or principles, and of its posture or circumstances; let us say that the link between thought and effect, the vessel of return-influence from the thinking-being to the field, is the contribution he must inevitably make to the posture of things in the present by his choice of intention and commitment.

Thus we have answered the first of our seven questions by saying that the choosables are *originated by the chooser*. They are not composable as free fictions or fantasies, since he requires them to be epistemically possible, that is, exempt from fatal obstacles discernible within his knowledge. Within the limits of such possibility, his arrangement of the elements suggested by the field, even his invention of these elements from the suggestions offered by the field, has the quality of a *beginning* in our extreme sense, the new existence of something not ascribable to antecedents.

In proposing this account of the provenance of the choosables, we have implied something concerning their essential nature. For what is to limit the number of distinct histories-to-come that the chooser can imagine as possible sequels of an elected scheme of commitment to personal action? In the nature of choice as a beginning, and in the need to suppose that any imagined sequel of present choice will include choices to be made in time-to-come by others, unforeknowable as to their occurrence or their own sequels, there seems to be an endless freedom to continue to originate further paths of possible history. This business of origination, however, cannot in practice go far, for choice must be made at a deadline. What we can conclude is that however much or little opportunity there has been for the chooser to proliferate the rival sequels in each skein, this skein must be treated as *incomplete and uncompleteable*. The rival skeins are originated by the chooser, they are each themselves composed of mutually rival hypotheses, and the plurality of these rivals within each skein is in principle infinite in some meaning of that word.

We asked thirdly what is the motive to undertake the business of choice? If all that *is,* exists in the transcience of the present, its continuous passage to a fresh creation of thoughts, must not the motive of choice be to participate to special effect in this creation, to achieve a state of thought of some particular kind? The economist has fastened the word equilibrium on a pattern of public interactions to do with things that are already reported from the field. But it is evident that interactions are in the first place actions of individuals, and that the choice of action by the individual is an activity of thought. For him, equilibrium is a good state of mind. What choice seems able to do is to affect the possibilities of time-to-come. Its concern is with history to come. A good state of mind, in relation to choice, must be a good state of imagination, a fabric of thoughts achieving present, immediate, and synchronous beauty, a whole that satisfies criteria that we must call aesthetic, but using as its means the need to fill, in some sense the calendar axis of time-to-come. If such is the motive of choice, if choice is the seeking of satisfaction in contemplation of time to come, we have a source of suggestions about the tests to be applied to the imagined sequels of present commitment.

Imagined sequels to commitment to some scheme of actions could not be supposed to afford the chooser satisfaction or concern in their contemplation if they seemed to him to be ruled out by some fatal obstacle. Sequels that he dismisses as impossible will not bear on his choice. But unless we can suppose him able to discern within his knowledge of circumstance or principle some fatal obstacle to all except one of the sequels that he can imagine for given conduct of his own, he cannot impose the requirement on any such sequel, before he will derive from it contemplative (anticipative) satisfaction, that it shall seem *certain* to be realized. The practicable test, at most, is epistemic possibility. Particular conduct of his own will seem to be a condition of this possibility for some imaginable sequels. But there is an essential consideration without which the business of choice, if necessary at all in any interesting sense, would at least be greatly simplified. The conduct that makes possible some desirable sequels will also usually make possible some counter-desired sequels. Choice of particular conduct can remove obstacles which would otherwise block a skein of sequels, and this skein may include strands of very various degrees of desiredness or its opposite. How can such skeins be compared with each other? We need to consider some properties of what I have been calling epistemic possibility.

If possibility, for some conceived path of history or some sequel of personal action, is to consist for the individual in the absence of fatal obstacles within his knowledge, then the rendering of such a path or sequel possible consists in the removal of such obstacles that may stand in the way. This removal may need to be effected by his commitment to some action. But once the path is clear, any satisfaction that this contemplation, the anticipation of this path, can give him is fully his. It further follows that this degree of satisfaction will not be made more fully and effectively his by the presence in his thought of *rival* paths or sequels of equal desiredness and equal freedom from epistemic obstacles. For he cannot take satisfaction from both of two mutually contradictory suppositions at one time. Thus we may say that *possibility is not additive.* The possibility of anticipative satisfaction can be conferred by one path of imagined history-to-come in whatever degree that path in itself, in its own content regardless of possibility, can afford it, provided this path itself is for him epistemically possible. We shall invoke this principle below in describing a mode of comparison of the rival skeins of imagined sequels.

What the chooser can directly achieve by his origination of rival choosables and his adoption of one among them as his incentive to commit himself to specific action and as the specifier of that action, is a state of mind, a state of imagination. If all that *is* exists only in its immediacy, in its taking shape in the transcience and transformation of the present, such a state of thought is the only effect and result that is within the actual grasp of choice. What will follow, when the action to which his choice commits him has been taken and has exerted an effect in the field, will exist for him only at a later moment when they are reported from the field. These events in the field, these reports of such events, cannot conceivably affect, induce, or guide that choice which is itself their source and their begetter, their *beginning* in our sense. Choice that begets action cannot be induced by the reported results of that action, only by the imagination of its possible results. Many rival such imaginations will form the skein of conceived sequels of the action. The only test they need pass for such inclusion, the only test which, in the nature of the human imprisonment in the solitary present they can pass, is to seem to the chooser possible. The test they must pass is to be possible on condition of his committing himself to the specific action from which the imagined sequels are conceived to flow. The incentive for choice is the satisfaction of contemplating the chosen skein of actions and sequels. What properties or character of this choosable will be the basis of this satisfaction?

The quality or character of this skein as a whole must be bestowed upon it by the properties of the individual strands, the imagined sequels. Any one of these will have in the chooser's eyes, in virtue of its form considered without regard to the question whether it can become in future time the recorded course of history, some degree of desiredness or counter-desiredness. It will also be in his judgment possible or impossible, it will be either exempt from fatal obstruction by obstacles which he can in some sense specify, or it will be subject to such obstruction. Let us suppose that the chooser, in view of a deadline when his choice must be made, divides all those sequels that he had imagined for some one choosable scheme of action, into the possible and the impossible without any other distinction of degrees of possibility.

Then he can consider this skein of rival sequels as allowing him to *contemplate as possible* (let us say to *envisage*) a sequel of a particular degree of desiredness, namely, the most desired of the "possible" sequels, but as also imposing on him, if he elects this skein, the obligation to consider as possible the most counter-desired of its "possible" sequels. These two sequels will be the only members of this skein relevant to his choice. For he is concerned with the best hope, and the worst threat, offered by the *skein as a whole,* since if he chooses it he must choose it as a whole, and the sequels whose desiredness lies in the interior of the range bounded by these two sequels can in no way render their respective degrees of desiredness or counter-desiredness more possible. The skein as a whole, being a choosable entity, offers at best an imagined course of history of some degree of desiredness, that of its most desirable member-sequel. If many sequels distinct from each other in form were equally desired, this plurality would not increase the possibility assignable by the chooser to this degree of desiredness offered by the skein as a whole. A parallel argument applies to the most counter-desired sequel.

If my theme be accepted, there is nothing among which the individual can make a choice, except creations of his own thought. When these are schemes of action and their supposed sequels, they cannot give anticipative pleasure, the pleasure of contemplating what *might be* in time to come, unless that might-be is interpreted as compatible, so far as the chooser can judge it, with the posture and the nature of the field. It is the field reported in the present, or held in the chooser's accumulated knowledge, which must supply the suggestions out of which the sanctioned building blocks of history-to-come are made by the chooser, and which must supply also the tests that he applies to such paths of history-to-come concerning their possibility. But it is inconceivable that such tests can eliminate all but one of the paths of relevant history that the chooser can conceive. There can be for him no settling on one such path, for each action-scheme, as its *certain* outcome. If the chooser deems his own choosing to be an origination, a beginning in our sense, undetermined by antecedents but making a difference to what can follow, there can be for him no settling on a uniquely possible, and therefore certain, sequel for such a choice. The sequel that history will record, when what is now time-to-come has been traversed, will have been partly formed by the originative choices which others, and he himself, will by then (as he must now suppose) have made. In short, there is unknowledge of the sequel of his (present) choice. This unknowledge is not for him unbounded. The present circumstances reported from the field, the nature of the field as he apprehends it, confine the possibilities. There is, then, *uncertainty*. How is the uncertain state of thought to be given a formal expression?

To say that the chooser's choice of action must be made in face of bounded uncertainty concerning the sequel is an expression of some lineaments of the conclusion which my argument has reached. But this expression fails to touch the nerve of the matter. For what I am seeking to describe is a conception of the engenderment of history, the notion of *continuously originated* history, of history taking form from *beginnings* in the extreme sense. *Uncertainty* conveys the suggestion that there is a determinate future preexisting choice and independent of it, needing only to be found out. If this were all, what meaning could be found in choice, what peculiar mechanism of error and ignorance would destiny be using in mockery of human effort, to bring about its preordained results? It seems plain that if the future merely waits to be revealed, the business of choice is merely a response to signals, a response which may be uncomprehending, even groping and blundering, but which is destined nonetheless to lead things into a course laid down from some once-and-for-all unique creation of history as an entirety. Choice which itself contributes in a fundamental sense, in the sense of an essential origination, to the form that history takes from moment to moment or from year to year, is a seeking to realize ambitions rather than to discover preexistents. The *gap of knowledge* that the word uncertainty suggests is, instead, if my theme has any truth, the *void of time*. The contrast I ultimately wish to present is between those constructions that exhibit uncertainty as a difficulty that can be overcome by an exercise of reason, and a view, utterly alien to that conception of remediable uncertainty, that sees in the void of time the indispensable condition of human originative freedom.

The exploitation of the void of time, the imaginative filling of it with a skein of rival strands rendered epistemically possible by the chooser's commitment to some scheme of action, is the conception for which we seek some formal frame. My theme has led to the notion that if all the strands of the skein are adjudged equally possible, and if among the strands of this skein there is one which the chooser more desires than any of the others, and one which he dislikes more than any of the others, these two will hold his interest and attention to the exclusion of all the others. In the conception where all imagined sequels of a chosen action are either epistemically impossible or else are equi-possible with each other, the attraction of this skein for the chooser will reside in these two *focus-outcomes.* Such a conception is evidently wholly at odds with any frame of thought that seeks a compromise among mutually exclusive rivals, that seeks, in other words, to add together the values of things only one of which, at most, can in time-to-come prove true, after adjusting these values, in some manner, for their mutual exclusiveness. If choice is originative, the inherent, essential, and irremediable unknowledge that must then pervade the business of choice must find some expression in our formal description of that business. There seem to be two classes into one or other of which such expression can fall. It can resort, as I have suggested in the foregoing, to the recognition of contrasting sequels as possible. Instead, it can entertain a single picture of the sequel, but give this picture a force or influence greatly reduced from what it would carry if it were treated as certain, as uniquely occupying by itself the entire field of possibility.

I have already made the suggestion that the presence in the chooser's thought of several imagined sequels of a choosable action-scheme, all equally desirable but rival and mutually exclusive to each other, will not increase this choosable's attraction for him in comparison with its having only one sequel of that degree of desiredness. The presence of one sequel of that degree of desiredness is sufficient to put that degree within epistemic reach of this choosable. When there is (as there must be) unknowledge of what *will* come to pass, what matters is what *can* come to pass. A desired possible sequel is all that is required to make its own degree of desiredness seem possible. There will be counter-desired sequels of equal possibility, and their possibility *cannot be annulled* by the presence of numbers of mutually rival desired sequels. The line of thought that supposes it meaningful to make a weighted average of valuations of mutually contradictory hypotheses is illicitly shifting the argument to a wholly different question. That question has to do with the means of extracting *knowledge* from evidence which is sufficient to provide knowledge. It has, therefore, nothing to do with *unknowledge,* with the irremediable presence of mutually rival hypotheses, all claiming possibility. The question to which the averaging of results, weighted according to some calculation of their frequencies, is legitimately applicable, is the question what will be the outcome of many trials of some system whose relevant conformation and use only change, from one trial to another, within specifiable limits, when all these trials are treated as one whole.

I have sought to show that in representing to himself the meaning for him of a skein of imagined sequels of specified action, as residing in the most desired and the most counter-desired of that class of these sequels that are unobstructed by any fatal obstacle within his knowledge, the class of sequels, that is, which in our terms are epistemically possible, the action-chooser is obeying the logic of his, the general, human, predicament. If so, the ultimate phase in his business of choice is the comparison of the choosable actions as pairs of focus outcomes. This comparison will be an exercise of *taste*. A possible success of some degree (a degree measured on a private scale) can be envisaged on condition of envisageing a possible misfortune of some degree; this pair can perhaps be compared by the chooser with another pair, namely, a greater success whose possibility depends on his making possible also a greater misfortune. Arbitraments of taste pervade the whole business of living. The economist has long since repudiated any concern with explaining taste, and when he can simplify its exercise to a comparison of two pairs of entities (no matter whether both members of each pair are desired, or one member of each pair is counter-desired) he can represent the chooser's taste by an indifference-map, and the choosable pairs by points appropriately distanced from the axes. Such visualizing can be the basis of much fascinating argument, but it leaves us with the need to accept taste as its own law.

Can taste then be excluded altogether from the business of choosing action, if we suppose the chooser to value each action-scheme by assigning to each of its envisaged sequels a *degree of belief* that this sequel will prove eventually to have described the recorded course of history in what now is time-to-come? What could be the meaning of such degrees of belief? On what ground and by what method could such a degree of belief be used to modify the value which the action-chooser would have put on some sequel if he had treated it as *certain* to prove true?

In the preface to his *Treatise on Probability,* John Maynard Keynes aligns himself with those writers in the English tradition who "are united in a preference for what is matter of fact, and have conceived their subject [of probability] as a branch rather of science than of the creative imagination." He proceeds in chapter 1: "If logic investigates the general principles of valid thought, the study of arguments, to which it is rational to attach *some* weight, is as much a part of it as the study of those which are demonstrative. The terms *certain* and *probable* describe the various degrees of rational belief about a proposition which different amounts of knowledge authorize us to entertain. It is often convenient to speak of propositions as certain or probable [but] this expresses strictly a relationship in which they stand to a corpus of knowledge, actual or hypothetical, and not a characteristic of the propositions in themselves. It is without significance to call a proposition probable unless we specify the knowledge to which we are relating it. To this extent, therefore, probability may be called subjective. But in the sense important to logic, probability is not subjective. When once the facts are given which determine our knowledge, what is probable or impossible in these circumstances has been fixed objectively. The Theory of Probability is logical, therefore, because it is concerned with the degree of belief which it is rational to entertain in given conditions. This involves purely logical relations between the propositions which embody our direct knowledge and the propositions about which we seek indirect knowledge.''[1]

What question, then, would be answered by the assertion that some stated degree of rational belief, other than certainty, in some proposition was justified by the evidence? Suppose this proposition described the consequences of the chooser's electing some specified course of action. Could the question be: Will these be the consequences? It could not, for the assertion is not: These *will be* the consequences. What *is* the assertion? What *use* is the assertion, if it does not amount to an injunction to the chooser to proceed *as if* the proposition were true? And if the chooser is so justified, what purpose is served by qualifying the "rationally justified" degree of belief as less than certainty? The claims of logic are appeals to an intuition. The claim is that of the cabinet-maker who "offers up" (in the carpenter's technical language) a structural member of the object he is making and demonstrates to himself that it fits. *Objectivity* is public and general acceptance. The question whether some idea is "objective" is itself a matter for subjective judgment. Rigid logic has a high score of success in conquering men's minds. What would be the nature of the claim that could be made by a logic that fell short of demonstration?

Keynes's view if it could be upheld, Keynes's program if it could be implemented, (they were the view and the ambition of Leibniz, as Keynes's quotation on his first page makes clear) would transform the situation of the theoretical economist. The Theory of Value rests on the supposition that men choose their conduct by *reason fully informed,* reason supplied with every datum of relevant circumstance, with every principle of the working of the cosmos in its aspect of Nature or of Man. Let us see, the value-theorist says, what will be to a man's best advantage in view of his tastes and his endowments, and that is what he will do. But men are not fully informed. How can they be informed of what their own choices in time-to-come have still to *originate* in the fundamental and extreme sense? The theoretician of value shows how men would choose, if there were no need for choice, if there were no possibility, no freedom, no meaning for choice. If some technique of probability could abolish the distinction between knowledge and unknowledge, Keynes's own ultimate position, that business and enterprise suffer disasters not because of moral or intellectual failure, not from lack of dedication and of effort, but because of the nature of things, would lose its force to explain the nineteen thirties and the nineteen seventies and all the anarchy of history. The world of meaningful choice, of choice as *beginning,* is the kaleidic world where imagination in action generates the unimagined.

Notes

1. John Maynard Keynes, *A Treatise on Probability* (New York: Harper & Row, 1962), pp. 3–4.

Comment: Radical Subjectivism or Radical Subversion?

S. C. Littlechild

Shackle in Context

G.L.S. Shackle has always seemed a man alone. By this, I do not mean he has lacked friends and admirers. A volume of essays in his honor,[1] which includes such distinguished authors as Arrow, Harrod, Hirshleifer, Harry Johnson, Hurwicz, Klein, and Shoup, is a testament to the affection and respect in which he is held. Nor do I mean that Shackle's work has lacked the critical attention of his fellow economists. An issue of the journal *Metroeconomica* was devoted to a symposium on his work,[2] and his books invariably call forth lengthy and sympathetic reviews.[3]

None can deny the insight and originality that Shackle brings to bear on a wide variety of topics, nor the elegance and style with which his case is stated. Not since Marshall, it has been remarked, has an economist had so splendid a command of language.[4] But to what school of thought does Shackle belong? In whose footsteps does he follow, and who follows in his? How far has he influenced, or been influenced by, the thoughts and writings of his professional colleagues? Is he not a man alone in his apparent independence of any conventional tradition?

No man, however, is an island. It would be strange indeed if there were no discernible influences on Shackle's thought, no links with writers of an earlier age, no seeds which may have flourished elsewhere too. And stranger still, if work of such brilliance failed to inspire the writings of others.

Shackle's influence is surely apparent in the title of Professor Loasby's recent book: *Choice, Complexity and Ignorance.*[5] With 27 citations in the index, Shackle is by far the most-quoted author. To list the other heavily cited authors (A. Marshall 17, K.R. Popper 15, H.A. Simon 15, G.B. Richardson 14) is to give some idea of the intellectual company Shackle is thought to keep.

Shackle himself has paid tribute to several writers, most noticeably to Myrdal and Lindahl, Keynes and Hayek. The latter was Shackle's supervisor at the London School of Economics, and "his brilliant study of the role of knowledge in economic affairs was an early source of inspiration for me."[6]

The same influence has recently been noted by others. In his mono-

In preparing this chapter, I have greatly benefited from conversations with I.M. Kirzner and A.L. Minkes and from correspondence with L.M. Lachmann.

graph *Cost and Choice*,[7] Professor J.M. Buchanan traces the evolution in Vienna and London of ideas in the conception of cost. Hayek is credited with introducing the subjectivist ideas of the Austrians to the L.S.E. "It is immediately evident," writes Buchanan, "that Shackle's treatment of the decision process is wholly consistent with the London doctrine of opportunity cost"[8]—though he finds it surprising that Shackle himself does not make this linkage. [9]

The most explicit attempt to place Shackle's ideas in context is by Professor L.M. Lachmann, who attempts to show

> that the body of economic thought that has come to be known as 'Austrian', and in particular that part of it which found expression in the seminal work of Ludwig von Mises, is not only less vulnerable to Shackle's attack than the main body of current orthodoxy, but that to a striking extent Mises and Shackle share a common outlook on the foundations of our discipline.[10]

Lachmann also argues that, in his emphasis on expectations, Shackle has made progress beyond the common ground he shares with Mises.

Given the origin and theme of this book, it seems appropriate to take this comparison of Shackle with the Austrians further. In chapter 2, Shackle proposes to us the vital role of imagination. What is meant by imagination, we shall ask, and to what extent is imagination consistent with Austrian economics? For concreteness we shall compare and contrast Shackle's approach with that of Professor I.M. Kirzner.[11] Our task is thus, in large part, to appraise the relation of imagination to the entrepreneurial market process that Kirzner has made so familiar.[12]

A Summary of Imagination, Formalism, and Choice

Choice, argues Shackle, represents an origin, a beginning. As such, it is neither determined nor caused, but it does have a sequel. It makes a difference to what comes after. This sequel cannot be foreknown, because subsequent events will depend partly upon other such choices yet to be made. But certain alternative sequels may be imagined, each regarded as more or less possible, and each having some power to attract the attention of the chooser.

Shackle's concern is to elucidate the nature and implications of such a theory of choice. He proceeds by posing and answering seven questions. The paper may best be summarized by sketching the answers to these questions:

1. By what means do rival choosable entities present themselves to the chooser?

The alternatives are not presented ready-made by "reports from the field."

Such reports concern what *is* whereas choice concerns what *might be*. The choosables must be *originated by the chooser,* they must be imagined, invented, created.

2.   What is the essential nature of such choosables?

They must not be "free fictions or fantasies," because they must constitute descriptions of the course of history–to–come that the chooser regards as *possible,* that is, "compatible so far as the chooser can judge it with the [present] posture and nature of the field." However, there is in practice no limit to the number of such possible paths which might be imagined. This list or skein must, therefore, be treated as *incomplete and uncompleteable.*

3.   What is the motive to undertake the business of choice?

It is to achieve *a good state of mind* which, in relation to choice, must be interpreted as a *good state of imagination.*

4.   What is the link between choice and its effect? and

5.   In the envisaging of sequels to choice, what test is applied?

Since the chooser is unlikely to find fatal obstacles to all but one of the sequels he imagines, he cannot require that a sequel be *certain* to be realized. An imagined sequel must, therefore, be seen as a *possible* consequence of the chooser committing himself to some action, perhaps with the help of further conduct of his own.

6.   How can choosables each itself consisting of rival imagined sequels be mutually compared?

Of the various possible sequels to any action, some desired and some disliked, two sequels (one of each type) will hold the attention of the chooser. Each action may thus be represented as a pair of *focus outcomes.* To compare such pairs is a matter of *taste.*

7.   What mode of engenderment of history would be implied by this conception of choice?

History is not predetermined, merely waiting to be discovered. Rather, history is continuously *originated* by the pattern and sequence of human choice.

Subjectivism, Expectations, and Imagination

Professor Lachman has argued convincingly, with supporting quotations, that Shackle and Mises share a similar subjectivist approach. "In their emphasis on the spontaneous, and thus unpredictable nature of human action, in the rejection of mechanistic notions of time and probability, our two authors are completely at one."[13] The chapter presently under discussion is fully characteristic of Shackle: there is no need to document with further quotation the affinity of its author to the subjectivist tradition.

Lachmann goes on to argue that Shackle has "made progress" beyond the common ground he shares with Mises, in that he has "extended the scope of subjectivism from tastes to expectations."[14] In doing so, he presents two challenges to Austrian theory. Can the market process diffuse expectations in the same way that it diffuses knowledge? And will not "restless asset markets," responding to daily changes in expectations, thwart the equilibrating forces in the economy as a whole?

In chapter 2, Shackle proposes to us the concept of imagination. Consider, for example, how he presents one aspect of what is conventionally called the theory of consumer choice.

> For [the individual], equilibrium is a good state of mind. What choice seems able to do is to affect the possibilities of time-to-come . . . . A good state of mind, in relation to choice, must be a good state of imagination.[15]

Here there is no invariant function determining the utility that the individual, given his tastes, will obtain from an objectively specified bundle of goods. Utility depends instead upon imagination. Of course, the individual must constrain his imagination to be consistent with his expectations of what is possible, which will partly depend upon his resources. Moreover, what constitutes for him a good state of imagination will depend upon his tastes. Nonetheless, it is imagination which provides the direct source of satisfaction.

What, then, is the nature of imagination? How does it differ from expectations? What role does it play? Our first task is to answer these questions.

The Nature and Role of Imagination

As they have come to be treated in conventional economic literature, expectations refer to the "outside world," to the environment in which an economic agent finds himself. The agent is allowed or required to have expectations about a predefined set of properties of a predefined set of entities—for example, the price of oil in 1984, or the distribution of wages on offer to him over the next six weeks. Expectations are thus a way of characterizing and dealing with uncertainty. For Shackle, however, "uncertainty conveys the suggestion that there is a determinate future, preexisting choice and independent of it, needing only to be found out.'' In this sense, expectations have been treated in the literature as a passive response to uncertainty.

Imagination, by contrast, knows no such bounds. It is the power of the human mind to conceive of an unending list or skein of alternative possible actions, each with an unlimited number of alternative possible sequels.

> . . . . however much or little opportunity there has been for the chooser to proliferate the rival sequels in each skein, this skein must be treated as *incomplete and uncompleteable*. The rival skeins are originated by the chooser, they are each themselves composed of mutually rival hypotheses, and the plurality of these rivals within each skein is in principle infinite in some meaning of that word.[16]

The role of imagination is thus an active and crucial one: to generate the elements from which choice is made.

> The future is imagined by each man for himself, and this process of the imagination is a vital part of the process of decision.[17]

However, imagination unconstrained is a necessary but insufficient basis for decision. A pure fiction can give pleasure, but is irrelevant for action unless it constitutes an imagined course of some possible history-to-come, a history whose possibility depends upon some action of the chooser. To be seen as possible, this imagined history must be consistent with the chooser's knowledge or beliefs about his own resources, the nature of the world, the likely actions of others, etc. For Shackle, only this special subset of imagined futures, the subjectively possible ones, attain the status of expectations.

> Imagination constrained to congruity with what seems in some degree possible we shall call expectation.[18]

We may now appreciate not only how expectations differ from imagination but also how expectations as used by Shackle differ from expectations as used by other writers. For Shackle, expectations do not refer to entities of the world as it *is,* nor yet to *predefined* entities of the world as it might be, but to entities existing in, and created by, the imagination of each decision maker. In other words, the raw material for expectations is provided not by the world directly, but by imagination at work on the world. For this reason, a man may have expectations about future events and actions that have not even occurred to anyone else.

It is this creative aspect of expectations, deriving from their source in imagination, that has not been incorporated in conventional work on expectations. With this important exception of Professor Lachmann, it would seem as though this might be equally true of Austrian economists. Our next task is to see whether this is indeed the case with respect to Professor Kirzner.

The Similarity of Entrepreneurship and Imagination

Professor Kirzner has developed with great clarity and insight the concept of entrepreneurship implicit in the work of Mises, and has argued that this concept is missing from the neoclassical (or "Anglo-American") discussion of individual decision-making exemplified by Lord Robbins. According to Kirzner, Robbinsian formulations of the economic problem are centered around the concept of "economizing." Economizing is the allocation of given (scarce) means to achieve as far as possible a set of given (competing) ends. Kirzner finds this analytical vision misleadingly incomplete. He proposes instead the broader concept of *human action* developed by Mises, which incorporates not only economizing but also an element of alertness to new opportunities which he calls enterpreneurship.

> Mises's *homo agens* . . . is endowed not only with the propensity to pursue goals efficiently, once ends and means are clearly identified, but also with the drive and alertness needed to identify which ends to strive for and which means are available."
>
> "Now I choose . . . to label that element of alertness to possibly newly worthwhile goals and to possibly newly available resources—which we have seen is absent from the notion of economizing but very much present in that of human action—the entrepreneurial element in human decision-making.[19]

Kirzner immediately goes on to describe the vital role which entrepreneurship plays.

> It is the entrepreneurial element that is responsible for our understanding of human action as active, creative, and human rather than as passive, automatic and mechanical.

It would thus appear that entrepreneurship plays precisely the same kind of role in Kirzner's approach to economics as imagination does in Shackle's. In either case, the effect is to extend the scope of individual decision-making from the passive selection among alternative actions that are somehow given (that is, economizing), to the active generation of actions from which a selection is to be made. In either case, again, the principal consequence is the same. Economic activity may be seen as a process taking place through time, as the exercise of entrepreneurial or imaginative abilities generates a succession of new choice-situations. For both writers, interest lies primarily in the nature and properties of this process rather than in the concept of equilibrium, which the Robbinsian economizing approach taken along inevitably emphasises.

This affinity between the approaches of Shackle and Kirzner (and, indeed, of the Austrians generally), and the contrast between the approach of all these writers, on the one hand, and the neoclassical theory of value, on the other, cannot be stressed too much. It is essentially the distinction between a world in which time plays a vital role, and one in which the passing of time may be ignored.

A Difference between Entrepreneurship and Imagination

Nevertheless, if we probe further to see whether entrepreneurship and imagination are held to be precisely identical, we find they are apparently not. There is one fundamental difference that is emphasized repeatedly. For Kirzner, entrepreneurship is the *discovery* of something *existing;* for Shackle, imagination is the *creation* of something *new.* Thus, Kirzner refers to "unexploited" opportunities which have a "prior existence"; the Kirznerian entrepreneur "responds to existing tensions and provides those corrections for which the unexploited opportunities have been crying out."[20] Shackle, on the other hand, associates imagination with originality; imagination generates a "beginning" in the extreme sense in which "we imply two states of affairs, one in which the originated thing is not present, and one [later in time] in which it is present."[21]

What are we to make of this distinction? Is it merely a difference of language or is there a fundamental difference of concept? In the later case, what is the significance of this distinction for economic theory?

It seems to me that there are (at least) three possible interpretations of the distinction between entrepreneurship and imagination as defined by Kirzner and Shackle. For reasons that will soon become apparent, I shall call these the "Chinese Boxes" interpretation, the "Dual Viewpoint" interpretation and the "Inherent Imagination" interpretation. We shall examine these in turn.

The Chinese Boxes Interpretation

If we accept that there is a fundamental difference between entrepreneurship and imagination, we appear to be led to the view that the two theories deal with different phenomena. Kirzner's theory of entrepreneurship deals with the discovery and spread of existing knowledge, techniques, and products, while Shackle's theory of imagination deals with the creation of new knowledge and with invention of new techniques and new products.

Shackle, for instance, is concerned with the invention of the jet engine, Kirzner with its adoption.

In this view, the two approaches are not mutually exclusive or competitive, but complementary. Shackle's approach may be seen as providing an "imaginative framework" of products, techniques, and ideas which the Kirznerian entrepreneur may proceed to discover. In a similar way the Austrian approach provides a framework of knowledge for the neoclassical economizer to work within. In other words, the three conceptions of economic theory developed by the neoclassicals, by the Austrians and by Shackle, are not to be seen as mutually exclusive paradigms, but as incorporating increasing levels of generality. They fit one into the next like Chinese boxes, each box providing a framework for the one within.

We do not, therefore, need to make an irrevocable choice between rival theories. Different levels of generality will have different advantages and disadvantages, each level providing some insights and obscuring others. What is important is to decide and agree, in any given economic analysis, at what level of generality we wish to operate.

However, the Chinese Boxes interpretation does present the following drawback. If the invention of new products and technologies is excluded from the scope of entrepreneurship, to what extent can entrepreneurship be held responsible, as Kirzner wishes, for the creative aspect of human action? How active is an activity limited to the discovery of existing products and technologies? The Chinese Boxes interpretation seems to imply that Austrian economic theory, at least as interpreated in terms of Kirzner's concept of entrepreneurship, cannot hope to explain the whole of economic activity, but only a part of it. Moreover, that which it cannot hope to explain comprises the really innovative, imaginative, and usually far-reaching manifestations of human activity. As Shackle himself asks "were Dante, Michaelangelo, Shakespeare, Newton and Beethoven merely alert?"[22]

The Dual Viewpoint Interpretation

A closer reading of Shackle's chapter suggests that the Chinese Boxes interpretation may not be a correct reflection of the point he is making. His emphasis on originality is not an insistence that decision relates only to major innovations. His central point is that choice is originating in the sense that it is not predetermined by previous events or experience. Choice is among thoughts that are conjured up by the chooser; these thoughts and subsequent actions are not confined to technical inventions: they may relate to matters as mundane as what to choose for Sunday dinner.

For his part, too, Kirzner does not seem to be excluding major innovations. It is true that a jet engine is in one sense a new invention, he might say, but it might equally be regarded as the discovery of a better means of satisfying an existing demand for fast air travel.

This suggests that our two authors are not so much looking at different phenomena as looking at the same phenomena from two different points of view. An example will help to illustrate this interpretation:

Suppose it occurs to a shopkeeper that his customers might like a certain product which he has never stocked before. From the point of view of the shopkeeper, this is an exercise of imagination, a new idea not implicit in his previous plans. From the point of view of the (omniscient) observing economist, this same act is the discovery of an existing opportunity, for the product was always available to be stocked, had the shopkeeper but realized this. In other words, the same act may simultaneously be interpreted as the imagination of something new *and* as the discovery of something existing, depending upon the purpose of the analysis.

Shackle's Approach as Psychological Rather than Economic

It is not precisely clear how far Kirzner's own interpretation of the relationship between entrepreneurship and imagination accords with either of the interpretations considered so far. The dual viewpoints interpretation would seem to be consistent with his approach, since in a brief comment Kirzner has noted that his own emphasis is "quite different" from that of Shackle, but that their two approaches "deal with different levels of discussion and *may* therefore both be simultaneously valid without coinciding at all.

However, Kirzner draws a further significant distinction. He suggests, in effect, that one of the viewpoints (Shackle's) is largely psychological in nature, and for that reason lies outside the scope of economics. It will be helpful to reproduce his comment in full.[23]

> In a number of writings, referred to earlier in this paper, Professor Shackle has called for a view of the decision as creative, rather than determined. Shackle wishes to see history as having injected into it at each instant of decision–making, a novel element not predictable from and not determined by previous history.
>
> The kernel of our own stress here on the entrepreneurial element in individual decision–making is rather different from what Shackle is seeking. The two approaches, Shackle's and our own, deal with different levels of discussion (and *may* therefore both be simultaneously valid without coinciding at all). Shackle is concerned with the psychology of decision–making. He regrets that economics developed at the hand of Smith, Ricardo and Marshall, instead of at the hands of psychologists. Much of Shackle's own contributions in this area are psychological in character.

> Our own emphasis is quite different. We remain content to stay at the purely formal level at which economic theorists have always aimed their discussion. We still see economics as a theory of choice; we merely seek to have it recognized that the appropriate notion of choice for this purpose is the Austrian one which we have identified as embracing also the entrepreneurial element. Entrepreneurs, too, make choices; our theory cannot afford to leave them out.[24]

On what grounds does Kirzner claim that the creative element of decision making belongs to psychology rather than economics? His claim appears to be based upon Mises' conception that economics is a science of human action. The essential element of human action is *purposeful behavior.*

> The core of the concept of human action is to be found in the unique property possessed by human beings of engaging in operations designed to attain a state of affairs that is preferred to that which has hitherto prevailed.[25]

Purposeful behavior requires the use of *human reason.*

> Sound logic will, in a given situation, point to one or several courses of action that give promise of most successfully securing the desired change. In so far as human behaviour is guided by logic, then, conduct will follow a path that has been selected by *reason.* This path of conduct is what is known praxeologically as *human action.*[26]

Reason has to operate under the pressures of physiological and psychological instincts, and these pressures may be strong, but nonetheless reason plays a role in every action. It is this element that separates the sciences of human action, such as economics, from the natural sciences such as psychology.

> The element in conduct that is the reflection of man's power to weight, arrange, and choose among courses of behaviour is the specifically human element in action. The investigation of this element of human action and of its manifestation in various particular situations forms a field of study unique by virtue of the nature of human action itself. Sciences of human action will be distinct from other sciences in that the former begin where the latter end, viz., in the implications of the rationality that governs purposeful behaviour."[27]

To summarize, Professor Kirzner argues that economics is a science of human action, that the essential element of human action is purposeful behavior, and that purposeful behavior is governed by reason. Insofar as Shackle is concerned with creativity and imagination rather than reason, to that extent he is concerned with psychology rather than economics.

The Inherent Imagination Interpretation

Shackle has not, to my knowledge, commented on Kirzner's view, but I take it he would consider himself an economist rather than a psychologist and would therefore, disagree with Kirzner's argument. In the light of his chapter, the basic source of disagreement is not hard to find. Assume, with Kirzner, that economics is a science of human action, which is in turn characterized by purposeful behavior. Assume, too, that reason is a central component of purposeful behavior. Shackle's point is that reason is not, and cannot be, the *only* such component. Reason cannot operate alone, for "expectation undermines the view of conduct as purely rational."[28] Reason must operate in conjunction with imagination. "Imagination and Reason," says Shackle, "are the two faculties that make us human."[29] It follows that economics, as a science of human action, must find a place for imagination alongside rationality, instead of relegating it to the realms of psychology.

Shackle is actually quite specific about the way in which imagination determines the mechanisms of choice. A choice must be made between rival imagined actions, each characterized by a skein of rival imagined sequels.

> My theme has led to the notion that if all the strands of the skein are adjudged equally possible, and if amongst the strands of this skein there is one which the chooser more desires than any of the others, and one which he more dislikes than any of the others, these two will hold his interest and attention to the exclusion of all the others.[30]

In other words, each action is characterized by two "focus outcomes" only. That approach is rejected which *averages* the sequels according to some probability distribution. Instead, each pair of focus–outcomes is compared with other pairs, and selection between these pairs is a matter of taste. Thus, Shackle claims in effect that the mechanism of focus–outcomes is logically implied by the properties of human action, properly interpreted.

Be that as it may, we are led to a third interpretation of the relationship between imagination and entrepreneurship. If all human action is based, in part, upon imagination, then a fortiori the exercise of entrepreneurial alertness must also be so based. That is, an element of imagination is *inherent* in entrepreneurship. For a shopkeeper to recognize the potential profitability of stocking a new product it is necessary for him to imagine the reactions of his customers. This act of imagination is an intrinsic part of the realization that an opportunity exists.

Kirzner has described his (and Mises') entrepreneurial theory of profit as an "arbitrage" theory.[31] An opportunity for profitable arbitrage exists whenever the same product is simultaneously being traded at different prices in the same market (or, by extension, when a consumption good is selling, or is expected to sell, at a price that exceeds the value of the necessary bundle of inputs).

In reality, as Mises emphasized, "one must never forget that every action is embedded in the flux of time and therefore involves a speculation . . . . There's many a slip 'twixt cup and lip."[32] For Shackle, the role of imagination is precisely to envisage the range of possible outcomes of any action, and to conjure up alternative outcomes, which may be more suited to the situation.

Kirzner recognizes that, in principle, "in a world of uncertainty every entrepreneurial decision . . . must to some extent constitute a gamble."[33] However, his "discussion of entrepreneurial alertness has deliberately avoided emphasising its speculative character."[34] Without uncertainty, there is no need for speculation, no role for imagination. Since there are no slips 'twixt cup and lip, there are no losses. A profit perceived is a profit secured.

Our last task is to explore the consequences for the entrepreneurial market process of relaxing Kirzner's assumption by acknowledging the presence of uncertainty and a role for the imagination inherent in entrepreneurial action.

Imagination and Market Process

Kirzner has shown that entrepreneurship is the source of a market process. He also claims more: that since entrepreneurship is a coordinating force the resulting market process is an equilibrating one. Thus he draws the following contrast between his own view and that of Schumpeter.

> for Schumpeter the essence of entrepreneurship is the ability to break away from routine, to destroy existing structures, to move the system away from the even, circular flow of equilibrium. For us, on the other hand, the crucial element in entrepreneurship is the ability to see unexploited opportunities whose prior existence meant that the initial evenness of the circular flow was illusory—that, far from being a state of equilibrium, it represented a situation of disequilibrium inevitably destined to be disrupted. For Schumpeter the entrepreneur is the disruptive, disequilibrating force that dislodges the market from the somnolence of equilibrium; for us the entrepreneur is the equilibrating force whose activity responds to the existing tensions and provides those corrections for which the unexploited opportunities have been crying out.[35]

It is immediately obvious that if uncertainty and imagination are admitted into entrepreneurship, then entrepreneurs may make mistakes and suffer losses. Insofar as they do, presumably they fail to coordinate the market—indeed, they may well constitute a disequilibrating force.

Furthermore, insofar as imagination generates a *new* opportunity, of whatever kind, rather than discovers an *existing* one, to that extent the entrepreneurial act cannot be described as equilibrating. The exploitation of an existing opportunity reveals that, from this later vantage point, the previous situation was lacking in coordination. But if the opportunity did not hitherto exist, the previous situation could, in principle, have been fully coordinated already, within the limits of the scope for coordination then available.

However, the very notion of full coordination is called into question. Hayek has defined the concept of equilibrium in terms of the mutual compatibility of plans. But he emphasizes that

> while such a position represents in one sense a position of equilibrium, it is clear that it is not an equilibrium in the special sense in which equilibrium is regarded as a sort of optimum position. In order that the results of the combination of individual bits of knowledge should be comparable to the results of direction by an omniscient dictator, further conditions must apparently be introduced . . . . One condition would be that each of the alternative uses of any sort of resources is known to the owner of some such resources actually used for another purpose and that in this way all the different uses of these resources are connected, either directly or indirectly.[36]

In his concept of equilibrium as embodying full coordination, Kirzner is evidently following this second concept of equilibrium as "a sort of optimum position." But note that this concept relies upon the possibility of knowing, or at least listing, "*all* the different uses" of a resource. More generally, the set of existing opportunities, whether discovered or not, must in some way be delimited. Contrast this with Shackle's insistence that the set of available actions is incomplete and uncompleteable, and therefore infinite. There is, in other words, no limit to the extent of coordination of plans. Equilibrium as an optimum, as full coordination, cannot logically exist.

We may now appreciate a difference between Kirzner and Shackle concerning the continuous character of the market process. For Kirzner, it is in principle possible to exploit fully the opportunities existing at any time, and the entrepreneurial process lasts only so long as some opportunities remain undiscovered. To ensure the permanent continuity of the market process, new opportunities ("fresh ignorance") must be introduced *exogenously,* in the form of changes in the "data" concerning tastes, resources, and technology.

> What is of importance is that as the result both of the ignorance existing in the market at any given point in time, and of the circumstance that spontaneous and continual changes (in human tastes, resource availabilities and technological knowledge) generate a ceaseless flow of fresh ignorance, as it were, into the market—that as a result of this there is continual scope for discovery by alert entrepreneurs of newly created opportunities.[37]

For Shackle, however, new opportunities are continuously created *endogenously* by the exercise of imagination; there is no need to introduce changes in the data to perpetuate the market process. As Lachmann points out:

> What emerges from our reflections [on Shackle's work] is an image of the market as a particular kind of process, a continuous process without beginning or end, propelled by the interaction between the forces of equilibrium and the forces of change.[38]

This leads finally to the question of the determinateness of the market process. Kirzner asserts that

> As an empirical matter . . . opportunities do tend to be perceived and exploited. And it is on this observed tendency that our belief in a determinate market process is founded.[39]

He is, therefore, able to claim that a situation of disequilibrium is "inevitably destined to be disrupted."[40]

Shackle rejects the notion that the course of history is predestined:

> Uncertainty conveys the suggestion that there is a determinate future, preexisting choice and independent of it, needing only to be found out . . . . It seems plain that if the future merely waits to be revealed, the business of choice is merely a response to signals, a response which may be uncomprehending, even groping and blundering, but which is destined nonetheless to lead things into a course laid down from some once-and-for-all–unique creation of history as an entirety.[41]

In this passage, Shackle is drawing a distinction between his own conception and that of the neoclassical (or theory of value) writers. But is he not equally distinguishing his own conception from that of the Austrians? Is not the entrepreneurial process ultimately concerned with "response to signals?" Of course, when Kirzner claims that the market process is determinate, he is not suggesting that its future course is already laid down in detail. But he is suggesting that, at any time, its general direction (or set of possible directions) is determined by the set of existing but unexploited opportunities, and that, in the absence of exogenous changes, its final resting place is precisely so determined. For Shackle, even this relaxed form of determinacy is unacceptable. It implies a degree of passivity to the buffeting of the world, which allows insufficient role for the active exercise of human choice.

> For what I am seeking to describe is a conception of the engenderment of history, the notion of *continuously originated* history, of history taking

form from *beginnings* in the extreme sense . . . Choice which itself contributes in a fundamental sense, in the sense of an essential origination, to the form which history takes from moment to moment or from year to year, is a seeking to realize ambitions rather than to discover pre–existents. The gap of knowledge which the word uncertainty suggests is, instead, if my theme has any truth, the *void of time*.[42]

A Summary of the Argument

Professor Lachmann has argued that "the first, and most prominent, feature of Austrian economics is a radical subjectivism."[43] In this sense, he suggests, Professor Shackle not only epitomizes the Austrian tradition, but has carried it further, for he has opened up an entirely new dimension of subjectivism, that of expectations in addition to that of utility.

In the present comment we have tried to show how the concept of expectations as proposed by Shackle differs from expectations as they have developed at the hands of mainstream economic theorists. The essential difference is that, for Shackle, expectations are not defined with respect to a preexisting set of entities but are generated by the imagination, and as such their scope is limited only by the creative power of the human mind. Our task has been to clarify the nature and implications of Shackle's insistence on imagination.

The concept of entrepreneurial alertness developed by Professor Kirzner shares many of the properties of imagination: both provide a vehicle for moving outside the static neoclassical economizing problem, and thereby provide the basis for a dynamic market process taking place over time.

However, upon further investigation, it appears that entrepreneurship, for Kirzner, comprises only alertness to existing opportunities: there is no role for imagination in the creation of new opportunities. Indeed, because economics is a science of human action, and human action is distinguished by the use of reason, Kirzner sees Shackle's theory of imaginative creation as belonging to psychology rather than economics.

Shackle's view, on the other hand, is that human action is distinguished by both imagination *and* reason: reason alone is insufficient. Imagination is, therefore, inherent in all human action, and in particular in entrepreneurship.

It follows that the market process as envisaged by Shackle differs in crucial respects from the envisaged by Kirzner. Kirzner sees the market process as coordinating or equilibrating, necessarily leading at all times toward a point of full coordination or equilibrium, but kept in perpetual motion by a series of exogenous changes in the data. Shackle, on the other hand, envisages a "kaleidic" process, heading at every instant in new directions, knowing no concept of full coordinated equilibrium, and generating within itself a perpetual motion regardless of exogenous changes. Whereas Kirzner sees the market process as determinate, inevitably destined to follow certain patterns in response to preexisting opportunities, Shackle sees it as developing into a "void of time," to be filled by the exercise of imagination and choice. The resulting kaleidic world is certainly not neoclassical, nor yet does it seem to be Austrian. "The world of meaningful choice, of choice as a *beginning,* is the kaleidic world where imagination in action generates the unimagined."[44]

Radical Subjectivism or Radical Subversion?

I have elsewhere argued that the Austrian theory of the market process differs crucially from various recent theories of behavior under uncertainty (such as the theory of search or the theory of temporary general equilibrium), in that "eventually all these [latter] models more or less run down as the agents discover all there is to know."[45] It would now appear that Kirzner's theory of the entrepreneurial process shares precisely this property. Paradoxically, perhaps one of the insights gained by expunging imagination from entrepreneurship is a better appreciation of the need to incorporate it again, for imagination apparently plays a vital role in any science of human action.

Shackle has elsewhere remarked that "Keynes's book [the General Theory] was an immensely more destructive subversion of received theory, a more absolute relegation, in particular, of the Theory of Value to irrelevance, than even his admirers have acknowledged."[46]

Shackle's subjectivism is clearly sympathetic to Austrians, and constitutes a subversion of neoclassical economics quite as radical as the work of Keynes. But is Shackle *too* subjectivist even for Austrians? If we have understood correctly his emphasis on the role of imagination, he calls into question not only their concept of the market process, but even their very definition of economics. Is Shackle's message to Austrians merely one of radical subjectivism, or is it one of radical subversion too?

Notes

1. C.F. Carter and J.L. Ford, eds. *Uncertainty and Expectation in Economics* (Oxford: Blackwell, 1972).

2. *Metroeconomica* 11 (April/August 1959).

3. For example, L.M. Lachmann, "Professor Shackle on the Economic Significance of Time," *Metroeconomica* 11 (September 1959): 64–73.

4. Carter and Ford *Uncertainty and Expectation,* p. vii.

5. B.J. Loasby, *Choice, Complexity, and Ignorance* (Cambridge: Cambridge University Press, 1976).

6. G.L.S. Shackle, *Epistemics and Economics* (Cambridge: Cambridge University Press, 1972), p. vi. The reference is to F.A. Hayek "Economics and Knowledge," *Economica* N.S. 4 no. 13 (February 1973), reprinted in F.A. Hayek *Individualism and Economic Order* (Chicago: University of Chicago Press, 1948).

7. J.M. Buchanan, *Cost and Choice* (Chicago: Markham, 1969).

8. Ibid., p. 36.

9. Lawrence White has argued that Shackle does not in fact endorse the concept of opportunity cost, and that for Shackle cost is the distressing prospect of loss accompanying a prospect of gain. "Comment on Shackle's Notion of Opportunity Costs" *Austrian Economics Newsletter* 1, no. 2 (Spring 1978): 10. It may be noted that Shackle seems to use the term cost in several different senses, including that of the subjective opportunity cost tradition, *see* for example *Expectation, Enterprise and Profit* (London: Allen and Unwin, 1970), p. 146.

10. L.M. Lachmann, "From Mises to Shackle: An Essay on Austrian Economics and the Kaleidic Society," *Journal of Economic Literature* 14, no. 1 (March 1976): 54–62. Quotation at p. 54. The reference is to L. Mises, *Human Action,* 3rd ed. (Chicago: Henry Regnery and Co., 1966).

11. I.M. Kirzner, *Competition and Entrepreneurship* (Chicago: University of Chicago Press, 1973).

12. It would appear that several of the topics discussed below have been examined by the Austrian Economics Seminar at New York, particularly in the discussion on March 9, 1976, of Lawrence White's paper (which I have not seen) entitled "Entrepreneurship, Imagination and the Question of Equilibrium". *See Austrian Economics Newsletter* 1, no. 2 (Spring 1978): 6.

13. Lachmann, "From Mises to Shackle," p. 58.

14. Ibid., p. 58. *See also* the valuable contributions of Lachmann himself, for example, "The Role of Expectations in Economics as a Social Science," *Economica* 14 (February 1943): 108–19.

15. Chapter 2, G.L.S. Shackle, "Imagination, Formalism and Choice"

16. Ibid., p. 13.

17. Shackle, *Epistemics and Economics,* p. 3.

18. G.L.S. Shackle, *Decision, Order and Time in Human Affairs,* 2nd ed. (Cambridge: Cambridge University Press, 1969), p. 13.

19. Kirzner, *Competition and Entrepreneurship,* pp. 34, 35.

20. Ibid., p. 127.

21. Shackle, "Imagination, Formalism and Choice," p. 19.

22. Shackle, "Professor Kirzner on Entrepreneurship" (manuscript May, 22 1978), p. 3.

23. Kirzner, "Methodological Individualism, Market Equilibrium and Market Process" *Il Politico* 37, no. 4 (December 1967): 787–99. Quotation at pp. 798–799.

24. Ibid. The reference is to Shackle, *The Nature of Economic Thought Selected Papers, 1955–1964* (Cambridge: Cambridge University Press, 1966), p. 13.

25. Kirzner *The Economic Point of View* 2nd ed. (Kansas City: Sheed and Ward, 1976), p. 148.

26. Ibid., p. 149.

27. Ibid., p. 150.

28. Shackle, *Epistemics and Economics,* p. xvii.

29. Ibid., p. xii.

30. Shackle, "Imagination, Formalism and Choice," pp. 27–28.

31. Kirzner, *Competition and Entrepreneurship,* p. 85.

32. Mises, *Human Action,* p. 253.

33. Kirzner, *Competition and Entrepreneurship,* p. 86.

34. Ibid.

35. Ibid., p. 127.

36. F.A. Hayek, "Economics and Knowledge."

37. Chapter 6, comment, I.M. Kirzner, "X–Inefficiency, Error, and the Scope for Entrepreneurship," p. 149.

38. Lachmann, "From Mises to Shackle," p. 61.

39. I.M. Kirzner "Equilibrium versus Market Process" in *The Foundations of Modern Austrian Economics* ed. E.G. Dolan (Kansas City: Sheed Andrews and McMeel, 1976), pp. 115–25. Quotation at p. 121. *See also* his paper "On the Method of Austrian Economics" in the same volume pp. 40–51.

40. Kirzner, *Competition and Entrepreneurship,* p. 127.

41. Shackle, "Imagination, Formalism and Choice," p. 27.

42. Ibid., p. 27.

43. L.M. Lachmann "An Austrian Stock Taking" in L.M. Spadaro, ed., *New Directions in Austrian Economics* (Mission, Kansas: Sheed, Andrews and McMeel, 1978).

44. Shackle, "Imagination, Formalism and Choice," p. 31.

45. S.C. Littlechild, *Change Rules, OK?* (Inaugural Lecture delivered at University of Birmingham on May, 28 1977), p. 7.

46. Shackle, *Epistemics and Economics,* p. xv.

3 Is Interest the Price of a Factor of Production?

Sir John R. Hicks

The question I am going to address would be thought by many to be a nonsense question; maybe we shall decide, in the end, that it is. I must admit that I have chosen it, not for its own sake, but as a peg on which to hang something much wider, not much short of a confession of faith of an economic theorist, which may begin, not inappropriately, with a personal story.

I was brought up as a Baptist. At that time there were (in England at least) two sorts of Baptists—Particular Baptists and Open Baptists. It used to be said of the Particular Baptists that when they went to Heaven (there was no doubt that they would go to Heaven) they would be put into a little corner with a curtain round it, so that they should not know that there was anyone else in Heaven! My parents, I am glad to say, were Open Baptists. When I began to grow up, I read a book in which it was said that the poet John Milton had been reported to be an "irregular and defective" Baptist; that, I thought, was just the kind of Baptist for me. Now, at the other end of my life, I find myself addressing a congregation of Particular Austrians, while I myself am no more than an "irregular and defective" Austrian. I have ventured to give the description "neo–Austrian" to the theory which has been developed in one of my books, and it has been stamped on for heresy. So I know that I have to defend myself.

It seems to me that Austrian economics has two distinctive doctrines. The first (I accept that Particular Austrians regard it as much the more important) may be described as the Supremacy of Demand, or, better perhaps, the Supremacy of Marginal Utility. This is opposed not only to the Classical (or Marxist, or even sometimes Keynesian) determination of value by cost, but also to the Marshallian halfway house, in which both Utility and Cost play a part, like the blades of a pair of scissors, as Marshall said. The second Austrian doctrine, not at all the same as the first, is insistence on the nature of production as a process in time, with the temporal relations between inputs and outputs occupying a similarly commanding position. There are relations between these two doctrines, but they are separate. It is possible to hold to one without attaching much importance to the other.

In the days when I learned my Austrian economics, when I was working with Hayek in London in the early thirties, it was the second which appeared to our group to be the characteristic Austrian doctrine; I am sure that the same would have held, at that date, for Hayek himself. Later on, we know, he has changed his emphasis. I myself have continued to be more interested in the second doctrine; it is an approach which, on some occasions at least, I still find myself wanting to use. It appears both in *Value and Capital*[1] (1939) and in *Capital and Time*[2] (1973). The latter book I would claim to be evidence that the two doctrines really are separate. For while it is truly "neo–Austrian" in the sense of the second doctrine, the simplifying assumptions (of the single final good and the homogeneous labor), which it maintains almost throughout, enable it to avoid, almost completely, any reference to the first.

I do however recognize that the two doctrines have something in common; a relation to time. The reason such stress is laid upon valuation by utility, not cost, is because it is held that utilities are future, though often very near future, while costs are past. Bygones are bygones; decision making refers to the future. The goods that are in the shops, even the unfinished goods that are in the pipeline, would not have been produced unless it had been thought that it would pay to produce them; but now they are there, the value that is set upon them reflects their utility now. And even when the decision to produce them was taken, it was taken with an eye to their saleability, and hence to their utility, in what was *then* the future. Since it was then future, the producers did not know it; we know it, but they did not.

All that is obvious. One need not be an "Austrian" to see it, even to attach importance to it. I am sure that Marshall attached importance to it; and so, surely, did Keynes. Where the "Austrian" diverges comes later.

Though, at the time the decision to produce was taken, the future was not known, something must have been presumed about it. If nothing was presumed, the choice of things to produce must have been entirely random; it is obvious that in the real world it is not entirely random. It is not sufficient to suppose, as some would do, that production to be undertaken must be covered by forward contracts; they do of course help, but surely much production is in fact undertaken which is not so covered. Further, why should anyone enter into a contract for future delivery? He will only do so if he has some expectation of what his wants will be at the delivery date. So, whether or not there are forward contracts, production will not be undertaken unless expectations are formed, and they must have been formed in some way. Just how are expectations formed?

All, I think, would agree that expectations must be formed from past experience. (That is where the past, after all does come in.) Past experience may well be quite various, and the distillation of expectations from a complex past must itself be a complex matter. (Think of all the projectors, econometrists, and others, who are nowadays engaged upon it.) Nevertheless, however complex and sophisticated the methods of projection that are used, there is something rather simple that is common to them. The only way of making the projection that is needed is to look for some pattern that has been *normal* in the past, and then to assume that it will continue to be normal in the future, for as far ahead as it is necessary to look. This does not mean that it is assumed that the projection *will* be realized; it will not, after all, have been true that the past experience was always normal. All that is needed is the assumption that future experience, on which some view has to be taken in initiating production, will not differ, very much, from what is projected.

What does one mean by "very much"? The answer, I think, is mainly as follows. If what actually happens does not differ *very much* from what is projected, the addition of the new information, which comes from the realized experience, does not alter the norm which has been distilled from past experience; if it does differ *very much,* the norm is altered. It is of course true that if we are thinking in terms of very short time–units, days or weeks, an extremely favorable, or extremely unfavorable outcome on some particular day, or in some particular week, is unlikely to affect the norm; the divergent outcome must continue for some time before the norm is affected. That can be granted and yet the principle still holds.

All that, I hope and indeed believe, is substantially common ground; it is at the next step after that that we come to the parting of the ways. A non-Austrian economist (of almost whatever "school") would hold that it is of the greatest importance to distinguish between a condition in which norms are unchanging (so that they are not being upset by current experience) and a condition in which they are being upset. The former he would describe as a condition of *equilibrium.*

I admit that when equilibrium is defined in that way, it is wider than many of the equilibria that are found in economic writings. It does not have to be a stationary equilibrium, in which inputs and outputs are unchanging; nor does it have to be a noninflationary equilibrium, in which prices are unchanging, or some index of prices is unchanging; it could even be a fluctuating equilibrium, with a built–in cycle, such as is beloved by market analysts. All these, however, are special cases of the general concept; and I believe that it is the general concept itself which is at issue. It is the general concept itself which, even as a tool of analysis, the "Austrian" rejects.

I have a good deal of sympathy with his allergy about it. I have myself become quite critical of equilibrium economics, especially when that is taken in the way so many economists take it. Of course we know that the real world is not an equilibrium system; plans do go wrong, expectations are cheated—but how much easier it would be to understand it if that were not the case! So how tempting it is to suppose that the system studied is in equilibrium, no doubt only approximately, but approximately enough. Then we can go straight ahead, setting our mathematical engines to work on it, churning it out.

It will be noticed that in equilibrium, since what happens now (and will happen in the future if equilibrium is maintained) is similar to what has happened in the past, we can in a sense dispense with time. One period of time is just like another. I fully agree that that is very dangerous.

Nevertheless I do not believe that we can dispense with equilibrium, though we must be careful not to overuse it. It has practical uses, which we cannot afford to be without.

Some of these concern projections, or predictions of the future, if one is bold enough to so call them. As I have explained, these can be no more than extrapolations, predictions of the path that will be followed on some hypothesis; that is to say, they are extrapolations of some assumed normality, hence of some assumed equilibrium. I do not think that such projections are useless, even though they so often go astray. It is necessary, for current decisions, to peer into the future; it is rational to do so with any means that are at our disposal. I shall nevertheless not discuss that use further here. For I think that there is another use, which is perhaps less controversial. It seems to me to be more revealing.

Business decisions are directed toward the future; but not all of the work of the economist (and here I mean the *applied* economist) is directed towards the future—though if he specializes in that direction he will no doubt be of more direct use to business and will earn a larger salary! There is a part of the economist's job that is similar to that of the historian— understanding the past. It could indeed be said that when he works in that way he is being a historian; for there does not seem to be any *logical* difference between the tasks of explaining the causes of the American Civil War, or of the English Civil War, and of explaining the causes of the abortive boom of 1972–1973. There are of course differences, vast differences, in the material available for study, so that different techniques are required for its analysis; in that respect the work of the historian and the work of the economist are different from one another. Each, however, is looking for explanations. The meaning of explanation, in the one field and in the other, cannot be very different. I doubt if it is different at all.

I must not indulge myself in a disquisition on the nature of historical explanation; but there are some things about it that need to be said. If one asserts that A was the cause of B, where A is some event occurring at some time, while B is some event (or sequence of events) occurring at some later time, one must at the minimum be asserting four things. First, that A existed and second, that B existed. Third, that a state of affairs in which A did not exist, but other things contemporaneous with A did exist (so that we can give a meaning to ceteris paribus) is conceivable. Fourth, that if that state of affairs (with A not existing) had been realized, B would not have existed. Though this last assertion is crucial, it has no meaning unless we can make the others.

Of these four statements the first two are, or can be, purely factual (one can indeed think of instances in which A and B are so stated that their existence is questionably factual, since they themselves are some kind of generalization, but let that pass). The third and the fourth, however, are clearly not factual. They imply some kind of theoretical construction, which may fairly be described as a model. The model must be such that *within it A* can be treated as an independent variable; and the consequences of its presence or absence, again within the model, must be predictable.

The demands that are made upon a model, if it is to be used in this way, are evidently severe; so it may be well to take a sceptical view, holding that we have no more than a few simple models that have any hope of meeting these requirements. If the Austrian position is interpreted as expressing this scepticism, I have a good deal of sympathy with it. I would, nevertheless, observe that similar scepticism can be found in the work of at least some others, who would not usually be labelled "Austrian." Marshall himself, with his preference for application to relatively simple problems of industrial structure, may be taken as an example. It is indeed true that there are many modern economists, Keynesians but not only Keynesians, who are more ambitious. It does no harm to remind them, now and then, how fragile are the foundations on which they build their high towers.

All the same, we cannot dispense with models. All of our concepts, even those that the most orthodox follower of Menger or Mises must insist on retaining, are dependent on models, though they may indeed be rudimentary models. It is meaningless, for instance, to associate market value with marginal valuation, unless something is implied about the valuation of a quantity greater or less than the quantity actually taken. Any such valuation is a theoretical construction. The same holds for it as for points on IS or LM curves, points other than that which is supposed to be actual. All alike are theoretical, or hypothetical, constructions; all alike refer to models.

Nevertheless, though the models are hypothetical, they need to refer to reality; and that means that they must have a time–reference, at least an implicit time–reference. The timeless, or static, models which abound in our text-books are at best unfinished business; they are not complete models, capable of being used in comparisons such as I have been describing; they can be no more than the stuff out of which complete models can be made. The historical application is in this respect clarifying. Any actual experience, which we seek to explain, will be set in history; it will be a story with a beginning and an end. The beginning must be in the past, and it is best to think of the end, also, as being in the past, though it is, of course, in principle possible for the story to be taken right up to the present day. But I have often reminded my students, who have wanted to do just that, that the present goes on moving while the research continues. Now if this is the standard form of the actual experience, the hypothetical, which is to be compared with it, should take the same form. One can in fact use an equilibrium model much more safely if one keeps firmly in mind that it also is to refer to a particular time–period, with a beginning and end.

Suppose that the period that is under examination is the year 1970. The actual events of the year are recorded; we may suppose, for the present purpose, that we know all the facts about them that we need to know. We then confront this actual experience with a hypothetical experience, in which something, which we are at liberty to choose, has been changed. Now we know that the actual experience was not an equilibrium experience; there were surprises, and unforeseen changes of course. But it is hardly possible that the hypothetical experience should not be an equilibrium experience, for it is under *our* control, so there can be no surprises in it. If then we compare the actual experience, which is *not* an equilibrium experience, with a hypothetical experience, which is, we are cheating; so to make the comparison fair we are bound to doctor the actual, suppressing the surprises, even though we admit that they are important. This, I suppose, is what the "Austrian" cannot take. I would answer that if he takes that line, he must confine himself to description. He cannot proceed to the further step, of finding explanations, even of searching for explanations. I am myself not prepared to refuse the task of looking for explanations, even though I am well aware how dangerous it is. I hope that what I have said has made it clear that I do not underestimate those dangers. I think that one should always be on the lookout for ways of taking precautions against them.

If one accepts that we should always be talking about a period, or year, with beginning and end, the standard scheme of an economic process, in a closed system, within a year, is ready for use. We shall need it in what follows, so, elementary as it is, it will be well to set it out.

The year begins with a stock of goods carried over from the past; to this, during the year, a flow of services is applied. As a result a flow of outputs emerges. There remains at the end of the year a stock of goods to be carried over to the next. So, looking at the year by itself, there is a stock input and a flow input; there is a flow output and a stock output. That, I believe, is the best way of classifying; it is certainly the safest.

It does indeed have its inconveniences. It is not very convenient to have two sorts of inputs—stock inputs and flow inputs; how much handier it would be if they could be reduced to one! So some people have sought to replace the initial stock by a flow of services derived from it; and others have sought to replace the flow of labor by a stock of "human capital." Neither device, however, is necessary; I feel myself, rather strongly, that much more is gained by distinguishing.

Much also is gained, much more than symmetry, by following von Neumann in treating the *whole* terminal stock as part of output. Additions to the stock are of course to be considered as part of output—investment output; but if investment is taken net, usings–up of the initial stock have to be deducted. Even if investment is taken gross, usings–up of working capital have to be deducted. It follows that either, if taken in value terms, is a difference between one total and another; even if we take the items separately, some are positive and some negative. When we come to making comparisons, comparing what was with what might have mean, it is awkward to work with negative items. That can be avoided if we adopt the von Neumann convention.

My preliminaries are now completed. I can turn, at last, to my title question.

You will have noticed that my question falls, almost grammatically, into halves; for there is a middle term that is missing. For the moment I shall not fill it in; I shall just call it Blank. "Is interest the price of Blank?" is the first subquestion; "Is Blank a factor of production?" is the second. If the title question is to be answered in the affirmative, we must find a meaning for Blank that will enable us to marry the subquestions, answering each in the affirmative.

It is the second subquestion that turns out to be the more tricky; it forces us to decide how we define a factor of production. Economists, in general, have just enumerated. The factors of production are Land, Labor, and Capital; or just Labor and Land; or just Labor and Capital; or just Labor. Enumeration, however, is not definition; the variety of enumerations itself shows that definition is called for. With the aid of the period-schema that I have been setting out, we can, I think, get a general definition. It would run as follows.

A factor of production is anything that can serve as an input into the productive process when that is taken as a whole. This sounds harmless, but there are three items in it that need notes.

1. *Input.* It is one of the advantages that we get from the period-schema, and from the von Neumann convention that I have associated with it, that the distinction between inputs and outputs is clear-cut. There are no negative outputs, so input has a clear meaning.

2. *Taken as a whole.* "Factor" is a macroeconomic concept. Since it refers to the economy as a whole, it is not to be interpreted in terms of transactions within the economy. So it is not necessary, in order that a thing should be a factor, that it should have a price. In order that a thing should have a price, it must be appropriable; but it is not necessary that a thing should be appropriable, for it to be a factor of production. What is necessary is that it should make a contribution to production, in the sense that if it were removed, production (or output) would be diminished. Or, more usefully, if a part of it were to be removed, production would be dimin-

ished, which comes to the same thing as saying that the factor must have a marginal product. (The marginal product need not be taken in terms of an index of production in general; it is sufficient to take it in terms of some particular product, or collection of products, which has value.)

3. *Can serve as an input.* It is not necessary, in order that a thing should be a factor, that it should *actually* be producing; what is necessary is that it should be producing in some of the hypothetical alternatives that are being considered. Take for instance the case of unemployed labor. If in actuality some labor is unemployed, we do not have to deny the title of factor to that labor, so long as conditions in which it would be employed are among the alternatives that are contemplated. Only the (so-called) labor that would not be employed, or used, in any such circumstances would not be a factor.

With these understandings, I think that the definition holds.

Now I can turn to fill in, or to try to fill in, my Blank. There are several candidates. Let us call them in for examination.

It is unlucky, and can be confusing, even extremely confusing, that so many of them have the same name—Capital. It will be essential to distinguish. But for the present, I shall just call them Capital I, II, III, and so on.

Capital I is the original meaning, the business sense of the principal of a loan. There is no doubt that interest is the price of Capital I. But Capital I is not a macroeconomic concept, so it cannot be a factor of production. It falls flat on the second subquestion.

Capital II, which surely is a factor of production (as appears from the period-schema) is the initial stock of goods having value, which is inherited by the current period from the past. Capital II does have a marginal product; if there had been more of it, more of any scarce constituents of it, production could have been increased; if there had been less of it, production must have been diminished. (Remember that the terminal stock is part of production.) But interest is certainly not the price of Capital II. Capital II does have a price that can at least be imputed to it, at its own date, the starting date; this is what we call its capital value in terms of something, presumably money. And it does have another price, the annual value that is attributed to it; and the rate of interest does play a part in associating this annual value with the capital value. Even so, it cannot be true that the rate of interest is the price of Capital II, considered as annual value. The annual value of Capital II, or of any piece of equipment that enters into it, is its annual earnings, a rent or quasi rent as Marshall called it. So Capital II, though it passes my second subquestion, falls down on the first.

Capital III is still the initial stock, but it is to be taken, now, in value terms. If what we call the price of this Capital is its annual value, then its price, per unit, is the rate of interest. So Capital III may perhaps be said to pass on subquestion one. There are indeed some qualifications to that that are rather obvious; but I shall not pause to consider them here.

For the trouble with Capital III, in my view, is on the other side; is it a factor of production? Many economists, including some Austrians, have wished to so regard it; but I cannot believe that that is right. The test of a factor of production, it has been shown, is that it has a marginal product; that is to say, a change in its quantity must be conceivable, *as* a change in an independent variable; an effect of that change on production must be conceivable. Now it is of course true that if Capital II is changed, and the prices at which it is valued are unchanged, Capital III will be changed; but why should those prices be unchanged? We would expect them to be changed, in consequence of the change in Capital II. They may also change in consequence of other changes, which themselves could indeed be regarded as primary changes. Suppose, for instance, that the (flow) supply of labor is increased. We should expect that this would increase production; that is all right; labor is a factor of production; no question about that. But among the consequences of the labor change are likely to be some changes in the values of the capital goods in the initial stock, so that even if Capital II is unchanged, Capital III is changed. Since Capital III is subject, must be subject, to these induced changes, it cannot be treated as an independent variable, and hence as a factor of production.

I am of course assuming that Capital III is being valued in what Austrians (and not only Austrians) would hold to be the correct manner; that is to say, in terms of its future productivity. That, of course, is not the value that "stands in the books" of the proprietors, at the opening date. Every student of economics knows that this book value should be rejected; but I think it will be useful to keep it on our list, as Capital IV.

The ratio between the annual value of a capital good and its Capital IV value is not a rate of interest, but a rate of profit, perhaps not even a "true" rate of profit. And Capital IV cannot be a factor of production *of the period,* if it is valued at historical cost, which has nothing to do with the values, or even with the events, of the period. Could it however be restored (it has in effect so often been asked) if replacement cost values are used, in place of historic cost values? That is quite an interesting question; if we try to answer it, in our terms, the result is rather revealing.

I begin with the obvious objections to replacement cost. How does one replace, within the "year," a ten-year-old machine? We have only got one year to "age" it in. And what do we do if the manufacture of similar machines has be discontinued? The "real" cost (whatever that is) of replacing it now may be far in excess of its original "real" cost; to the actual events of this year that must be quite irrelevant. The objections are in practice insuperable; but in theory they could perhaps be avoided. Suppose that we allow ourselves to assume that the system has been in equilibrium (in one of the senses previously outlined) during the *whole life* of the machines in question, back to the date of their original construction. If such an assumption could be granted, it could be true that the forward–looking value (Capital III sense) would be equal to the replacement value (Capital IV), so that the "annual" price of Capital IV would be the rate of interest. Capital IV, in equilibrium with Capital III, would have won.

It will be clear, from what I have said already, why in my view that cannot be granted. I have (I think) shown that, so far as hypothetical constructions are concerned, the economy, during the period (or year) must be supposed to be in equilibrium. We cannot manage it otherwise. But to go on from that to suppose that it has *always* been in equilibrium is quite a different matter. It is a "relapse into statics," as I have called it in another place, a relapse into timelessness. It must surely be avoided.

Where then are we left? Do all candidates fail? Can Blank not be filled in? Perhaps there are some other candidates.

One, for whose appearance you may well have been waiting, does not properly come into sight until the period–schema has been elaborated a little further. I have said that the inputs of the period should comprise both stocks and flows; and that the outputs should comprise both stocks and flows. Now a stock, with reference to time, is quite determinate; the value of that stock is what mathematicians would call a scalar quantity. If we are measuring it in money, it is just so many dollars.

A flow, however, even in value terms, is not a scalar; it is not sufficiently described by its total over the period, or by its average over the period. It must have a distribution over time, which cannot be adequately specified by a single number. It must have a time–shape.

The time–shapes of the flows (of input and of output) is chiefly relevant to our problem when the period considered is rather long. Suppose we make it quite long, say ten years; that is as long a period as it is sensible to take. The lengthening increases the size of the flow output (regarding it as a total) relatively to the terminal stock; but it also makes the time–shape of the flow output more variable. That is to say, it increases the variety of time–shapes that can usefully be introduced into our hypothetical constructions. In particular, a flow output that starts low and rises rapidly, as against a flow output that starts higher but rises less rapidly, are effective alternatives. It could be that the initial stock is the same in each, that the flow input of labor (including its time–shape) is the same in each, even that the terminal stock is the same in each; nevertheless, especially if the period is long enough, the time–shape of the flow output, within the period, could be different. We have then to consider how we should describe the change from the one time–shape to the other.

It could happen that on the faster growing path, the total of output (which we must assume to be measurable in some invariable standard), when it is taken over the whole period, is greater than it is on the slower path. The faster path, therefore, by sacrificing some earlier outputs, has substituted later outputs, which are larger. So, looking at the total of production over the whole period, there is on the faster path an increase in production; an increase that is not to be attributed to increase in the initial stock, nor to increase in the flow of labor. To what is it to be attributed? We have to invent a factor of production to which to attribute it. There has been no agreement on the name of that factor. Senior called it Abstinence; Marshall and Cassel called it Waiting; Böhm-Bawerk roundaboutness; Barone and Wicksell just Time. It is quite hard to resist calling it Saving! But since all these terms are so "loaded," I shall refrain from using any of them. I shall just call it ITSO, for Intertemporal Switch in Output. I dare say that that will be sufficiently mysterious!

ITSO, then, can be a factor of production, under suitable conditions, if the switch is in the right direction. But it is only at the margin, in the comparison of one hypothetical path with another, that we can find a place for it. It is not like Labor, or like Capital II, which can be thought of as responsibil for the whole of production, so that if they were removed (either of them, indeed, were removed) production would be zero. It is essentially comparative. (This is where Böhm–Bawerk, with his Subsistence Fund, and the early Hayek, with his Average Period, went wrong.) It does nevertheless satisfy what we have seen to be the crucial test. It does have a marginal product.

And, still thinking in terms of hypothetical constructions, we can say that its price is the rate of interest. Any such hypothetical path, as we have seen, must be an equilibrium; that is to say, it must proceed as if there were perfect foresight *within the period*. In that equilibrium, the marginal product of ITSO and the rate of interest (in competitive conditions, if we allow ourselves to suppose them) will come together. So, perhaps, after all it is ITSO who is the successful candidate. But what an odd candidate he is!

He cannot put in an appearance unless the period that is under consideration is fairly long. For his switch, when we look at it in detail, involves first the tranference of some elements in the labor flow and of the initial stock, from the production of current flow output to the production of instruments; and second, the use of the instruments to produce additional flow output, all to be accomplished *within the period*. (It will be noticed that the *whole* of the additional flow has to be realized within the period.) On the other hand, the longer the period, the harder it is to tolerate the assumption of equilibrium over the period, the assumption on which (as we have seen) he relies. For remember what I said before about historical comparisons. We have to compare the actual sequence of events, over what is now to be a long period, say 1965–1975, with a hypothetical process, which is in equilibrium. If the comparison is to be at all fair, we have to assume that the actual experience does not differ *very much* from what it would have been if it was to be in equilibrium. Over a short period, that may be tolerable; but over ten years?

So, if we give ITSO a pass mark, we do not congratulate him upon it. Indeed there are many who would throw mud at him for it. I think I can hear them making a noise outside. You will recognize them; they are a crowd of Keynesians. We must attend to them, for they have a candidate of their own.

They have, of course, been jumping to the conclusion that I have been saying that saving is a factor of production; and that, in their view, is terrible. But I have been careful to talk about ITSO, not about saving. One can certainly recognize that there are models in which an increase in saving will not result in an increase of output at a later date, but will just result in a fall in current employment, that is to say, in current flow input. And that is certainly not productive! Our increase in ITSO, with other things equal, must imply that there is no change in current flow input; so in their terms it is an increase in saving that is matched by an increase in investment.

We still have to examine their candidate, His name is Liquidity. To say, as Keynes did, that the rate of interest depends on Liquidity Preference, and to say that rate of interest is the price of Liquidity, may be accepted to be much the same thing. So they may claim to have their Master's authority for giving Liquidity a pass on my subquestion one. Keynes did not say that Liquidity is a Factor of Production, for he did not use that language; but on our definition of Factor is that not implied in what he did say? He would certainly have said that in conditions of "involuntary unemployment" an increase in Liquidity would increase production. So it would seem that in Keynesian terms, Liquidity passes, on both counts.

It would be wrong to attempt, at the end of this paper, any serious statement of my own view of Keynesian Economics. I think I may be excused it, for I have done it elsewhere at some length: in my *Crisis in Keynesian Economics*[3] and in *Economic Perspectives*[4]. All I will say in this place is just this.

I still have the greatest admiration for many parts of Keynes's construction; but there are two critical points on which he invited misunderstanding. Or perhaps one should say that they are qualifications that are indeed present in his work—they are formally stated by him—but which, no doubt because of the time at which he was writing, during the Great Depression of the thirties, he did not feel called on to stress to the extent that (we can now see) they deserve.

The first is concealed by that unfortunate phrase *involuntary unemployment,* which does not, in Keynes, carry at all the same meaning as the ordinary man (including so many economists) would naturally attribute to it. We would now do much better to call it *Keynesian unemployment,* defining it by the consequence that he drew from its existence. Keynesian unemployment is unemployment that can be reduced by an increase in Liquidity.

The second concerns Liquidity itself. It is not the case, as a casual reading of the *General Theory* might suggest, that Liquidity can always be increased by an increase in the supply of money. Keynes is really quite clear on that. In formal statement, Liquidity is defined as money supply measured in "wage–units," that is to say, money supply deflated by a wage-index. Whether that is the correct adjustment to make, I shall not pause to consider. But we have Keynes's own authority for saying that some adjustment is necessary. It is confirmed by my own inflationary experience that circumstances are possible in which an increase in the supply of money does not increase Liquidity. Mises, you will no doubt be wanting to remind me, knew that long ago; but he was not good on Keynes's case, as Keynes (I recognize) was not good on his. *Now* we need both.

Dennis Robertson, one of whose gambits I have been imitating in the structure of this paper, had a favorite quotation from *Alice*—"everyone has won, and all must have prizes." I have been distributing prizes, but also a few slaps. You will, I fear, feel in the end that I am too Open to be an Austrian; for I am an Open Marshallian, and Ricardian, and Keynesian, perhaps even Lausannian, as well. I put perhaps to the last, for I think I have shown why I now rate Walras and Pareto, who were my first loves, so much below Menger. I hope I have shown how much I have got from him, and from thinking about him.

Notes

1. John R. Hicks, *Value and Capital,* 2nd. ed. (Oxford: Clarendon Press, 1967).
2. John R. Hicks, *Capital and Time, A Neo-Austrian Theory* (Oxford: Clarendon Press, 1973).
3. John R. Hicks, *Crises in Keynesian Economics* (New York: Basic Books, 1975).
4. John R. Hicks, *Economic Perspectives* (Oxford: Clarendon Press, 1977).

Comment: Austrian Economics Today

Ludwig M. Lachmann

In commenting on the chapter of my old teacher and friend of more than forty years, Sir John Hicks, I find myself confronted with a set of circumstances some of which make my task easier, while others make it rather harder than expected. Foremost among the former ranks the simple fact that there is so much common ground between us, so much in this chapter with which I entirely agree. At the same time, though the points on which we disagree may be few, the sources of our disagreement run rather deep.

As Hicks has told us, his subject was chosen "not for its own sake, but as a peg on which to hang something much wider, not much short of a confession of faith of an economic theorist." In this spirit, I shall confine what I have to say about his subject to a few words at the end of this comment.

For one economist to comment on another economist's *confessio fidei* may not seem quite proper, and I must keep this in mind throughout. But even such a confession cannot but refer to some facts and, as regards facts, it is always right and proper to set the record straight. Moreover, the student of Hicksian faith will surely gain a deeper understanding of it if he is able to see it in juxta-position to other faiths. A statement, however succinct and inadequate, attempting to clarify the nature of the Austrian style of thought will, not be altogether out of place in commenting on Sir John's chapter.

Let us start with what we agree on. Open-mindedness is a virtue, like other virtues more easily proclaimed than practiced. We can all agree that in our present inflationary dilemma we need both Keynes and Mises. Moreover, the time dimension of production raises fundamental problems, Böhm-Bawerk's work badly needs to be brought up-to-date, and the distinguished author of *Capital and Time* has a claim to our gratitude.

On a matter of possible misunderstanding let me set the record straight. Hicks said, "I have ventured to give the description 'neo-Austrian' to the theory that has been developed in one of my books, and it has been stamped on for heresy. So I know that I have got to defend myself." What I wrote was, "It is futile to quarrel about labels. A thinker who carries on Böhm-Bawerk's work cannot be gainsaid the predicate 'Austrian' if he claims it."[1] Stamped on for heresy? Really?

Labels, if we can agree on them without quarrel, serve a useful purpose. They help us to find our way through the thicket of ideas. It is valuable to be able to distinguish ideas by origin and timbre. To explore the relationships between the ideas of different groups of thinkers is often worthwhile and sometimes imperative.

Sir John tells us "that Austrian economics has two distinctive doctrines. The first . . . may be described as the supremacy of demand, or better perhaps, the supremacy of marginal utility . . . . The second Austrian doctrine, not at all the same as the first, is insistence on the nature of production as a process in time, with the temporal relations between inputs and outputs occupying a similarly commanding position. There are relations between these two doctrines, but they are separate. It is possible to hold to one without attaching much importance to the other." Later on he adds, "I myself have continued to be more interested in the second doctrine."

In *Capital and Time,* however, we were told, "The concept of production as a process in time . . . is not specifically 'Austrian.' It is just the same concept as underlies the work of the British classical economist, and it is indeed older still—older by far than Adam Smith."[2]

It seems to me that Sir John is inclined to underrate the unity of thought and style underlying his two Austrian doctrines. Austrian economics rests on subjectivism, a view of the social world in which human action occupies the central place. The social world consists of facts and the perspectives in which its inhabitants see them. We cannot study the former without paying heed to the latter. All action presupposes ends and means. Action, in the shape of a project, a means–end scheme, must exist in the minds of actors before it manifests itself in observable facts. Hence, it seems natural to want to explain the latter in terms of the former, and hence the Austrian insistence that all models be constructed in such a way as to make means and ends conspicuous.

Böhm-Bawerk, the most Ricardian of the Austrians, found it necessary to bring time preference, a subjective magnitude, into his explanation of the rate of interest, thus providing a link between the two doctrines. The eminent economist who in 1934 told the London Economic Club "that the marginal utility analysis is nothing else than a general theory of choice"[3] must have shared the Austrian belief in certain universal principles of action transcending specific doctrines.

Hayek has said that "it is probably no exaggeration to say that every important advance in economic theory during the last hundred years was a further step in the consistent application of subjectivism."[4] The extension of subjectivism in this century from preferences to expectations is an obvious example. Hicks seems to agree. "All, I think, would agree that expectations must be formed from past experience. . . . Past experience may well be various, and the distillation of expectations from a complex past must itself be a complex matter." No doubt it is, and perhaps the most important aspect of this complexity from the point of view of subjectivism is the divergence of expectations between individuals, between "bulls" and "bears."

Different men, sharing the same experience, will derive very different expectations from it. The divergence of expectations is as much a natural feature of the economic landscape as is the divergence of human preferences.

We now must turn to what is probably a major issue of contention, Sir John's view that in economics all explanation requires not merely a model, but an equilibrium model. Let me explain the background.

In my review of *Capital and Time,* I wrote "Economics has two tasks. The first is to make the world around us intelligible in terms of human action and the pursuit of plans. The second is to trace the unintended consequences of such action. Ricardian economics emphasized the second task, the 'subjective revolution' of the 1870s stressed the urgency of the first, and the Austrian school has always cherished this tradition. The pursuit of the second task, to be sure, need not, in principle, impede that of the first. Experience has shown, however, that formal analysis on a fairly high level of abstraction is indispensable to accomplishing our second task, in particular where the number of possibilities is large and, in order to reach any firm conclusions, we have to limit this number by restrictive assumptions which may hinder us in the pursuit of our first task."[5]

Now Hicks is in fact telling us that even our first task, that is, to understand the past and the present, cannot be accomplished without the use of equilibrium models. "If, then, we compare the actual experience which is *not* an equilibrium experience with a hypothetical experience which is, we are cheating; so to make the comparison fair we are bound to doctor the actual, suppressing the surprises, even though we admit that they are important. This, I suppose, is what the Austrian cannot take. I would answer that if he takes that line, he must confine himself to description. He cannot proceed to the further step, of finding explanations, even of searching for explanations, even though I am well aware how dangerous it is."

Nobody will deny that equilibrium models have their uses. The question is precisely where the limits of their usefulness are to be found. Equilibrium of the individual is not at issue. Austrian economists, like others, have to believe that human beings are capable of consistent action. And I know of no strong objection to Marshallian particular market equilibrium. For Austrians only the general equilibrium model of Walras and Pareto is the real stumbling block.

Hicks says, in fact, that there can be no causal imputation without a presumption of normality. It is certainly true that all causal imputation of change requires something unchanging that can serve us as a measuring rod, as time and space did in the older natural science. But why does this have to be a general equilibrium model?

Hicks tells us that "If one asserts that *A* was the cause of *B,* where *A* is some event occurring at some time, while *B* is some event (or sequence of events) occurring at some later time'' one needs a model of explanation ''such that within it *A* can be treated as an independent variable; and the consequences of its presence or absence, again within the model, must be predictable.''

The accent is here heavily on determinateness and necessity, and the question arises of how we are to deal with those many cases where economic relationships are contingent and not necessary. We surely must find some looser form of model to account for them. Our greatest difficulty is, of course, that human action, in its more interesting forms, cannot be pressed into this mold without losing most of its distinguishing characteristics, so that our attempt at ''causal explanation'' ends with our inability to understand anything worth knowing.

The causal scheme of explanation here presented clearly applies to observable events such as *A* and *B*. It is less clear that it can apply to circumstances in which ''the cause of *B*'' (in the sense of antecedent circumstances), is not an observable event, but a project, a plan envisaging events that may take place much later than *B,* that is, where we have to deal with causality not a tergo but a fronte.

We should also remember the amount of damage that has been done in the history of our discipline by ill–considered attempts to turn contingent relationships into apparently necessary ones by blocking all alternative outcomes by means of restrictive assumptions until only one was left for us to contemplate. This is what Schumpeter, as ''open'' an Austrian as you might wish for, called the Ricardian vice. Before we embrace the belief that necessity is the only admissible ground of explanation, let us remember his description of it: ''[Ricardo] cut that general system to pieces, bundled up as large parts of it as possible, and put them in cold storage—so that as many things as possible should be frozen and 'given.' He then piled up one simplifying assumption upon another until, having really settled everything by these assumptions, he was left with only a few aggregative variables between which, given these assumptions, he set up simple one–way relations so that, in the end, the desired results emerged almost as tautologies.''[6]

Sir John, to be sure, did not mean to turn Ricardian vice into Hicksian virtue, but he has provided its practitioners with at least a plausible defense. They may now claim that all they have done is, to the best of their ability, to follow the Hicksian injunction to construct schemes of strict causation.

In the passage quoted earlier, I used the words ''making the world around us intelligible in terms of human action and the pursuit of plans.'' Perhaps I was fortunate to avoid the word ''explanation,'' now seen to be surrounded by some ambiguity.

The Austrian plea for a widening of our terms of explanation is an obvious response to the situation in which economic theory finds itself today. There are hardly any empirical laws to provide us with enough fuel and power to keep an impressive number of causal schemes of explanation going. The economic world is full of contingent relationships, and we must surely make some attempt to come to terms with them and understand them as best we can. To insist on the finding of sufficient conditions in all cases is to leave us impotent to deal with the many cases in which all we shall ever know about the causes of a phenomenon are a few necessary conditions. Models are indeed indispensable, and even models precariously held together by ceteris paribus conditions have their uses, provided we acknowledge, at an early stage, our obligation to look into circumstances in which some cetera are not paria.

Professor Hicks wrote, "There is a part of the economist's job which is similar to that of the historian–understanding the past." I quite agree. Who would want to quarrel with the eminent author of "A Theory of Economic History"? Good historians, however, use the notion of necessity sparingly and with some caution. They shun "historical inevitability" and smile at predictability. When they have to explain a complex situation, they often take great pains to make us understand what alternatives were open to the actors on the scene *as they saw it*. Why should we not follow them in this?

At last I ask, "Is interest the price of a factor of production?" I think we should accept the conclusion that ITSO, intertemporal switch in output, may be regarded as a factor, and the cogent argument on which it is based, as in the spirit of the modern Austrian school. It is true that Böhm–Bawerk would probably reject ITSO, as he rejected Senior's abstinence, but we may ascribe his reluctance to excessive devotion to the Ricardian faith.

" 'Factor' is a macroeconomic concept" we are told. Austrians would probably like to see it reduced to microeconomic terms. I need hardly tell Hicks that they are all committed "catallactists," so they naturally distrust the vocabulary of plutology.

The rate of interest is a price. We would all very much like to know something about the market forces that shape it and the structure of the markets in which these forces operate. Sir John must have felt some such need himself when he said of ITSO that in Keynesian terms "it is an increase in saving which is matched by an increase in investment." So he seems to feel that an explanation of the phenomenon in terms of subjectivism, of the convergence of individual plans, is called for. Austrians therefore will probably be inclined to see in the conclusion of his chapter the starting point of a promising research program rather than a settled conclusion to be wrapped up and taken home.

Austrian economists do not need to be reminded that they are not alone in the world. Those of them who are old enough can remember a time when they were not even supposed to exist. The opening page of the "Hayek Story" reflects this situation: here the author found it necessary to tell the reader (in 1967) who Hayek, the economist, was. Things have changed since then. When Sir John tells us that he now rates Walras and Pareto, his "first loves," so much below Menger, it is possible to feel that the long era of neo-classical ascendancy is drawing to a close. In the new situation a dialogue of the various schools, and of members of various schools, is possible and deserves to be encouraged.

An open mind is a virtue but not everybody is a Hicks. It is not merely that few of us can aspire to the level of Hicksian virtue as none of us can to his other achievements. Within the community of scholars different parts are played by different players.

For forty years Hicks has been the great broker of ideas who has regarded it as his main task to accomplish a synthesis of the ideas of the age. And how successful he has been! It may well happen that when, a few decades hence, the history of economic thought in the twentieth century comes to be written, the last forty years will be described as the *age of Hicks*. I think it would be an apt description. But if all of us were to set up as brokers of ideas, the outcome could hardly be other than disastrous, and not merely because viable markets cannot consist of brokers only.

A broker of ideas needs an open mind before everything, but his clients may have other needs. There are those humble souls who find it easier to let their thought grow and take shape within the narrow confines of a "school," with the needed encouragement of kindred spirits, than they would within a wider and more open, but also less companionable world. Ideas may have to pass many and diverse minds before becoming negotiable objects for our brokers, and the virtues which Sir John, in the splendor of his office, ranks highest may be accorded a somewhat lower status by some of the more humble minds among his clients.

Notes

1. Ludwig M. Lachmann, *Capital, Expectations and the Market Process* (Kansas City: Sheed, Andrews and McMeel, 1977), p. 261.

2. Ibid., p. 12.

3. John Hicks, *Critical Essays in Monetary Theory* (Oxford: Clarendon Press, 1967), p. 63.

4. F.A. Hayek, *The Counter-Revolution of Science,* (Glencoe 1952), p. 31.

5. Lachmann, *Capital Expectations,* pp. 261–262.

6. Joseph A. Schumpeter, *History of Economic Analysis* (Oxford: Oxford University Press, 1954), pp. 472–473.

4 Uncertainty, Subjectivity, and the Economic Analysis of Law

Mario J. Rizzo

The economic analysis of law is a new and growing field within the domain of applied economics. Yet, as in the case of all applied fields, from time to time, it has fallen prey to some of the profound confusions and misapprehensions of economic theory. In addition, it has been overly selective in the choice of legal doctrines used to illustrate the alleged efficiency of the common law.

Our task will be twofold: (1) we shall try to demonstrate the legal inconsistencies and problems involved in the efficiency claim for common law doctrines; and (2) we shall attempt to shed light on some of the economic difficulties of the claim by an excursion into the world of disequilibrium economics. This task is as much constructive as it is critical, for in alerting us to some very common pitfalls, we shall have taken a great step in the direction of enhancing the important contributions economics can indeed make to the study of law.

Ambiguity of the Efficiency Idea

If the claim that the common law is "efficient" is to have any useful meaning, an alternative possibility must be specified. The alternative hypothesis implicitly refuted in most of the economics of law literature appears to be that the common law promotes some nonoverlapping standard of "equity."[1] But can we make a distinction between these two concepts in a way that is not largely arbitrary? A moment's consideration will show this to be impossible. Efficiency exists only in relation to certain ends or objectives. Narrowly conceived, it can be defined in terms that amount to little more than maximizing gross national product. This, however, immediately breaks down once externalities are introduced into the system. The standard

I am indebted to Professors Israel Kirzner, Ludwig Lachmann, and Fritz Machlup of New York University, and to Mr. Frank Arnold of Harvard University for helpful discussions. I am particularly indebted to Mr. Michael Becker of the New York University School of Law for a great deal of assistance on the discussion of legal doctrines in the second section. I also wish to thank the Scaife Foundation for financial support of my research. None of the above are responsible for the views expressed or errors committed.

then used is the maximization of national product as it would look in a world of zero transactions costs, net of the costs involved in "properly" distributing legal liabilities. Therefore, to attain the minimization of the sum of accident and accident prevention costs, legal liability ought to be placed on the least-cost avoider of the accident—a result that would be already achieved in a world of costless transactions.[2]

What happens, then, if the common-law courts decide that in some kinds of cases liability will be placed on the greatest-cost avoider or, still more generally, if the allocation of liability is made without regard to cost considerations? Is the common law to be deemed inefficient? The answer to this depends, of course, on the relevant objective functions in the model being used. If the ends with respect to which maximization is hypothesized to take place do not include the dictates of the equity standard then, obviously, the answer must be in the affirmative. Yet, to the extent that common-law judges reflect the equity standards of the society in which they live, what possible justification can there be for excluding some "social" objectives? In economics, at least, all effective demands are created equal. The systematic exclusion of certain ends would require the intrusion of external values into the analysis.[3]

Efficiency is a concept that has no meaning apart from the model that happens to be in use. Efficiency is always relative to the objectives and subject to the constraints specified in a theoretical framework.

Simply, the point is this: the question is not whether the common law is efficient or not. Of course, it is efficient. The question is rather whether it is efficient relative to some set of arbitrarily preselected objectives or whether it is efficient in terms of the effective demands (or revealed preferences) of the common-law judges' "constituency" (analogous to consumers). The latter is necessarily the only relevant benchmark. Along these lines, it may be contended that common-law courts don't reflect the interests of *all* members of society but, rather, only those who utilize resources in an effort to affect case law (for example, through litigation, influencing those who appoint judges, and so forth). This is readily admitted but of no importance from the economic perspective. To repeat, only *effective* demands count and those who sit at home wishing things were otherwise will not affect the law.

The common law, then, is necessarily efficient in relation to any relevant (that is, internally imposed) standard. This follows from the rationality of the maximizing framework itself (and if an exception were ever to be observed, it would only mean that we hadn't understood what we were doing). It is only by arbitrarily excluding certain objectives (for example, equity) from the model that the possibility of finding the common law to be inefficient emerges. If we try to avoid this arbitrariness, we then find ourselves trapped in what turns out to be an empty box. If in any relevant sense the common law can *never* be inefficient, how interesting is the claim that it is efficient? At bottom, what is really being claimed has nothing at all to do with efficiency. In fact, to the extent that the common law is said to ignore society's views of equity, the claim is really being made that the law is *in*efficient. This, of course, is not how we choose to look at it and such a conclusion stems from the original arbitrariness involved in specifying the model.

Inconsistencies and Problems

Let us now put aside the argument of the previous section, and examine the internal coherence of the claim that the common law promotes "efficiency." To examine these matters in some depth, we shall confine ourselves to a study of some important doctrines in the law of torts. There are two major aspects of our argument: (1) in a number of important areas the courts have behaved in a way that is inconsistent with the (narrowly construed) efficiency hypothesis; and (2) in other important areas this "economic principle" is more generally incapable of dealing with the observed behavior of the courts.

1. The good Samaritan problem is, perhaps, the classic case of the law's refusal to apply narrow efficiency criteria to situations of nonfeasance.[4] *B,* a stranger, sees *A* drowning in a pool. Assume that *B* could, at minimal cost to himself, save *A.* Clearly, it will be said, if transactions costs were zero, *A* would have been willing to pay *B* more than enough to compensate his costs in order to be rescued. Hence, the economic approach would conclude that *B ought* to be held liable for *A*'s injuries or death. Yet the law does not see the matter in this way. It has, of course, been admitted by at least one proponent of the "efficiency" view "that the law is out of phase with economic analysis in the matter of warnings and rescues."[5] Nevertheless, it is asserted that "affirmative duties to avert him to strangers are frequently imposed" and hence, "the law's handling of the Good Samaritan case [is not] quite so inconsistent with the basic logic of economic analysis."[6] The doctrine of the last clear chance is proffered as an example.

To examine this, consider a paradigmatic last clear chance situation. A man is negligently sitting on the subway tracks and the driver of the train could have (or might have) been able to save the man's life by taking reasonable action.[7] He doesn't; the man is killed. The law holds the driver or his employer liable in such situations. Clearly, however, the negligent man could have avoided the whole incident at little cost by not sitting on the subway tracks in the first place. "The economic rationale of this rule, we are told, "is that . . . *at the moment* when the train is bearing down upon [the victim] it is the engineer who can avoid the accident at least cost and this cost is substantially less than the expected accident cost."[8]

Compare now the doctrine that "in general the negligent act of a third party is not held to negative causal connection."[9] The driver of an oil truck, for example, finds that, because of his negligence, oil is spilling out into the street. A passerby then negligently throws a lighted cigarette into that street. A fire starts as a consequence and a building is seriously damaged. The law finds that the driver is liable because the negligence of the passerby does not break the causal chain. Yet, obviously, *at the moment* of the oil spill the passerby is the least-cost avoider of the (further) accident.

This is more than perhaps an inconsistency between two important legal doctrines, although it is true that the argument that demonstrates the efficiency of the last clear chance demonstrates the *in*efficiency of the causation doctrine. The most relevant issue, however, is the difference in results one gets by looking at different time frames. The least-cost avoider may be different depending on the run chosen by the analyst. Consider that the immediate-run least-cost avoiders are the trainman and the passerby in the above cases. The longer-run avoiders, on the other hand, should be the trespasser and the truckdriver. Which, then, is the correct time frame? Some may think that the law should concern itself with the long time-frame.[10] However, the longer the time frame, the more important will be the possibility of technological changes. A development in technology can transform a least-cost avoider into a greatest-cost avoider by altering (unequally) the marginal costs of accident prevention. Placing liability on the (immediate or short-run) least-cost avoider may well be uneconomic in the longer perspective. It eliminates or reduces the incentives for appropriate research and development. Yet the future course of technology cannot be predicted.[11] Furthermore, it is not possible to draw up for each party a (presumably) complete list of the possible technological advances and, therefore, optimal (court) decisions in a probabilistic context are also out of the question.[12] To speak of an efficient allocation of liability in such situations is surely a misnomer.

There is, additionally, an element of tautology involved in the distinction between long- and short-run efficiency. *Any* state of affairs can be efficient if the run is taken as long or short enough. Efficiency, as we have previously indicated, is relative to a model. It is not surprising, then, that by manipulation of the time frame one can transform an inefficient situation into an efficient one.

Recent developments in the area of medical malpractice are possibly inconsistent with the hypothesis that the common law is efficient. Prior to 1972, the state of the law that the customary standard of care was permitted as a defense in negligence actions. If a physician could show that he had acted in accordance with the prevailing practice in the medical profession, he could thereby adequately defend himself against accusations of negligence. This can be rationalized as an economically sound outcome.[13] In buyer (patient) and seller (physician) relationships, the latter has an economic incentive to provide the standard of care for which people are willing to pay. Therefore, it is efficient to make the physician liable for only subcustomary care. Presumably, the average consumer thought he was buying the average degree of care, and it is only when he gets *less* than this that there is any damage.[14]

The law changes, and this rationalization of the custom-defense in medical malpractice was rudely unraveled. In *Canterbury* v. *Spence* (1972) the court held that a physician has a duty to disclose to his patient the risks of an operation *even where* it is not customary to do so.[15] Later in *Helling* v. *Carey* (1974) the court reinforced this duty-of-disclosure position in a glaucoma case.[16] It was the custom among ophthalmologists not to give tests for glaucoma, as a general rule, to patients under forty. As the number of cases of glaucoma in young patients amount to 1 in 25,000 it was presumably thought that patients preferred not to undergo such tests in the absence of any indications of the disease. Yet the court knew better, claiming that the test was relatively inexpensive and hence ought reasonably to be given. Again, a clear case of custom proved an ineffective defense.

If the pre-1972 situation was efficient as claimed then, by the same argument, the post-1972 law cannot be. This, however, is not the main lesson to be drawn from the above illustration, especially since we can rationalize the inconsistency as being merely apparent. We can quite plausibly claim that, in the absence of advertising by physicians, consumer information is not adequate to ensure that they will indeed be able to purchase the degree of care that they desire. Yet, on the other hand, even without advertising, information travels in the form of a doctor's reputation. So there is *some* information; consumers are not making decisions in the dark. How are we to know if the information they do have is inadequate enough to warrant this intervention by the legal system? How much information is too little? Without direct observation of the quantity and quality of information possessed by patients, one can rationalize any result in the law by appropriately adjusting the presumed information component. Furthermore, the answer to our question is not at all obvious because the consumers need not possess the technical knowledge of the physicians to make efficient choices. One can choose as between paternalistic doctors and high-disclosure doctors, if there is knowledge of their existence. Finally, even if we had direct observation of the informational component, how would we know when it is inadequate?

2. In a number of other areas the courts have developed doctrines that are not so much in conflict with the efficiency interpretation of common law as they are irrelevant to it. There are important classes of situations in which the "economic interpretation" does not yield a determinate implication for legal doctrine.

Consider, first, cases in which *neither* party can economically avoid an accident. Situations such as these should not be hard to imagine since even in an optimal world some accidents will occur. In *Vincent* v. *Lake Erie Transport,* for example, the defendant kept his boat tightly fastened to a dock during a violent storm.[17] The winds drove the boat into the dock causing $500 worth of damages. Both parties would probably have incurred more than $500 in costs to avoid the accident and hence the outcome was an economic one. Nevertheless, the court placed liability on the *causal* agent,[18] that is, the boat's captain, rather than letting the losses fall where they may.[19] From the efficiency point of view the court ought to have found no reason for making the captain liable since the allocation of resources would not thereby have been improved.

The degree to which an accident is foreseeable has assumed an enormous importance in the tort law. The courts usually consider an event "unforeseeable" if the expected value of losses is very low.[20] "If the defendant could not reasonably foresee any injury as the result of his act," Prosser tells us, "or if his conduct was reasonable in light of what he could anticipate, there is no negligence, and no liability."[21] From an efficiency standpoint, however, it makes no difference who bears the liability in cases of unforeseeability. Resources will not be utilized to avoid an accident when its expected losses are very low.[22]

In all such cases where the determination of liability does not affect the allocation of resources, the "economic interpretation" does not produce determinate result for court behavior. Yet the outcomes in such cases do not appear to be random. In situations of unforeseeability the damages are permitted to fall where they may, but, on the other hand, in circumstances such as those in *Vincent* v. *Lake Erie Transport* the causal agent is made to shoulder liability. Furthermore, it seems implausible that the considerations operative in these cases would be entirely absent in all others.

Both the legal and the economic issues are confused somewhat by the important distinction between the kind of damage and the extent of damage (of a given kind).[23] Although an individual is not to be held liable for unforeseeable kinds of harm he will be held liable for unforeseeable extents of harm. Even if there were some affirmative economic rationale for the allocation of liability in situations of unforeseeable consequences, there is certainly no economic rationale for the distinction just cited. For example, suppose that because of the driver–defendant's negligence there is a car accident during which the plaintiff, the driver of the other car, suffers an epileptic seizure as a result of the accident. Is the defendant liable for the damages brought on by the (presumably unforeseeable) seizure as well as the other damages? According to the principle discussed above, he is completely liable. The epileptic seizure is within the scope of the risk, constituting as it does an extent of damage within a (given) kind of damage. Economically, however, the distinction is irrelevant as no resources will be utilized to prevent unforeseeable losses, whether they are dubbed "extent" or "kind."

In intentional torts the applicable rule is "You take your victim as you find him." All that is required for full liability is that the damage be causally related to the intended "offensive touching." Foreseeability plays no role here in establishing liability. Clearly, some of the consequences of an intentional interference with another person will not be foreseeable. For example, if *A* intentionally kicks *B*, who unbeknown to *A* is a hemophiliac, then *A* is still fully liable for *B*'s death due to the resultant bleeding.[24] It is hard to argue that *A* should have foreseen the possibility of *B*'s hemophilia. Nevertheless, the law assigns liability to *A*. This is in sharp contrast to the "let the damages fall where they may" attitude with regard to unforeseeable *types* of damage in negligence cases. To distinguish between negligence and intentional torts by claiming that the former consists of accidents while the latter are intended harms is terribly superficial. The unforeseeable consequences of an intentional torts constitute the *accidental component* of the act. Economically, the two ought to be viewed as identical. The law, however, sees things otherwise.

Causation

In the previous section our discussion of *Vincent* v. *Lake Erie Transport* alluded to the importance the court seemed to place on the issue of causality. We have not, though, even scratched the surface of the legal and philosophical complexities of this subject nor, fortunately, do we intend to. Our purpose is far more modest: we intend to show that elimination of the causal framework from the economists' approach to questions of law has serious economic consequences.

Let us first establish the "economic" standpoint on this matter. Guido Calabresi, for example, claims that he "does not propose to consider the question of what, *if anything,* we mean when we say that specific activities 'cause,' in some *metaphysical* sense, a given accident."[25] Ronald Coase wishes to view costly interactions as being reciprocal in nature.[26] Both the railroad and the farmer are responsible for the damages in his famous "spark" cases.

This reciprocity view will become clearer if we consider a simple example. *A* emits smoke onto *B*'s property and thereby soils *B*'s laundry, which is hanging on a clothes line. Now *A could* stop the emission or *B could* buy a clothes dryer. On commonsense principles, though, we say that *A caused* harm to *B*. However, in economics the refusal to act when one has the opportunity is as much an "action" as any "positive" act.[27] Purposeful noninterference in the course of events is still action. Hence, it is claimed that from the economic perspective, the distinction between misfeasance and nonfeasance vanishes.[28] *A* and *B* are both just as responsible and the only question becomes who is the least–cost avoider. Unfortunately, this conclusion, while embodying a substantial amount of truth, is seriously misleading. Rejection of the economic importance of causation leads quite reasonably to the treatment of costs and benefits as disembodied entities. From this perspective, the perception of costs (benefits) by the particular parties to, say, an accident is an unimportant intermediary step. Costs and benefits are viewed as having an existence that transcends the perceptions of those individuals: costs are *objective* "social" phenomena. It is this view that we must reject.

The Nature of Costs

As we have previously indicated, the conventional economic analysis of law sees the body of tort doctrine as aiming at the minimization of accident costs to society. Until now, we have assumed that if one arbitrarily narrows the meaning of the term "efficiency" it is at least *possible* for a tort law to be efficient. There are, however, some fundamental considerations of economic theory that make it highly questionable that the law can ever be efficient *in the sense of* a judicial balancing of costs and benefits.

The issues to be discussed in this section constitute an elementary lesson in economics but, for reasons that will become clear later, this lesson has not been fully appreciated. From at least the time of Stanley Jevons, economists have known that historical costs have no influence on price. They have furthermore understood (assuming they have read Böhm-Bawerk) that production takes time. From this it follows that only *expected* costs can influence price: the value that needed resources are expected to have in alternative endeavors will determine the amount that producers intend to produce for any given expectation of price. The distinction between expected and historical magnitudes is, of course, largely unimportant in a world of general equilibrium. In such a world, mistakes are not made and all expectations prove correct. More importantly, in general competitive equilibrium the prices of resources will accurately reflect the value of alternative uses of these resources to society.[29] If this were not so, these prices would be bid up or down until such equality is obtained.

Alas, we do not live in a world of general competitive equilibrium. In fact, we must be outside such a world in order to have any of the problems that the law of torts itself is designed to remedy. The coexistence of nonpecuniary externalities and general competitive equilibrium is impossible.

General equilibrium presupposes a market in every commodity so that all benefits and costs are incorporated into the price mechanism. The law of torts enters the picture precisely because the actual system (otherwise) permits uncompensated costs to be imposed involuntarily on individuals. In other words, we need tort law because the price system is, so to speak, "limited."

We live in a world of continual change in the underlying data that define a general equilibrium position (that is, in tastes, resources, and technology) as well as one in which there is a great deal of uneradicated, and perhaps uneradicable, ignorance. As a consequence, not all prices are correct general equilibrium prices since, at the very least, they will be based on erroneous expectations. (Here we are not even mentioning the existence of static monopoly.) For example, the prices of flow inputs will not be equal to their true alternative-use values because the latter will not be known. What we *expect* that these resources would be worth in alternative uses is not an objective datum. Indeed, as Ronald Coase has reminded us, "costs are not necessarily the same as payments. It is this fact that makes the 'costs' disclosed by cost accountants something quite different from 'opportunity cost'."[30] In addition, the opportunity cost of the services from stock inputs (for example, machines) will be affected by the subjective factors that determine user cost. Use of a machine in a particular way in the present, Coase further remarks, "means that profits that would have been earned at the end of its life will now no longer be received."[31] What these profits are and how much will be sacrificed is again dependent on subjective estimates of the future. Finally, the alternative cost of the *sources* of flow services will reflect divergent and conflicting expectations of future opportunities for their use. Therefore, in a world where expectations of the future may be contradictory the external observer will find it impossible merely to choose a consistent subset and pronounce them objective.

In general *dis*equilibrium individual agents try, as it were, to out-guess market prices: at the very least, some factors will be underpriced and undercapitalized while others will be overpriced and overcapitalized relative to their "true" general equilibrium values. In such an environment agents will (correctly and incorrectly) perceive many pure profit opportunities, but only to the extent that their guesses turn out to be accurate will their activities be corrective of disequilibria.

When, therefore, profit opportunities are perceived as available, the genuine opportunity cost of any activity must include those *expected* foregone profits available elsewhere in the system.[32] The cost of an investment is not merely the direct outlay cost (plus, say, the interest or normal rate of "profit" return on it); it includes also the pure profits perceived as possible in the next best alternative. The existence of these profits does not constitute a certain objective datum. If this were the case, then the opportunities would be *immediately* eliminated or, better yet, they would never have come into existence at all in such a world.

We are now in a position to shed some further light on the issue of accident cost minimization in general and the least–cost avoider question in particular. Recall that efficiency requires liability to be placed on the least–cost avoider of a costly interaction.

Suppose that two individuals, *A* and *B,* can both economically avoid an accident between them. *A* can avoid it by an expenditure on resources that have a disequilibrium market value of $50, while *B* can do the same by an expenditure of $75 on different resources that are also disequilibrium-priced. Assuming that we possess this information with certainty, can we then say that social costs will be minimized if liability is placed on *A*? We cannot. It does not follow that the social opportunity cost of *A*'s resources exceeds that of *B*. Even if we knew the *subjective* opportunity costs (direct outlays—$50 or $75—plus perceived alternative profit opportunities) of the two individuals (and we do not), we still would not be any closer to the true social opportunity costs. This is because individual estimates of foregone profit opportunities elsewhere in the system can and will be wrong. If this were not the case, there could never be any losses.

There are then essentially two points. First, agents try in disequilibrium to outguess existing market prices. As a consequence opportunity costs must include a subjective estimate of profit available elsewhere in the system. Direct outlays do not represent true opportunities foregone. Second, even the full costs as perceived by the market participants do not represent accurate social opportunity costs because of the likelihood of incorrect estimates.

Although it may be granted that the system is never in a state of general competitive equilibrium and that the subjective estimates of agents about foregone profit opportunities could be wrong, it may be asked: will they be wrong by a "significant" amount? This question confuses estimates about events that *will* take place with those about events that *could have* taken place, but did not. Since the alternative courses of action were, by definition, not undertaken, there will be no direct evidence against which one can check the accuracy of entrepreneurial judgments.[33] The alternative revenues will not materialize. Statements about foregone profit opportunities are *counterfactual* and hence are, in principle, not directly falsifiable.

Let us now return to the disequilibrium market prices themselves. The "virtue" of dealing with prices of resources, even if they are in disequilibrium, is that they are objective. So perhaps the status of disequilibrium prices deserves some further investigation.

Since, presumably, individuals are doing the best they can in estimating the divergence from general equilibrium prices (that is, they are searching for profit opportunities), can we say that disequilibrium market prices represent society's best guess of the alternative value of resources? Remember that this is not a simple case of agents trying their best to hit an ordinary target; here we are dealing with a "moving target," that is, the underlying data are undergoing change as these agents try to adjust.[34] The answer to our question must, unfortunately, be no. This is because the market disequilibrium price (or, more likely, prices) of a resource is the result of *inconsistent* estimates of its alternative uses. Outside of general equilibrium, only a single individual's estimates of the values of resources can be consistent (that is, self-consistent). It does not matter whether that individual is a particular market participant or a central planner. A disequilibrium price is the result of inconsistent or divergent expectations; it is, in a sense, the homogenization of contradictory forecasts. In what sense, then, can that be a useful approximation of general equilibrium prices?

At any given point in time, the market *process* does not take resource prices "literally". The expectations of participants—*upon whom the consequences of the inaccuracy of these expectations fall*—will serve to "correct" the misinformation of disequilibrium prices. The market, unlike the efficiency motivated common-law judge, is not a literalist.

The root of the problem here lies in the hopeless ambiguity that enshrouds the whole concept of social cost in a disequilibrium world. Strictly speaking, outside of general equilibrium, the word *social* as it is generally used has no coherent meaning. In a world of complete plan consistency society is, as it were, an integrated organism. Introduce now the inconsistency of plans ("general disequilibrium") and we have many individuals pursuing incompatible ends and possessing contradictory expectations. In such a world there is no single, unambiguous social cost: not everyone perceives the alternatives sacrificed in the same way.

Whither General Equilibrium?

We have insisted that the implications of disequilibrium analysis for judicial cost-benefit calculations are indeed profound. It casts serious doubt on the ability of the common law to promote efficiency by attempting to minimize objectively measurable costs. The judge ought not to be confused with the entrepreneur who reaps the rewards of correct decisions.

Those who deal in social cost-benefit analysis implicitly view the world as if it were in general equilibrium. Aside from the contradiction involved in trying to reconcile the existence of tort problems and general competitive equilibrium, this viewpoint does grave injustice to the nature of conceptual frameworks in economics. Indeed, as Fritz Machlup has commented, "To characterize a concrete situation 'observed' in reality as one of 'equilibrium' is to commit the fallacy of misplaced concreteness."[36] In fact, Frank Hahn has recently admitted that there is "no presumption that a sequence of actual economic states will terminate in"[37] general competitive equilibrium. Furthermore, he is not willing to claim that general equilibrium can be viewed as even the asymptotic outcome of real world processes.[38] Alan Coddington has made the point still more explicitly, that "equilibrium is not a state of the economy, any more than the long-run is a point in time."[39]

What, then, *is* general equilibrium? It is a conceptual tool designed to help us "tackle one problem at a time,"[40] and to ensure that we have analytically traced out *all* of the consequences of a given change.[41] Frequently, although not always, we begin from a state of general equilibrium so as to make sure that no more than one (disequilibrating) change is occurring at once, and we end up in a general equilibrium so that all of the adjustments will be analytically fully worked out. General equilibrium exists in the mind of the economist and not in the real world. Remember that not every conceptual tool need be directly operational. It is this failure to distinguish between a conceptual apparatus that assists us in organizing our thoughts and one that refers to something directly observable that is responsible for the inability to comprehend our elementary economics lesson.

Uncertainty

In our previous discussion of general disequilibrium we have, of necessity, already addressed the question of uncertainty. However, we have not yet directly focused on the precise nature of the concept and on its drastic implications for most forms of cost–benefit analysis. This is what we must now undertake.

The utilization of resources to prevent accidents necessarily involves decision making in an uncertain world. Individuals, for example, will be found negligent if they fail to take accident-prevention measures when the cost of those measures, however determined, falls short of or equals the *expected value* of losses. (This is the famous Hand formula.) Typically, then, economists have handled the issue of uncertainty with probability theory.[42] The probability calculus is, in turn, applicable to both an objective and subjective conception of the content of probability statements. We shall divide our analysis into a brief consideration of each of these viewpoints.

Objective probability statements—in the sense of the limit of a sequence of relative frequencies—are in principle unfalsifiable. For example, if we say that when a fair coin is tossed the probability of heads is 0.5, do we consider the proposition falsified if in a hundred tosses heads comes up only forty-two times? Of course not. We merely say that the number of tosses must, strictly speaking, approach infinity and so we haven't tossed the coin enough. In addition, we may even say that the coin was not "fair" or the conditions of the toss were not just right, and so forth. It was precisely this problem that led Karl Popper to introduce a convention or methodological rule that would permit falsification of probability statements.[43] In essence, his convention says that if in a relative-frequency sequence there are predictable, reproducible, and systematic deviations from the hypothesized probability, we shall consider it falsified. The most relevant criterion for us is the *reproducibility* of the deviation. This immediately sets up the requirement that the event in question must be repeatable if the probability assigned to a specific outcome is to be falsifiable and, hence, objective. For example, hypothesize that the probability of a certain outcome in a game of chance is 0.5. Now, if the game is played a hundred times and that outcome appears in only thirty percent of the cases, do we then proclaim the hypothesis falsified? Not quite yet. If we continue to play the game and the observed relative frequency of 0.3 persists, then we ought to seriously reconsider. The rule "does not forbid the occurrence of a-typical segments; neither does it forbid the *repeated* occurrence of deviations," rather, what it forbids is "the occurrence of segments which are a-typical in a *definite* way."[44]

The reader's patience may now be exhausted: What does this have to do with judicial cost-benefit analysis? The relevance is immediate. Unless we are dealing with *reproducible* stochastic phenomena the objectivity claim of probability statements disintegrates. Assignments of probability without reproducibility are strictly nonfalsifiable. Hence, insofar as they refer to empirical (and not ideal) processes, we have no way of judging their truth or falsity.

In some situations, of course, reproducibility is an actual feature. When, for example, millions of coca-cola bottles are being produced, we doubtless have a good idea of the probability that at least one bottle in the series will explode. Similarly, the evidence of mortality tables seems to provide useful information to insurance companies since they can pool individual cases.

In circumstances such as these, there is no great problem in deciding how a "reasonable man"[45] would view the likelihood of certain outcomes. He would merely accept the objective (and falsifiable) probability. This, of course, does not solve the problem, discussed above, of measuring social opportunity costs but it does tell us what the "correct" probability weights are to plug into the Hand formula.

Many situations, however, are what Shackle has called "self-destructive" experiments.[46] In these a crucial part of the initial conditions of the experiment is the state of the human agents' knowledge. When the outcome of a single experiment (for example, the failure of a business) changes the state of knowledge, that experiment can never be repeated. As Shackle reminds us: "in a great multitude and diversity of matters the individual has no record of a sufficient number of sufficiently similar acts, of his own or other people's, to be able to construct a valid frequency table of the outcomes of acts of this kind. Regarding these acts, probabilities are not available to him."[47]

The widespread availability of objective frequency ratios presupposes equilibrium just as does the availability of objective measures for the social opportunity cost of resources. In the former case, however, the equilibrium is of a different kind. For universally objective probability we require a stochastic stationary equilibrium: a world in which probabilistic events eternally reproduce themselves so that we all know what the relevant probabilities are. Until such a world comes about, and most of us are not waiting for it, we will have to deal with circumstances of "insufficient" information.

The problem of nonrepeatability leads us logically to consider *subjective* probability. Yet this issue will not detain us very long. Subjective probability is merely the name we give a set of personal decision weights that satisfy the formal rules of combination known as the probability calculus. These weights have no directly objective content except insofar as they may, in part, be based on some objective information. Essentially, however, they are the individual's own personal degree of belief as manifested in his behavior. This view of probability, though, can be of little value to the law. Here, every man is the best judge of what the probability of a given event is because there is no underlying objective frequency distribution: nothing that we can even approximate in our efforts to discover what the "reasonable man" would do.

The Crude Approximation Thesis

We have so far, hopefully, demonstrated that the kinds of data needed by a common-law court to balance costs and benefits are subjective in nature. Outside of general competitive equilibrium, there is no objective measure of the social opportunity costs of resources. Outside of stochastic stationary equilibrium, there is no objective measure of probability. In what sense, then, can we say that the common law promotes efficiency when the necessary data are, in the first case, unavailable and, in the second, nonexistent?

An advocate of the conventional economic approach to law *might* agree with much of what we have said but, nevertheless, maintain that we have ignored a fundamental point. Richard Posner, for example, has remarked that "the negligence system produces, *at best,* crude approximations of the result one could expect if market rather than legal processes were operative. But why despise crude approximations?"[48] This is an important, if undeveloped point, so let us undertake to examine it.

The theoretical underpinnings of what we can call the "crude approximation thesis'' have not been laid, so in much of what follows we shall have to struggle with the precise meaning implied.

There is immediately an important ambiguity here for we are told that "the negligence system produces, *at best*, crude approximations." Hopefully, it would not be thought a mere quibble over words to ask what is meant by "at best"? If "at best" we get a *crude* approximation, what do we normally or typically get?

The problems, however, are much deeper than this. In the absence of knowledge about the general equilibrium position, we cannot possibly know when resource prices are near or far from their general equilibrium values. Furthermore, since the relevant probabilities in most important situations are subjective, we cannot know what decision weights people, in fact, *would* use if market transactions were possible in cases now covered by the tort law (that is, if transaction costs were zero). Therefore, since we do not know how the market would operate if it could, we can say little about just how crude our approximation really is. Where is the benchmark?

If the crude approximation thesis is to be considered a positive scientific one then it must, at least in principle, be falsifiable. Yet to be falsifiable we must be able to imagine the kind of evidence that, if produced, would either refute or lend support to the thesis. Clearly, an approximation to the "efficient" solution would be better the closer resource prices are to their general competitive equilibrium levels. But could we recognize a general equilibrium if we saw one? Recall that equilibrium is not an operational or observable concept. Most importantly, a position of general equilibrium is defined in relation to a set of expectations. To the extent that these expectations are not directly or indirectly observable, we could not know whether a real world state of affairs is a general equilibrium or not. The empirical identification of a position as near or at equilibrium requires knowledge of subjective states. Could we then perhaps *infer* equilibrium from stability of prices? This, of course, rests on a confusion between equilibrium and stability; these are not identical concepts. A stable price can be a disequilibrium price if the underlying data are changing; its stability may be a function of a sluggish adjustment process rather than of equilibrium. Furthermore, we are talking about *general* equilibrium so a partial–equilibrium price is not enough save, perhaps, in the Marshallian tea markets. There seems, then, no way in principle of finding evidential support for the crude approximation thesis, and hence its scientific status is open to question.

To view the behavior of the courts as crudely approximating efficiency does not by itself reveal very much. What ought to concern us is how crude is the approximation *relative* to some alternative. For example, instead of an elaborate system of negligence law, the courts could adopt a "let the damages fall where they may" attitude in all but, say, the most grotesque cases. Initially, there would doubtless be an increase in the number of accidents but clearly this would eventually be reduced as other institutional arrangements developed. The main, and considerable, saving would be in court and litigation costs, as well as in the elimination of those decisions that reduce efficiency. In a world of general disequilibrium, the evidence of market prices can (and will) mislead us. Another possibility is for the courts to decide on the basis of strict liability. Is this more, less, or just as crude an approximation? Finally, some standard of—dare we speak its name?— "justice" might be applied that could possibly approach efficiency less crudely than any attempt to aim directly at it. Judicial cost–benefit analysis, to the extent that courts actually do engage in it, may not be more promotive of economic efficiency than some other standard.

We have talked about the necessity of the courts using (disequilibrium) market prices in arriving at a weighing of social costs and benefits. Yet even this is easier said than done. Consider the situation where both A and B can avoid an accident between them. To determine the relative potential expenditures (even at disequilibrium prices) on accident prevention is not always feasible. Sometimes even the array of market disequilibrium prices for a resource is not available. An example of this is the case where a shopper in the supermarket is able to prevent a can from falling off the shelf onto someone's foot by pushing the person out of the way. The disequilibrium price for his services is not available since there is, presumably, no market in such services. Who, then, is the least–cost avoider?

The crux of the issues, however, is this: efficiency is normally defined in terms of the preferences and expectations of the market participants. In much of the economics of law literature a different notion of efficiency has been implicitly smuggled into the picture. This is the efficiency conception of the central planner: he tries to minimize or maximize objectively measurable costs and benefits using either his own subjective or some pseudo-objective probability distributions. In any event, these are not the magnitudes that are relevant to market participants and, hence, use of the term "efficiency" is a misnomer.

Conclusions

In all of the foregoing we have been at great pains to demonstrate both the legal and economic difficulties involved with the claim that the common law is efficient. Many of these difficulties rest on fundamental conceptual confusions, while others are the result of internal inconsistencies. All of them serve to illustrate the serious incoherence of the view.

In summary, we have made seven basic points:

1. The idea of efficiency is hopelessly clouded in ambiguity, and clear thinking might better be served by complete elimination of the notion.

2. The claim that the common law promotes efficiency is internally inconsistent. We illustrate this contention by reference to at least six fundamental common-law doctrines.
3. The elimination of causation from the economic approach leads to the fallacy of objectifying costs and benefits.
4. Outside of general competitive equilibrium, direct outlays do not represent true social opportunity costs.
5. Failure to recognize this previous point is an example of the fallacy of this misplaced concrete. General equilibrium is a mental construct and not an operational concept.
6. In most interesting contexts, probability is subjective, and the search for what a "reasonable man" would do in uncertainty is not a factual question but a value judgment.
7. It is quite doubtful that the common law is capable, except by chance, of crudely approximating an efficient solution through judicial cost-benefit analysis.

Notes

1. "Not only are justice and fairness not economic concepts, but the economist is not interested in the one question that concerns the victim and his lawyer: who should bear the cost of *this* accident." Richard A. Posner, *Economic Analysis of Law* (Boston: Little, Brown and Company, 1972), p. 7.

2. Harold Demsetz, "When Does the Rule of Liability Matter?" *Journal of Legal Studies* 1, no. 1 (January 1972).

3. Mario J. Rizzo, "Equilibrium and Optimality: Do We Live in the Best of All Possible Worlds?" (Unpublished paper, New York University, 1977).

4. Richard A. Epstein, "A Theory of Strict Liability," *Journal of Legal Studies* 2, no. 1 (January 1973): 189–190.

5. Richard A. Posner, "Strict Liability: A Comment," *Journal of Legal Studies* 2, no. 1 (January 1973): 220.

6. Ibid., 219.

7. Kumkumian v. City of New York, 305 N.Y. 167, 111 N.E. 2d 865 (1953).

8. Posner, *Economic Analysis of Law,* p. 75. Emphasis added.

9. H.L.A. Hart and A.M. Honore, *Causation in the Law* (Oxford: Clarendon Press, 1959), p. 143. See also Epstein "Theory of Strict Liability," p. 180.

10. "Since any ruling of law will constitute a precedent, the judge must consider the probable impact of alternative rulings on the future behavior

of people engaged in activities that give rise to the kind of accident involved in the case before him." Posner, *Economic Analysis of Law,* p. 7. This position is not easily reconciled with his argument on the last clear chance. See note 8, *supra.*

11. Karl R. Popper, *The Poverty of Historicism* (New York: Harper Torchbooks, 1964), pp. vi–viii.

12. Brian Loasby has stressed the importance of incomplete listability in another context. See Brian J. Loasby, *Choice, Complexity and Ignorance* (Cambridge: Cambridge University Press, 1976), pp. 7–10.

13. Posner, *Economic Analysis of Law,* p. 72.

14. Can it be argued that this is a quasi–contract?

15. Canterbury v. Spence, 464 F. 2d 722 (D.C. Cir. 1972).

16. Helling v. Carey, 83 Wash 2d 514, 519 p. 2d 981 (1974).

17. Vincent v. Lake Erie Transport Co., 109 Minn. 456, 124 N.W. 221 (1910).

18. See the next section below.

19. For a discussion of this, see Epstein, "Theory of Strict Liability," p. 157.

20. The expected value takes account of *both* the probability of the harmful event and the losses if it occurs ($p \cdot l$). Therefore, if the probability is low but the losses would be very high, the event still might be foreseeable.

21. William L. Prosser, *Handbook of the Law of Torts,* 4th ed. (St. Paul, Minn.: West Publishing Co., 1971), p. 250.

22. Assuming that some indivisibilities prevail, a "very small" expenditure on prevention will have a zero marginal product.

23. Hughes v. Lord Advocate, [1963] A.C. 837.

24. *See,* for example, Vosburg v. Putney, 80 Wis 523, 50 N.W. 503 (1891). I am indebted to Prof. R.A. Epstein of the University of Chicago for this citation.

25. Guido Calabresi, *The Cost of Accidents* (New Haven: Yale University Press, 1970), pp. 6–7, n. 8. Emphasis added.

26. Ronald Coase, "The Problem of Social Costs," *Journal of Law and Economics* 3 (October 1960).

27. Ludwig von Mises, *Human Action: A Treatise on Economics* (Chicago: Henry Regnery Co., 1966), p. 13.

28. Posner, *Economic Analysis of Law,* p. 77, n. 4.8.1.

29. The existence of nonpecuniary advantages or disadvantages doesn't really change this conclusion. For example, if a person will work in industry X for $5.00 per hour because the work is pleasant, while he could receive $5.50 in industry $Y,$ the true (social) opportunity cost of his time is $5.00, *not* $5.50. This is because the opportunity foregone by working in Y includes a nonpecuniary advantage worth $0.50.

30. Ronald Coase, "Business Organization and the Accountant," *LSE*

Essays on Cost, ed. James M. Buchanan and G.F. Thirlby (London: Weidenfeld and Nicolson, 1976), p. 108.

31. Ibid., p. 115.

32. Ibid., p. 108. *See also* James M. Buchanan, *Cost and Choice* (Chicago: Markham, 1969), p. 28.

33. G.F. Thirlby, "The Ruler," *South African Journal of Economics* 14 (December 1946): 264.

34. This task is, of course, greatly simplified if the underlying data change slowly relative to the speed of the adjustment processes.

35. William J. Baumol in his review of Buchanan's *Cost and Choice* claims that there is a "strong presumption that the available [cost] figures often approximate reasonably the information we really want." *Journal of Economic Literature* 8 no. 4 (December 1970): 1210–1211. Baumol offers no evidence to support this contention. On this issue, see the section below, "The Crude Approximation Thesis."

36. Fritz Machlup, "Equilibrium and Disequilibrium: Misplaced Concreteness and Disquised Politics," *Essays in Economic Semantics* (New York: W.W. Norton and Company, 1967).

37. Frank H. Hahn, *On the Notion of Equilibrium in Economics* (Cambridge: Cambridge University Press, 1973), p. 7.

38. Ibid., p. 9.

39. Alan Coddington, "The Rationale of General Equilibrium Theory," *Economic Inquiry* 13 no. 6 (December 1975): 550.

40. Ibid.

41. Machlup, "Equilibrium and Disequilibrium," p. 48.

42. Although G.L.S. Shackle has consistently refused to do this. *See,* for example, G.L.S. Shackle, *Decision, Order and Time* (Cambridge: Cambridge University Press, 1961), pp. 47–113.

43. Karl R. Popper, *The Logic of Scientific Discovery* (New York: Harper Torchbooks, 1965), p. 205.

44. Ibid. Emphasis added.

45. See further discussion below.

46. Shackle, *Decision, Order and Time,* p. 56.

47. Ibid., p. 55. Original emphasis.

48. Posner "Strict Liability," p. 218. Emphasis added.

Comment: The Myth of Efficiency

Murray N. Rothbard

I am delighted that Dr. Rizzo, in chapter 4, is calling the highly touted concept of "efficiency" into grave question. I would like to carry his critique still further.

One of Rizzo's major points is that the concept of efficiency has no meaning apart from the pursuit of specified ends. But he concedes too much when he states, at least at the beginning of his paper, that "of course it [the common law] is efficient" relative to certain specified goals. For there are several layers of grave fallacy involved in the very concept of efficiency as applied to social institutions or policies: (1) the problem is not only in specifying ends but also in deciding *whose* ends are to be pursued; (2) individual ends are bound to conflict, and therefore any additive concept of social efficiency is meaningless; and (3) even each individual's actions cannot be assumed to be "efficient"; indeed, they undoubtedly will not be. Hence, efficiency is an erroneous concept even when applied to each individual's actions directed toward his ends; it is a fortiori a meaningless concept when it includes more than one individual, let alone an entire society.

Let us take a given individual. Since his own ends are clearly given and he acts to pursue them, surely at least *his* actions can be considered efficient? But no, they may not, for in order for him to act efficiently, he would have to possess perfect knowledge—perfect knowledge of the best technology, of future actions and reactions by other people, and of future natural events. But since no one can ever have perfect knowledge of the future, no one's action can be called "efficient." We live in a world of uncertainty. Efficiency is therefore a chimera.

Put another way, action is a learning process. As the individual acts to achieve his ends, he learns and becomes more proficient about how to pursue them. But in that case, of course, his actions cannot have been efficient from the start—or even from the end—of his actions, since perfect knowledge is never achieved, and there is always more to learn.

Moreover, the individual's ends are not *really* given, for there is no reason to assume that they are set in concrete for all time. As the individual learns more about the world, about nature and about other people, his values and goals are bound to change. The individual's ends will change as he learns from other people; they may also change out of sheer caprice. But if ends change in the course of an action, the concept of efficiency—which can only be defined as the best combination of means in pursuit of given ends—again becomes meaningless.

If the concept of efficiency is worthless even for each individual, it is a fortiori in far worse straits when the economist employs it in an additive way for all of society. Rizzo is being extremely gentle with the concept when he says that it amounts "to little more than maximizing gross national product" which "immediately breaks down once externalities are introduced into the system." The problem, however, is far deeper. For efficiency only makes sense in regard to people's ends, and individuals' ends differ, clash, and conflict. The central question of politics then becomes: *whose* ends shall rule?

The blindness of economic thought to the realities of the world is systemic, and is a product of the utilitarian philosophy that has dominated economics for a century and a half. For utilitarianism holds that everyone's ends are *really* the same, and that therefore all social conflict is merely technical and pragmatic, and can be resolved once the appropriate means for the common ends are discovered and adopted. It is the myth of the common universal end that allows economists to believe that they can "scientifically" and in a supposedly value-free manner prescribe what political policies should be adopted. By taking this alleged common universal end as an unquestioned given, the economist allows himself the delusion that he is not at all a moralist but only a strictly value-free and professional technician.

The alleged common end is a higher standard of living, or, as Rizzo puts it, a maximized gross national product. But suppose that, for one or more people, part of their desired "product" is something that other people will consider a decided detriment. Let us consider two examples, both of which would be difficult to subsume under the gentle rubric of "externalities." Suppose that some people pursue as a highly desired end the compulsory equality, or uniformity, of all persons, including each having the same living conditions and wearing the same shapeless blue garment. But then a highly desired goal for these egalitarians would be considered a grave detriment by those individuals who do not wish to be made equal to or uniform with everyone else. A second example of conflicting ends, of clashing meanings allotted to the concept of "product," would be one or more people who greatly desire either the enslavement or the slaughter of a disliked ethnic or other clearly defined social group. Clearly, the pursuit of product for the would-be oppressors or slaughterers would be considered a negative product, or detriment, by the potential oppressed. Perhaps we could jam this case into an externality problem by saying that the disliked social or ethnic group constitutes a "visual pollutant," a negative externality, for the other groups, and that these external "costs" can be (should be?) internalized by forcing the disliked group to pay the other groups enough to induce the latter to spare their lives. One wonders, however, how much the economist wishes to minimize social costs, and whether or not this proferred solution would really be "value-free."

In these cases of conflicting ends, furthermore, one group's "efficiency" becomes another group's detriment. So that the advocates of a program—whether of compulsory uniformity or of slaughtering a defined social group—would want their proposals carried out as efficiently as possible; whereas, on the other hand, the oppressed group would hope for as *in*efficient a pursuit of the hated goal as possible. Efficiency, as Rizzo points out, can only be meaningful relative to a given goal. But if ends clash, the opposing group will favor maximum *in*efficiency in pursuit of the disliked goal. Efficiency, therefore, can never serve as a utilitarian touchstone for law or for public policy.

Our cases of clashing ends bring us to the question of minimizing social costs. The first question to raise is: why *should* social costs be minimized? Or, why *should* externalities be internalized? The answers are scarcely self-evident, and yet the questions have never been satisfactorily addressed, let alone answered. And there is an important corollary question: even given the goal of minimizing costs, for the sake of argument, should this goal be held as an absolute or should it be subordinated, and to what degree, to other goals? And what reasons can be given for any answer?

In the first place, to say that social costs *should* be minimized, or that external costs *should* be internalized, is not a technical or a value–free position. The very intrusion of the word *should,* the very leap to a policy position, necessarily converts this into an ethical stand, which requires, at the very least, an ethical justification.

And second, even if, for the sake of argument, we consent to a goal of minimized social costs, the economist still must wrestle with the problem: how absolute should this commitment be? To say that minimized social costs must be absolute, or at least the highest–valued goal, is to fall into the same position that the cost–benefit economists scorn when it is taken by ethicists: namely, to consider equity or rights heedless of cost–benefit analysis. And what is their justification for such absolutism?

Third, even if we ignore these two problems, there is the grave fallacy in the very concept of "social cost", or of cost as applied to more than one person. For one thing, if ends clash, and one man's product is another man's detriment, costs cannot be added up across these individuals. But second, and more deeply, costs, as Austrians have pointed out for a century, are subjective to the individual, and therefore can neither be measured quantitatively nor, a fortiori, can they be added or compared between individuals. But if costs, like utilities, are subjective, nonadditive, and noncomparable, then of course any concept of social costs, including transaction costs, become meaningless. And third, even within each individual, costs are not objective or observable by any external observer. For an individual's cost is subjective and ephemeral; it appears only ex ante, at the moment before the individual makes a decision. The cost of any individual's choice is his subjective estimate of the value ranking of the highest value foregone from making his choice. For each individual tries, in every choice, to pursue his highest-ranking end; he foregoes or sacrifices the other, lower-ranking, ends that he could have satisfied with the resources available. His cost is his second-highest ranking end, that is, the value of the highest ranking end that he has foregone to achieve a still more highly valued goal. The cost that he incurs in this decision, then, is only ex ante; as soon as his decision is made and the choice is exercised and his resource committed, the cost disappears. It becomes an historical cost, forever bygone. And since it is impossible for any external observer to explore, at a later date, or even at the same time, the internal mental processes of the actor, it is impossible for this observer to determine, even in principle what the cost of any decision may have been.

Much of chapter 4 is devoted to an excellent analysis demonstrating that objective social costs make no sense outside of general equilibrium, and that we can never be in such equilibrium, nor could we know if we were. Rizzo points out that since disequilibrium necessarily implies divergent and inconsistent expectations, we cannot simply say that these prices approximate equilibrium, since there is an important difference *in kind* between them and consistent equilibrium prices. Rizzo also points out that there is no benchmark to enable us to decide whether existing prices are close to equilibrium or not. I would simply underline his points here, and make only two comments. To his point that tort law would not be needed in general equilibrium, I would add that torts themselves could not be committed in such a situation. For one feature of general equilibrium is certainly and perfect knowledge of the future; and presumably with such perfect knowledge no accidents could possibly occur. Even an intentional tort could not occur, for a perfectly foreseen tort could surely be avoided by the victim.

This comment relates to another point I would make about general equilibrium; not only has it never existed, and is not an operational concept, but also it could not conceivably exist. For we cannot really conceive of a world where every person has perfect foresight, and where no data ever change; moreover, the general equilibrium is internally self-contradictory, for the reason one holds cash balances is because of the uncertainty of the future, and therefore the demand for money would fall to zero in a general equilibrium world of perfect certainty. Hence, a money economy, at least, could not be in general equilibrium.

I would also endorse Rizzo's critique of attempts to use objective probability theory as a way of reducing the real world of uncertainty to certainty equivalents. In the real world of human action, virtually all historical events are unique and heterogeneous, though often similar, to all other historical events. Since each event is unique and nonreproducible, it is impermissible to apply objective probability theory; expectations and forecasting become a matter of subjective estimates of future events, estimates that cannot be reduced to an objective or "scientific" formula. Calling two events by the same name does not make them homogeneous. Thus, two presidential elections are both called "presidential elections," but they are nevertheless highly varied, heterogeneous, and nonreproducible events, each occurring in different historical contexts. It is no accident that social scientists arguing for the use of the objective probability calculus almost invariably cite the case of the lottery; for a lottery is one of the few human situations where the outcomes are indeed homogeneous and reproducible, and, furthermore, where the events are random with no one possessing any influence upon its successors.

Not only is "efficiency" a myth, then, but so too is any concept of social or additive cost, or even an objectively determinable cost for each individual. But if cost is individual, ephemeral, and purely subjective, then it follows that no policy conclusions, including conclusions about law, can be derived from or even make use of such a concept. There can be no valid or meaningful cost–benefit analysis of political or legal decisions or institutions.

Let us now turn more specifically to Rizzo's discussion of the law, and its relation to efficiency and social costs. His critique of the efficiency-economists could be put more sharply. Let us take, for example, Rizzo's discussion of the Good Samaritan problem. As he poses the problem, he supposes that B could save A "at minimal cost to himself," and he concludes that, from the point of view of the efficiency theorists, B should be liable for injuries to A if B doesn't save A. But there are more problems with the efficiency approach. For one thing, there is the characteristic confusion of monetary and psychic costs. For, since B's costs in this case are purely psychic, how can anyone but B, say a court, know what B's costs would entail? Suppose indeed that B is a good swimmer and could rescue A easily, but that it turns out that A is an old enemy of his, so that the psychic costs of his rescuing A are very high. The point is that any assessment of B's costs can only be made in terms of B's own values, and that no outside observer can know what these are.[1] Furthermore, when the efficiency theorists put the case that, in Rizzo's words, "Clearly . . . A would have been willing to pay B more than enough to compensate his costs in order to be rescued," this conclusion is not really clear at all. For how do we know, or how do the courts know, if A would have had the money to pay B, and how would B know it—especially if we realize that no one except B can know what his psychic costs may be?

Furthermore, the question of causation could be put far more sharply. Rizzo's quotation from Mises on nonaction also being a form of "action" is praxeologically correct, but is irrelevant to the law. For the law is trying to discover who, if anyone, in a given situation has aggressed against the person or property of another—in short, who has been a tortfeasor against the property of another and is therefore liable for penalty. A nonaction may be an "action" in a praxeological sense, but it sets no positive chain of consequences into motion, and therefore cannot be an act of aggression. Hence, the wisdom of the common law's stress on the crucial distinction between misfeasance and nonfeasance, between a wrongful aggression against someone's rights, and leaving that person alone.[2] *Vincent* v. *Lake Erie Transport* was a superb decision, for there the court was careful to investigate the causal agent at work—in this case, the boat, which clearly slammed against the dock. In some ways, tort law can be summed up as: "No liability without fault, no fault without liability." The vital importance of Richard Epstein's strict liability doctrine is that it returns the common law to its original strict emphasis on causation, fault, and liability, shorn of modern accretions of negligence and pseudo-"efficiency" considerations.

I conclude that we cannot decide on public policy, tort law, rights, or liabilities on the basis of efficiencies or minimizing of costs. But if not costs or efficiency, then what? The answer is that only *ethical principles* can serve as criteria for our decisions. Efficiency can never serve as the basis for ethics; on the contrary, ethics must be the guide and touchstone for any consideration of efficiency. Ethics is the primary. In the field of law and public policy, as Rizzo wittily indicates, the primary ethical consideration is the concept that "dare not speak its name"—the concept of justice.

One group of people will inevitably balk at our conclusion; I speak, of course, of the economists. For in this area economists have been long engaged in what George Stigler, in another context, has called "intellectual imperialism." Economists will have to get used to the idea that not all of life can be encompassed by our own discipline. A painful lesson no doubt, but compensated by the knowledge that it may be good for our souls to realize our own limits—and, just perhaps, to learn about ethics and about justice.

Notes

1. Marc A. Franklin, *Injuries and Remedies* (Mineola, N.Y.: Foundation Press, 1971), p. 401.

2. "There is no distinction more deeply rooted in the common law and more fundamental than that between misfeasance and non-feasance, between active misconduct working positive injury to others and passive inaction, a failure to take positive steps to benefit others, or to protect them from harm not created by any wrongful act of the defendant." Francis H. Bohlen, "The Moral Duty to Aid Others as a Basis of Tort Liability," *University of Pennsylvania Law Review* 56, no. 4 (April 1908): 219-221; cited in Williamson M. Evers, "The Law of Omissions and Neglect of Children," *The Journal of Libertarian Studies* (Winter 1978).

5

Ethics and Efficiency in Property Rights Systems

Harold Demsetz

Introduction

Frank Knight, who was neither antagonistic toward capitalism nor one of its more romantic supporters, in some ways was one of its more interesting critics. Knight never seemed in much doubt about the superior capabilities of the capitalistic system to efficiently satisfy those wants and preferences expressed in the market by consumers, although he readily recognized the imperfection in all human institutions. But he was concerned about the kind of person who emerges from the competitive milieux of capitalism.

> Is emulation as a motive ethically good or base? Is success in any sort of *contest,* as such, a noble objective? . . . In America particularly, where competitive business, and its concomitant, the sporting view of life, have reached their fullest development, there have come to be two sorts of virtue. The greater virtue is to win. . . . The lesser virtue is to go out and die gracefully after having lost.[1]

The question raised here implicitly assumes that economic organization has a detectable impact on our basic psychological drives. There is room for reasonable doubt about the validity of this assumption. There is some evidence from modern sociobiology that our inner motivations derive from many centuries of evolution, that short of direct genetic engineering or selective breeding there is no way for this genetic endowment, and hence these inner drives, to be modified significantly by the choice of institutional environment; economic organization may have very little to do with competitive drive, altruistic sentiment, or the propensity to *ape*.

Be that as it may, it seems difficult or impossible to define, isolate, and measure true inner qualities, and so we are left with no basis other than human action, or the consequence thereof, by which to judge the ethical properties of alternative economic organizations. In this chapter I wish to critically examine some ethical questions about the private property rights system from the perspective of human action, an especially appropriate viewpoint since so much of Austrian economics centers on the praxeology of human action. Ethical judgments about economic organization, however, frequently rest on some unspecified, usually vague concept of "justice" or "morality," often stated quite independently of an examination of the human action implied by that economic organization. "It is immoral to allow owners of factories to put smoke into other people's air," or, "it is immoral not to assess the person *causing* damages with the liability for those damages"; these are typical of the statements I have in mind. My first task is to expose the weakness of this religious or intuitive approach to moral problems. This could be done rather easily by attacking the overriding faith of socialists in the correctness of a holistic view of society, or in their belief that altering economic organization alters the inner qualities of man, but, before this audience, I choose what for me is the more difficult task of attacking the simplistic faith of a few libertarians in their notion of the ethical superiority of particular private property arrangements. A target is needed. Walter Block, writing critically about work by R.H. Coase and me in a recent issue of the *Journal of Libertarian Studies* (Spring, 1977), has inadvertently volunteered.

The Ethical Superiority of Private Property Rights

Block raises a substantive positive issue as well as a moral one about property rights systems. It is necessary to examine both if our perspective on ethical matters is to derive from the implied outcomes of alternative property right assignments. The substantive issue has to do with whether or not the assignment of right ownership will alter the mix of output when "bargaining transactions . . . are costless [and] changes in the distribution of wealth . . . can be ignored." Coase and I (with a proviso about "free riders") say no; Block says yes. Block then presents some examples that appear to refute our analyses, but which really only violate our explicitly made assumption that there are no wealth effects on the demands for the commodities being discussed. We both recognize that there will be allocative effects when this assumption does not hold.

He considers a case involving "psychic income" wherein a smoke prevention device can be installed for $75,000 by a factory which, in the absence of such a device, will ruin a neighbor's flower bed because of smoke pollution. The flower bed is worth nothing to anyone else, but to the neighbor it is worth $100,000 because of sentimental value. The factory would not be willing to pay its neighbor more than $75,000, the cost of a smoke cleaning device, for his permission to pollute the air, so, if the neighbor has a right to a soot-free garden, the factory owner would elect to install the smoke cleaning device rather than pay the $100,000 demanded by its neighbor. But if the factory owner has the right to use smoke-producing fuel, the neighbor, being so poor, would be unable (unwilling) to pay the factory owner the $75,000 required to install the smoke cleaning device. With the first assignment of rights, there is a flower garden and no smoke (and there

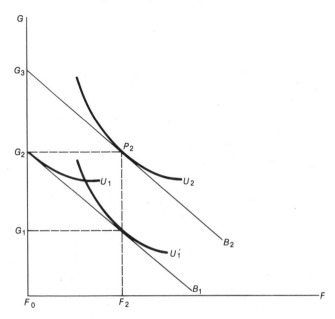

Figure 5-1. Rights Assignments and Income Effects.

also is less factory output). With the second, there is smoke (more factory output) and no flower garden. The mix of output is contingent on the assignment of rights. True, but only because of the income effect, as can be seen with the aid of figure 5-1.

The horizontal axis of figure 5-1 measures quantity of flower garden, and the vertical axis quantity of other goods. The indifference curves and budget lines picture the neighbor's situation in each of the rights assignment situations. If the neighbor has the right to soot-free air, he consumes P_2 containing F_2 of flowers and G_2 of other goods. But since he can sell the right to pollute the air for $75,000, he also can consume no flowers, F_0, and G_3 of other goods, where $G_3 - G_2$ equals $75,000 worth of other goods. He therefore confronts a budget line, B_2, that passes through P_2 and G_3.

The second rights assignment alters the budget line on which he can operate. Given his income and no right to soot-free air, he can consume G_2 of other goods and enjoy no flowers or he can give up $75,000 of the other goods, consuming only G_1 of these but increase his garden to F_2. The second right assignment, therefore, has reduced his budget line to B_1. This alteration in income alters the mix of goods produced in Block's example because the indifference curve relevant to the new budget line is U_1; if it had been U_1', he would have purchased the same quantity of flowers, F_2, as he enjoyed with the first rights assignment. The alteration in the mix of output reflects an implicit wealth effect on the demand for flowers, as can be seen easily if a compensating increase in income is given to the garden owner when the factory owner has the right to use smoke–producing fuel, and, therefore, is in no way acceptable as a refutation of Coase's analysis. An identical explanation lies behind the allocative difference Block sees between a "buy–him–in" voluntary army and a "let–him–buy–his–way–out" type of draft. In the Coase analysis, to assume no income effect is not to assert the unimportance of such an effect, but merely to keep the discussion within the Pigouvian tradditional analysis of externality problems; that analysis was critical of the ability of competitive economic organization to produce efficient resource allocations quite aside from income distribution problems.

It is clear from the emotionalism of Block's discussion that he has strong ethical feelings as to how property rights *should* be defined in such cases. It is the gardner who should have the right to soot–free air, and the potential recruit who should have the right to his freedom. One is entitled to an explanation of why these assignments of property rights are ethically superior to their alternatives. A volunteer army undoubtedly has great intuitive appeal as superior even to a draft in which a person has the right to buy his way out, but the ownership by the gardner of the right to control the soot content of air does not. A general ethical resolution of the problem of property right definitions cannot be supported by the definiteness of one's view about some intuitively easy case.

Tougher examples can be found easily. Consider the following analog to Block's gardening problem. Let there be an island that contains all the known stock of Austrian Pure Snow trees. The island is inhabited by a religious sect, the first to mix their sweat and blood with the island's soil, thus satisfying Rothbard's principle of "original ownership." They worship these trees as if they were God. Never would they let them be tampered with in any way. Unknown to anyone, these trees contain an ingredient that is a sure cure for cancer, and when this is discovered a question of the ownership of this ingredient, unavailable elsewhere, arises. The religious sect will in no way, for any compensation, allow that ingredient to be extracted. Is it "evil and vicious" to believe that it would be preferable for someone else to own the right to this ingredient, requiring instead that the religious sect purchase the inviolability of this ingredient? Might not "our most cherished and precious property rights" be still more cherished and precious if the private ownership of this new resource was not confined to those who own the rest of the island? Would the answer be much different if this ingredient not only was known to the island dwellers, but was precisely that part of the trees that they worshipped? Would the answer be different if the islanders were very poor?

The instrumental nature of property rights is made clear in this example. The multidimensionality of human want virtually guarantees that a sufficient alteration in the gains and losses of alternative definitions of property right structures can dim the ethical aura that surrounds any specific structure. I do not believe that it is possible to defend effectively a particular property right structure by appealing to some supposed overriding concern for freedom, or for equality, or for wealth, or for "original ownership." Lexicographic orderings crumble in the face of scarcity. The general constraint of scarcity imposes substitutability at the margin, even when one speaks of substituting alternative property right definitions for present ones or for those that would derive from "original ownership."

Consider the problem of reconciling the demand to play tennis with the demand for peace and quiet. These often conflict, especially when there is a desire to play tennis at night on lighted courts. The conflict is similar to that of the factory owner and the gardener discussed by Block, both of whom wish to put airspace to competing uses. Noise, like soot, can envelope a neighbor's home.

A private property rights system, in recognition of this conflict, may assign the right to determine nearby noise levels to those who would sleep or to those who would play tennis. *Both* rights assignments are equally private and both seem equally productive of individual freedom. Neither exhibits any obvious ethical superiority over the other even when one's preferences are highly weighted in favor of individual freedom. The same can be said of a third alternative wherein the right to control noise levels during daytime hours belongs to those who would play tennis and during nighttime hours to those who would sleep.

The instrumental advantage of the third alternative can (but need not) be measured in terms of its consequences for resource allocation. The dollar value of benefits of assigning rights over noise levels during nighttime hours to would-be sleepers *plausibly* exceeds the dollar value of costs thereby imposed on would-be nighttime tennis players, so that even if the cost to these parties of negotiating with each other were prohibitive, resources would tend to be utilized in an "efficient"[2] manner. Similarly, the assignment to tennis players during daytime hours of the right to control noise levels yields a dollar value of benefits that exceeds the dollar value of costs imposed on neighbors. The property rights system could be complicated further but not at zero cost; persons who are seriously ill might be allowed to control noise levels during daytime hours, while those who work at nighttime might not.

The fine tuning is left largely to market negotiations. If a nighttime tennis player is willing to pay enough to his neighbor, his neighbor will give permission for tennis to be played. Once a private property rights system is defined, especially with respect to who owns the right to offer to sell specific entitlements to use resources, it can be expected that subsequent negotiations will *tend* to tolerate only efficient uses of scarce resources. If the cost of transacting were zero, and if there were no "free rider" or "holdout" problems, any private rights system, once it is defined, will do this.

If there are significant transaction costs, then the choice of a private rights system will have direct consequences for resource allocation in addition to any indirect impact this choice may have through wealth distribution effects. To take an extreme case, suppose that the cost to neighbors of negotiating with each other is prohibitively high relative to the gains to be expected from such negotiations. No matter what the distribution of wealth, assume this remains true. If tennis players have the right to use tennis courts at night, they will play tennis even when the dollar value to them of doing so is less than the dollar value of sleep to their neighbors. Similarly, if would–be sleepers have the right to quiet all day, tennis players who would choose to play daytime generally will be barred from an activity that they value more than their neighbors value quiet. Plausibly, when transaction costs are significant, a system of private rights that assigns entitlements to control nighttime noise levels to sleepers and daytime noise levels to tennis players would be "superior" to either of these simpler assignments if the objective is to achieve an efficient use of resources.

Efficiency Considerations

Substitutability at the margin suggests that efficiency considerations may be relevant to the problem of choosing property rights definitions, and I will argue that this is the case, both normatively and positively. The instrumentalism of property rights systems can be recognized, although perhaps not completely, by employing the criterion of maximization of the real values of the resources whose uses are affected by the assignment of rights. I do not refer to simple maximization of recorded market value, which inappropriately reflects leisure/labor tradeoffs, pecuniary/nonpecuniary tradeoffs, and monopoly/competition tradeoffs, but to the efficiency with which it is expected that resources will be deployed as a result of one right assignment as compared with another.

This criterion undoubtedly will be suspect among both Austrian economists and libertarians, the first because it seems to imply that values are not subjective, that they can be measured objectively, and the second because it suggests that private property rights might not survive the efficiency criterion. Neither suspicion is completely unfounded; neither is completely warranted. I will turn to these issues below. But, first, let us eschew problems of state intervention in the exercise of rights, and also the pragmatic problem of just how certain information would be known and acted upon, confining attention for now to the question of which of two (or more) individuals should control the private right to use some resource—that is, to the problem typified by gardener and factory owner.

I wish to begin the analysis of this case assuming zero transaction cost and no income effects on the demands for cleaner air or for the product of the factory, but then move quickly to more relevant assumptions. With these assumptions, the right to control the soot content of the air will have no impact on the quantity of soot, flowers, or the factory's output, since the contesting parties will negotiate to the identical quantity of soot, that which is efficient, no matter who pays whom to reach this level of soot content. (If there are third parties affected by the soot content, they simply are brought into the negotiation.) The only aspect of the situation that can be affected by the choice of owner of the right to control soot content is the distribution of income (or wealth), since with one rights assignment, that in which the gardener controls soot content, the factory owner pays his neighbor for permission to put more soot into the air, while in the other case the neighbor pays the factory owner to take soot out of the air. It would seem awkward for libertarians to argue for the ethical superiority of one distribution of income over another when no issue of freedom or resource allocation is involved. Moreover, if income distribution were the desideratum, there would be no clear ruling on the merits of the *situation,* only on the merits of the relative incomes of the two parties standing before the court, or likely in the future to stand before the court. Nonetheless, in such a hypothetical situation there is *only* the comparison of resulting income distribution to guide the ethical decision. In such a case, it might will be thought the person denied control of soot content should receive a compensating increase in income, but more about this later.

Real situations will seldom fit this hypothetical case. Generally there will be transaction costs and also income effects on demands for commodities. But let us proceed a step at a time, assuming still that transaction cost is zero but that income effects are present. As in Block's example, an assignment of the right to control the soot level to the gardener, if we assume the preferences implied in that example, now yields more flowers and less soot (and less factory output) than does the alternative rights assignment. A choice between different mixes of output is now possible, but on what grounds is it to be made since the efficient mix of ouput is itself dependent on the distribution of income? More flowers and less soot (and less factory output) maximizes the real value of resources when the neighboring gardener owns the right to control soot content, and more soot (and more factory output) and fewer flowers maximizes the real value of resources when the factory owner owns the right (always noting that third parties should be included in negotiations over soot content in the absence of transaction cost if they have any interest in the outcome). We seem to be back to the ethical superiority of alternative income distributions, although in this case the mix of output will not be invariant with respect to the right assignment. Of course, if a compensating increase in income is granted to the person denied the right to control soot content, then the mix of output will be invariant with respect to the decision as to who owns the right.

This will not be the case if the cost of transacting is significant. To make the point as easily as is possible, let it be assumed that transaction cost is so high relative to the gains from exchange that no exchange between the interested parties will take place once the assignment of rights is made, but that the party denied ownership of the right receives a compensating increase in income. The assignment of rights affects the mix of goods for a reason other than income distribution. Assuming that full income compensation accompanies the decision about who should control the soot content of air, can a reasonable statement be made as to which output mix is superior, and hence, about which right assignment is to be preferred?

If the right to control soot content is acquired by the gardener, there will be no soot, less factory output, and more flowers than if the factory owner receives the right because the party denied the right cannot (because of transaction cost) economically bring his preferences for altering soot content to bear on the decision of the party who acquired the right. Monopoly aside, why not assign the right to that party who would find it most valuable? The second party is made whole through income compensation (still to be discussed), and the required compensation would be less than would be required by the first party if it was the second who had received the right; moreover, the air is put to a higher value use with this right assignment than with the reverse.

Questions about this criterion will surely arise in the minds of some readers. Does this violate the notion that values are subjective and unknowable to second parties? Does this involve interpersonal utility comparisons? My answer to these questions is that the criterion of efficiency assumes no more than does the criterion of the marketplace. For, after all, all that has been done is to auction the right off to the party who would have been the highest bidder (assuming no problems of monopoly are present). Suppose the right to control soot content belonged to some original settler, who was himself indifferent as to the soot content of air, that he was soon joined by two neighbors, one a factory owner and the other a gardener, and that he offers to sell the right to control soot content to that neighbor submitting the highest bid. Assuming negligible transaction costs, the problem of the identity of the ultimate controller of air quality would be resolved in a manner identical to that implied above by the efficiency criterion. Why not adopt the criterion of the market place in those situations in which the question of ownership arises? It is not as if that question need not be answered. In one way or another it must be answered before negotiations can take place; clearly identifying the owner through legal processes merely reduces the cost of negotiating by making clear who must pay whom. Absent such a legal determination, other methods, possibly violent, such as in a range war, will be adopted to settle the question of ownership. If settlement is to be made through legal processes, some criterion must be used. Attempting to use the market's criterion of placing resources in their highest value use seems difficult to improve upon.

To adopt the criterion of the marketplace in the court room is *not* to assert that values are objective or that it is possible to compare utility across individuals. The method of the market and the method proposed here for the court both adopt the *convention* that willingness to pay serves well as a *substitute* for utility comparisons in the resolution of conflicts over the use of scarce resources.

The specification of the underlying private rights system ultimately defines who has the right to impose harmful effects on whom, or, more accurately, how to identify who has such a right. The imposition of costs is inescapable given that our desires to use resources often conflict. But even after a private property rights system is in place, it is incorrect to claim as does Rothbard that "the free market always benefits every participant, and it maximizes social utility *ex ante*." The maximization of "social" utility implies interpersonal comparisons of utility, a notion fraught with pitfalls and arbitrariness, but it is the idea that everyone benefits from free market activities that must be rejected, for it completely misinterprets the function and the operation of free markets. The market weighs and compares the beneficial *and* harmful effects, measured in the money that people are willing to pay, and filters out situations that would yield a net loss in this metric. The free market does not prohibit harmful effects. Indeed, a system that did, such as one based on the unanimity principle, would be so intolerably impractical (*inefficient*) that it would soon give way to other arrangements.

That harmful effects are borne through the operation of free markets can be illustrated clearly when a new product is marketed. However beneficial a new product is to consumers, its purchase imposes harmful effects on producers of the old product that it displaces. One seller invents a new marketing technique that allows him to reach potential customers at a lower cost than his competitors. The introduction of this technique yields beneficial effects for customers by allowing them to satisfy their demands at a lower price, but it also imposes harmful effects on the firms losing these customers. The open market will allow the innovation to succeed only if customers and new product producers, including the owners of inputs used to produce the new product, are benefited more than competitive sellers are harmed. If the customers experience a gain worth $100 by shifting their trade to the innovator while the sellers they leave suffer a loss of only $80 as a result, then these sellers will be unwilling to cut prices sufficiently to hold their customers. Whereas, if these sellers suffer a loss of $150 if customers switch, they would be willing to cut prices sufficiently to retain patronage. The innovation succeeds only if the gains it confers, measured in dollars, exceeds the cost it imposes.

It is this aspect of the private property rights system that is one of its great strengths. In the absence of individualized voluntarily given consent to a transfer of resources, it would seem difficult to know whether the transfer yields a net gain since such transfers also impose harmful effects. The net gain so measured, it is worth repeating, is an index based on willingness to pay, not on some global utility maximization. Since the market does not forbid activities that impose costs on some individuals, some such index is desirable. It is amazing how tolerant we are of such costs when they are embedded in a private property rights system in which willingness to pay is the index. Perhaps one of the more redeeming features of such a system is its apparent ability to attenuate the degree of group conflict that seems to infect those socialistic systems in which collective decisions on resource allocation and wealth distribution are made through democratic political institutions.

The definition of rights by the legal system, which preceeds market negotiations, of course, does not have the benefit of market–revealed information when ownership decisions are made, and so any prescription that courts adopt the efficiency criterion is likely to find its application blunt and susceptible to error. The fact that efficiency considerations should perhaps influence the choice of private property rights systems therefore should not be misinterpreted to endorse frequent involuntary reassignment of such rights. It is precisely because it is so difficult to know what the underlying efficiency considerations are that it is useful to allow transactions in the free market to fine tune the ownership and use of resources. Frequent involuntary reassignment would destroy confidence in the longevity of property rights and all long-run consequences of resource use will tend to be neglected, at least in a world of uncertainty and positive transaction cost. Efficiency calls for a high degree of stability in property rights definitions, but it does not necessarily forbid all involuntary reassignment, especially when high exchange cost or free–rider type problems reduce the efficacy of allocations through the market.

Should compensation actually be paid? The producer of a new product receives the right to offer it for sale to all potential buyers; producers of rival old products are denied the right to the trade of their customers, and these producers therefore suffer an uncontemplated loss. (There is good reason for this rights assignment. It would be too costly to ascertain who is harmed by how much, or who would be harmed by how much, when a new product is to be introduced.) The payment of compensation to losers is itself a question of instrumentalism. If all losers in conflicts of rights were compensated, every one would have an incentive to contend all right determinations, whether or not they are at all likely to be accorded the right by courts. A "moral hazard" problem arises that will be worth bearing only in certain cases.

The choice criterion proposed by Rothbard, that "everyman has the absolute right of property in his own self and the previously unowned natural resources which he finds, transforms by his own labor, and then gives or exchanges with others," is hopelessly superficial and vague.[4] How would such a criterion be applied to the conflict over decibel levels between would-be tennis players and sleepers? One person desires to exercise his rights in himself by playing tennis, the other by sleeping, and the exercise of these rights conflicts. What does it mean to say "everyman has the absolute right of property in his own self"? It certainly cannot mean that everyone has the right to use his person as he pleases, for the very question of defining private property rights is that of determining what can and what cannot be done by one's self. When the use of one's self comes into conflict with someone else's use of himself, both cannot continue to exercise absolute property rights in themselves. The question is what are the property rights one has, not whether he can exercise those that he has. The uncritical substitution of words for analysis in much property right literature merely postpones the careful attention that this complex question deserves.

The above discussion does *not* address the institutional problem of how to implement property rights systems, nor does it defend absolutely any particular criterion for defining property rights, but I did hope to demonstrate that (1) conceptually there are an infinite number of alternative private property systems, (2) one can conceive of better or worse private property arrangements, (3) the instrumental impact of a system on efficiency has a significant role to play in any such ranking, and (4) until this or other choice criteria are made explicit there is no way to determine which definition of private rights is best, that is, whether the gardener or the factory owner should control the soot content of the surrounding air.

Private Property Rights and Efficiency Considerations

I have attempted to argue for the relevance of efficiency to definitions of better rights systems within the confines of private property rights systems. In fact, we frequently encounter notions of fairness, equity, and justice that seem derivative from efficiency considerations. These notions are particularly conspicuous for situations in which transaction cost is likely to be high, and, therefore, in which rights assignment clearly has efficiency implications.

In a rear-end collision involving two cars, there is a prima facie case that the driver of the second car is liable. Could this be "because" in the general case the driver of the second car can avoid such accidents more *cheaply* than the driver of the first car? This rule of law is especially applicable at the slow speeds of city traffic, but for high speed expressways it is not applied so rigorously. The driver of a second car has a more difficult time avoiding rear-end collisions at expressway speeds, and we often observe minimum speed limits on expressways.

If the owner of a factory considers locating next to an existing laundry, and the owner of that laundry protests in court that soot from the factory will raise the cost of laundering, the factory owner is more likely to be held liable for damages than if it is the laundry that contemplates locating next to an existing factory. Although the reason for this difference in treatment might be ascribed to Rothbard's notion that every man has the absolute right of property in the previously unowned natural resources which he finds, it is more likely traceable to the generally correct judgment that he who has not yet located his business can move his business to another location at less cost than he who has already fixed his assets into a particular location.

The very notions of fault and accident seem inextricably tied to the cost of avoiding damaging interactions. A person is more likely to be held at "fault" when he could have avoided a damaging interaction with another person at relatively little cost to himself; and he is more likely to be held the innocent victim of an "accident" in which no one is at fault when neither party could have avoided the interaction at relatively low cost. Comparative negligence, in which both parties bear part of the damages of a costly interaction, seems associated with situations in which both parties could have contributed to the avoidance of the interaction at relatively little cost.

The idea of causation is also difficult to separate from the notion of the cost of avoiding damaging interactions. A boat is moored to a dock. A storm arises in which the dock is damaged by the boat. The boat owner is held liable for damages "because the boat caused the damages by striking the dock." However, all motion is relative, and it could equally be thought that the dock struck the boat, and it would probably be the dock owner that was held liable if the accident took place during gentle breezes if the dock was rotten for want of proper maintenance. In the latter case, it is the dock owner who could have prevented the damaging interaction at least cost, and it is likely to be him, or his dock, that is viewed as "causing" the accident.

The last clear chance rule, which would hold a railroad liable upon striking a trespasser is the engineer did not attempt to warn the victim, would seem to violate the notion of efficiency. Since the trespasser could avoid the accident at less cost than the railroad, it would seem that efficiency would call for liability to rest on the trespasser even if the railroad made no attempt to warn. But that is a superficial view of the problem. The accident itself is very likely to kill the trespasser, a condition in which it would be difficult in any case to make the victim whole, so there is much deterrent already in the situation, although undoubtedly some additional deterrent could be purchased by never holding the railroad liable. If, because of deafness, drunkenness, or daydreaming, the trespasser is nonetheless wandering carelessly on the tracks, then it is unlikely that this dangerous situation would have been otherwise even in the absence of the last clear chance rule of liability. After all, with the last clear chance rule, the railroad could easily escape liability by making sure that its engineers blew the whistle and applied the brakes. The trespasser, therefore, can be but little encouraged by the uncertain probability of his estate being enriched by his carelessness. Recognizing that not much deterrent is lost by the last clear chance rule, the law weighs the likelihood of saving a man's life, and the value of doing so, as sufficiently great to warrant holding the railroad liable if it fails to take the last clear chance at warning the trespasser.

The legal rules of thumb we adopt, and even our use of such words as fault and accident seem to reflect basic efficiency considerations. Efficiency seems to be not merely one of many criteria underlying our notions of ethically correct definitions of private property rights, but an extremely important one. It is difficult even to describe unambiguously any other criterion for determining what is ethical.

In some situations, such as in the development of common–law precedents, a conscious choice of assignment of private property rights is being made, but, although I have discussed this and several other matters as if such choices were straightforward and simple, I do not mean to miscalculate the difficulty of the problem, to suggest that mistakes are not made, or to underestimate the complexity of the real institutions used to resolve the problem. Just how a preferred system of property rights is to be achieved is an important matter about which we know little. There is reason to believe that a series of common–law type decisions will tend to converge on efficient definitions of rights because a legal decision that generates inefficiency is more likely to set in motion a stream of appeals and new cases designed to upset that decision than would be the case had the decision been correct form the viewpoint of efficiency. "Losers" generally have more to gain from upsetting a decision than "winners" have in defending that decision when it has produced an inefficient allocation of resources, and just the reverse when it has produced an efficient allocation. This is particularly true when the damages are largely confined to the contesting parties, as would be true with regard to a conflict between neighbors over noise levels, or the bearing of collision damages as between drivers of the two involved cars, or the conflict between a factory and a laundry over nearby air quality. For such problems, common–law legal processes seem capable of converging on precedents and property rights definitions that tend to solve conflicts over resource use efficiently. In such cases, we are essentially dealing with problems for which the resolution can be found within the confines of alternative definitions of private property rights.

Private vs. Communal Property Rights

However, when the gains or costs associated with particular interactions are not confined to a few parties, but, instead, are spread thinly over large numbers of individuals, then "high" transaction costs and "free rider" problems may be serious, even when utilizing the best of private property rights definitions, and some attenuation of private rights may be rationalized to achieve a more efficient solution to resource allocation problems. The traditional examples of providing national defense, national foreign policy, and cleaner air come to mind.

To rationalize a role for the state in this way, of course, does not insure that the state will confine its attention to such matters or even that it will improve the situation when it does. So much of the requisite information, let alone the motivation, is lacking precisely because private property based markets can function only with difficulty when such problems are serious. High transaction costs and free rider problems sometimes can be resolved by substituting private rights for communal property rights arrangements, that is, those in which there is an individual right of use but not a right to exclude others from use. The conversion of a freeway to a tollway would be an example. But this is practical only when the cost of excluding nonpayers is not too high. When dealing with national defense and air pollution problems this does not seem to be the case, and when it is not, a rationalization for action by the state in the name of efficiency becomes available.

My point is not to argue on behalf of or against state intervention in such cases, but to call attention to the ethical distinctions that seem to exist in principle between state intervention in these cases and in other cases where high transaction costs or free rider problems do not exist.

Where it is difficult to see how costs and benefits can be internalized at practical cost, as would be true with regard to air pollution in any private property rights system that I have been able to envisage, government intervention may be thought to be clumsy, costly, and misdirected, but it is seldom thought to be unethical. Similarly, the opposition to the government's use of defense forces may be based on its involvement in an immoral war or its use of an immoral draft, but it is seldom based on the immorality of the principle of using the government to provide for the "common" defense. But when a government confiscates property rights that could have been obtained through the market, as with condemnation proceedings, the military draft, or the nullification of gold clauses during the recession of the 1930s, there is more than a hint of belief that an unethical theft of rights has been perpetuated.

The problem of obtaining accurate measures of benefits and costs is not restricted to free rider–externality problems. Especially in the case of young children, but possibly also in that of serious mental cases, the state intervenes to invalidate individual actions. The usual argument in such cases is paternalism pure and simple. The intervention is required if the interest of particularly incompetent groups are to be served.

It is difficult to resist an appeal to paternalism in some cases while it is easy in others. The danger latent in the "paternalism" rationalization no doubt is great. The issue is whether a person should always have the right to act for himself when it is believed that he is incompetent to judge the costs and benefits of his actions. On what basis is the line drawn beyond which an ethical system of property rights no longer endorses coerced denial of normal contracting rights? Clearly, the greater the reliance on paternalism, the more extensive the use of coercion and the more likely it will infringe on the decisions of those who are in the best position to judge their own interests. But it is not clear from this line of reasoning that there should be no paternalism, nor how far paternalism may be carried while yet not reducing the ability of the economic organization to deliver the net gains possible through free choice.

A possible way out of this quandry is offered by modern biology. The innate propensities of man, especially when he deals with day–to–day problems of living, may not allow for a very great supply of effort or inclination to aid others. A genetic endowment producing large amounts of such helping in individual behavior, it is thought by some modern biologists, would be (and presumably was) competed out of existence by genetic varieties that confined altruism close to home. A generally altruistic genetic endowment must succumb to genetic free riders who take without giving. The selfish genetic endowment tends to displace the altruistic genetic endowment on which it rides free,[5] but it does not displace altruism completely. Biologists have found that limited amounts of such aid even in the absence of reciprocity confer survival ability to genetic endowments. To a large extent altruism is limited to kinship relations. Genetic endowments have greater survival ability if they encourage the helping of others when it can be expected that by doing so the survival power of that genetic endowment is enhanced. A person who willingly sacrifices himself to save two siblings, eight cousins, and so forth, who but for his sacrifice would surely die, increase the probability that "his" genes, idependently of which body contains them, will survive, because "his" genes also exist, with descending probability, in the bodies of siblings, cousins, and so forth. The arithmetic of genetic inheritance guarantees that relationships more distant than uncles, aunts, and first cousins are not reliable sources of paternalistic care. Similarly, a culture generous only to its own will be more resistant to freeloading and to its displacement by freeloading cultures. (There are special situations, particularly in the insect world, for which this need not be true.)

Although these findings of sociobiology are still quite speculative and subject to debate, their implication for the problem at hand is direct and dramatic. Reliable paternalistic feelings between strangers are largely ruled out by evolutionary processes. It is unlikely that net gains from exchange can be enlarged by coerced intervention in the name of paternalism if the trustee is not closely related to his charge or if there is difficulty in setting up an incentive system that more or less makes the trustee's interests coincide with those of his charge, in which case we are no longer dealing with altruistic behavior. Paternalism is, in fact, largely limited by natural selection to intrafamily relationships. Altruistic behavior toward offspring or siblings is not an anomaly in nature, and in some circumstances it may be relied upon to improve the gains from exchange, but its reliability for doing so diminishes rapidly once the coerced interaction is determined outside the immediate family of the person coerced. Adam Smith puts it neatly in his famous statement about benevolence and in his less well known one about friendship that follows closely on the first.[6]

> It is not from the benevolence of the butcher, the brewer, or the baker, that we expect our dinner, but from their regard to their own interest. We address ourselves, not to their humanity but to their self-love, and never talk to them of our own necessities but of their advantages.

> In civilized society [man] stands at all times in need of the cooperation and assistance of great multitudes, while his whole life is scarce sufficient to gain the friendship of a few persons.[7]

The limits to paternalism based on benevolence, however, do not arise only from an abhorrence of coercion; since coercion is a cost much like other costs, there is a practical inability of paternalism to deliver benefits above its cost except within narrow circles.

More fundamental than the problem of paternalism is that of competition itself. There are a multitude of methods for competing, ranging from a brick through a rival's place of business to a reduction in price to the introduction of a superior product. All these impose harmful effects on rivals but not all are viewed as equally ethical. The distinction along the ethical dimension between alternative methods of competing is peculiar to the social sciences and the humanist philosophers. Biologists in their analyses of life make no such distinction. There is only competition and natural selection of the fittest, and although biologists may distinguish descriptively one form of competition from another, they do not do so ethically.

The ethics of competition is a viable subject for students of social organization precisely because we view our situation as one where we can choose to encourage or discourage particular forms of competition. This element of volition in choosing among social organizations is not a view that biologists bring to their subject, although it is not a view that is precluded by natural selection theory. The property rights system is in large part a set of definitions and rules of behavior that specify which forms of competition are approved and encouraged and which are not.

I believe there is a strong correlation between the efficiency consequences of various forms of competition and the degree to which they are judged to be proper or ethical. Competition via violence is generally frowned upon, partly because toleration of violent competition would obscure an assessment of underlying net benefit calculations. The thief who steals an automobile does not necessarily value it more than its original possessor, but the person who purchases it does. Competition via "voluntary" negotiations, as in the case of product innovation discussed above, is more likely to yield an increase in the real wealth of a society than is competition via violent "involuntary" methods precisely because the former offers a superior technique for weighing benefits and costs, as these are measured in the market, and for filtering out net loss situations.

Methods of competing are not always easy to judge from the viewpoint of efficiency. Competition via patent procurement or by "predatory" tactics are unclearly evaluated because it is not obvious whether such forms of competition are likely to yield more gains than costs. Competition designed and executed solely to secure monopoly would be easy to frown upon if it could be detected and if it were not generally the case that it usually fails and, in the process, as with Schumpeter's "creative destruction," yields gains that greatly exceed cost. The securing of monopoly through legislated protection, however, seems much less likely to yield these gains than the securing of monopoly through superior products. It is difficult for me to see how to distinguish these two sources of negatively sloped demand curves other than by judging their likely contributions to real wealth, and it is only when judging that ethical considerations become relevant.

The general favoring of private rights of action when these can be expected to yield more accurate assessments of benefits and costs is revealed by our willingness to intervene when such expectations are not present. Competition between auto firms to reduce automobile exhaust emissions is not likely to succeed since emission controls impair the privately enjoyed services of an automobile to its owner and also raise the cost of obtaining these services. No amount of rivalry between automobile producers is likely to yield an efficient amount of smog control. A producer who incurs the cost of devising emission controls will only lose customers to his rivals if he places these controls on his automobiles. Competition based on usual notions of private rights is an ill-designed institution by which to foist private costs on consumers even if the collective benefits so obtained is greater than these costs. Intervention by the state is not viewed as unethical in such cases.

Conclusion

The legal and market implications of efficient resource allocation is no less arbitrary normatively than the preferences and tastes of the population of decision makers upon which it rests. People are willing to pay for what they *want*. The ethical weight accorded efficiency in property rights assignments is thus dependent on the ethical properties of prevailing tastes and preferences unless freedom of choice occupies the lead position in a lexicographic ordering of such preferences. An uneasy feeling of arbitrariness is inevitable when basing normative prescriptions on efficiency (but no more so than when other criteria are proposed). This is so only so long as our preferences and tastes are thought to be arbitrary. In a scientific sense, they are not arbitrary but, rather, are explainable by variations in income and relative prices. Such explanation has just begun,[8] but, for example, there undoubtedly is much consistency across time and geography in the types of wants that arise out of higher income.

Although these regularities are not without use when adopting efficiency as a normative criterion, they do not themselves provide ethical justification. Such justification cannot be provided from outside, as by divine revelation, and, in a real sense, it must be as arbitrary as is our history. But that history cannot be completely arbitrary. We have survived. Preferences, tastes, and other life-style perspectives that seriously impair the survival capability of individuals cannot themselves easily survive. Competitive preferences and life-style views, whether these are held within or outside a particular social organization, provide competition for any set of existing preferences. Life-styles that promote survival come to be viewed as ethical, and those that fail in this respect come to be viewed as in poor taste, if not as unethical. Our present preferences and tastes must reflect in large part their survival promoting capabilities. (Such capabilities, of course, may not be good enough to insure survival.) Is there much doubt that a life-style of law and order within an extensive framework of individual choice has arisen from the constraints imposed by survivability? No large society today finds itself in a much different situation in these respects; it is in the details, some of which are no doubt important, that differences are found. In a loose and general way our life-styles, preferences, and ethical beliefs are not arbitrary but are the product of thousands of centuries of biological and cultural evolution.

There is, of course, error. An efficient, that is, a high probability of survival, social organization never reduces error or experiment to zero. Moreover, what has survival capability in one environment, or century, may not do so well in another. A command social structure is likely to do better in small tribal societies than in large complex societies. War and peace are likely to bring forth different ethical precepts. A society of plenty can tolerate more altruism toward special hardship cases than can a society of poverty. We are bound to view the proper resolution of legal problems from the perspective of what presently seems efficient, whether or not efficiency is explicitly applied. Our genetic and cultural endowment contains elements of ethical preference that have survived dramatically different environments. It undoubtedly contains some ethical preferences not well suited to present conditions, but then the present is not long with us.

I began this essay in disagreement with Knight. I now end it in similar fashion.

> It seems to the writer almost superfluous to deny the appropriateness of the term "ethics" to any such [biological] conception. The conditions of survival are merely the laws of biology. It may well be the part of prudence to act in accordance with them, assuming that one *wants* to survive, but it can hardly be associated with the notions of right or duty, and if these have no meaning beyond prudence the whole realm of ethics is illusory. Ethics deals with the problem of choosing between different kinds of life, and assumes that there is a real choice between different kinds, or else there is no such thing as ethics.[9]

Those who do not *want* to survive generally have not, and neither has their genetic stock, so that most of us, under the usual conditions in which we find ourselves, do want to survive. To say that survival has brought with it (or inculcated) a general view of the good life (that style of living that has survived with us) is not to say that choice is ruled out. The ability to choose, or our lack of reliance on instinct, has itself promoted survival and has in turn been promoted by survival. Evolutionary forces do not equate to determinism, nor are evolutionary forces necessarily the only ones at work. We can exercise choice over the ethics by which to guide our lives, but it does not follow that all such choices are equally likely to survive and prosper. The competition between ethical criteria is meaningful because our condition and environment changes, but in that competition it is the set of ethics that does survive and prosper that will identify what is efficient and what is not. If the environment does not change frequently or drastically, the set of tastes and preferences that emerge will have some guiding merit. A criterion of efficiency merely proposes that this merit not be ignored when choosing among alternative property rights systems.

This does not mean abandoning efforts to alter preferences or ethical beliefs. Today's mainstream beliefs may have lagged behind today's conditions or they may be poorly attuned to tomorrow's. However, the debate over ethics can be carried out at many levels. Those who value freedom highly would seem to be wasteful of their efforts and of those of others to issue a call to debate where no substantial issue of freedom is involved; the choice between alternative private property definitions would seem a case in point. Here there is no conflict between efficiency (even narrowly defined) and freedom. And there are ample instances where *both* freedom and efficiency can be served by debate, as in arguing for deregulation. Here the criterion of efficiency reinforces the appeal of freedom. Where freedom and efficiency seem to clash, as where paternalism, free riders, and hold-out problems seem important, those who delight in pressing the cause of freedom hopefully serve some purpose other than diverting efforts from where the competition between ethical beliefs is most easily won for freedom.

Notes

1. Frank H. Knight, *The Ethics of Competition* (N.Y.: Harper and Brothers, 1935), p. 66.

2. The meaning I attach to "efficiency" is clarified later in this chapter.

3. Murray N. Rothbard, *Power and Market* (Menlo Park, Calif.: Institute for Humane Studies, 1970), p. 11.

4. Ibid., p. 1.

5. For a discussion of the growing interface between economics and biology, see Jack Hirshleifer, "Economics from a Biological Viewpoint," *Journal of Law and Economics* 20, no. 1 (April 1977): 1–52.

6. See R.H. Coase's excellent discussion of "Adam Smith's View of Man," *Journal of Law and Economics* 19, no. 3 (October 1976): 529–546.

7. Adam Smith, The Wealth of Nations (New York: Random House, 1937), p. 14.

8. George J. Stigler, and Gary S. Becker, "De Gustibus Non Est Disputandum," *American Economic Review* 67, no. 2 (March 1977): 76–90.

9. Knight, *The Ethics of Competition,* p. 71.

Comment: Efficiency Is Not a Substitute for Ethics

John B. Egger

Professor Demsetz has presented us with a characteristically insightful study of the relationship between his concept of economic efficiency and the manner in which property rights are enforced. I propose to divide this critical comment into three sections: first, my attempt at an evenhanded summary of Demsetz's principal conclusions; second, a critical interpretation of these findings from an Austrian perspective; and third, some suggestions for reconciling or integrating the view of Demsetz with those of Hayek and of Rothbard, and other "natural rights" theorists. My general conviction is that Demsetz has, indeed, something valuable to offer, but that his interpretation of it is improperly identified.

Demsetz on Efficiency, Ethics, and Property Rights

Demsetz argues that while the only effective way in which we can "judge the ethical properties of alternative economic organizations" is by examining the actions promoted by these different systems, advocates of one system or another frequently make recourse to "some unspecified, usually vague concept of 'justice' or 'morality', often stated quite independently of an examination of the human action implied by that economic organization."[1] These tactics appear to be based upon *faith* and seem ineffective to Demsetz because they imply an absolutism in property rights, which he believes clashes with commonly held ideas of right and wrong: "a sufficient alteration in the gains and losses of alternative definitions of property right structures can dim the ethical aura that surrounds any specific structure."[2] As a substitute for the "simplistic *faith*" approach to comparison of the ethics of different rights systems,[3] Demsetz proposes that we compare instead the economic efficiency of the actions and resource allocation promoted by different types of property rights. He informs us that not only does such an hypothesis "explain" the way rights are actually developed, it also sets up rules by which rights structures *should be* developed. By arguing this normative position, Demsetz maintains that our views on ethics are in fact also determined by efficiency considerations.

> The legal rules of thumb we adopt, and even our use of such words as fault and accident seem to reflect basic efficiency considerations. Efficiency

seems to be not merely one of many criteria underlying our notion of ethically correct definitions of property rights, but an extremely important one. It is difficult even to describe unambiguously any other criterion for determining what is ethical.[4]

It is significant that Demsetz sees comparisons of costs and benefits as determining not merely what kinds and degrees of property rights will be *enforced:* he sees such comparisons as actually determining what rights people *have.*

Demsetz proceeds to discuss a number of specific cases that appear to justify his contention that courts do base decisions on efficiency considerations, and he suggests that any property right that violates such a criterion in an obvious and dramatic way would soon cease to be enforced (which he seems to equate to "cease to exist"). As further evidence, he points out that different kinds of societies, facing different geographical (economic) conditions, do in fact enforce (again, he reads "have") different property rights.[5] The economic realities facing a society thus appear to Demsetz as the principal determinant, via the concept of efficiency, of both that society's ethical beliefs (and, consequently, the system of property rights which should be enforced) and the structure of property rights it actually develops and enforces.

Although he is careful to attempt to exclude his own political and ethical preferences from his analysis, Demsetz is a prominent advocate of the market system, and he leaves us with the conclusions that his "efficiency" approach does in fact generally support the free market and that it offers libertarians a much more solid and convincing case than do arguments based on "simplistic *faith*" in some absolute, overriding general ethical rule.

An Austrian View of Efficiency and Property Rights Evolution

Because his paper is presented before a group assembled to hear about "current Austrian perspectives," Professor Demsetz is entitled to an Austrian-style critique.[6] The unique outlook of the Austrian school can be identified in any of a number of ways.[7] A favorite way of Professor Ludwig Lachmann is to emphasize "radical subjectivism," a phrase that means to the Austrian not merely avoiding the explicit specification of utility function arguments but, more generally, interpreting the world through the eyes of the acting economic agent. From this viewpoint follows not merely the subjective nature of value and cost, but also a meaningful role for learning and hence for time, error, and uncertainty, and the verbal causal-genetic method (as opposed to that of mathematical simultaneous determination).

From these follow the unique outlooks on capital theory, business-cycle theory, and entrepreneurship—all the specifics for which the Austrian school is known.

If we think back over the gestalt of Demsetz's paper, we are struck with a crucial question: where, in the nature and characteristics of the Austrian school, is the "simplistic *faith*" in some general natural-law principle from which all ethics are derived and which dictates to us the proper property rights structure? The answer: absolutely nowhere. Indeed, the commonly held ideal of value freedom in economics was an early Austrian-school development, and as Richard Ebeling has pointed out there have been prominent Austrian economists who were socialists, fascists, and communists.

Although the relation between Austrian economics and property rights will comprise a major topic of this section of my critique, we might note that Demsetz, whatever his intent, succeeds in confusing the issue by criticizing the ethical foundations held by two prominent Austrian economists. In fact, although their economic understanding undoubtedly had some effect on their ethical attitudes, the ethics adopted by Professors Block and Rothbard cannot be derived from Austrian-school principles and are not necessary to Austrian economic analysis. Professor Demsetz has invited confusion of the ethical positions of two Austrian economists with the completely value-free nature of Austrian economics itself. As Walter Block himself observes, Austrian economics and libertarianism, although often found together, are distinct both in principle and practice.

What role does one find for property rights in the works of the Austrian economists? Very little mention is made of the things except when these economists—Professors Hayek and Rothbard spring to mind—have put on their political scientist hats. There is good reason for this; it isn't just that the major Austrian treatises were written before the modern "economic analysis of property rights" developed. The fact is that the acting economic agent does not see the property rights structure in which he acts as a choice variable. It is a datum to him, fully as much as is the weather, and is significant because it determines the pattern of benefits and costs resulting from particular actions. In any situation, the individual can choose to violate the tenets of the prevailing structure—he can steal, for instance, or avoid paying taxes—but he must recognize, and take into account, that if he is detected certain large sacrifices may be required. Actions chosen under one rights structure (for example, "buy him in") might not be desirable under another (for example, "let him buy his way out"), and to point this out and examine its implications is as far as Austrian economics per se can go.[8]

What function is served by a property rights structure? Once we determine an acceptable answer to that question I think we expose the central flaw in Professor Demsetz's analysis, and in some of the "economics of property rights" literature in general. As long as this literature is confined to comparison of the different cost–benefit judgments governing individual action under alternative rights systems, there can be no quarrel with it— indeed, it plays a valuable role. The problems arise when one attempts, as does Demsetz, to rely on economic arguments alone to rank rights systems according to their desirability.

Property rights define the nature of the things individuals use and exchange. When I acquire a bass drum, along with it comes the freedom (the right) to use it in many ways. But one of these is *not* to beat on it outside my neighbor's bedroom window at 4:00 A.M.; if I want to do that, I have to buy the right from him. A list of examples could be extended indefinitely. My point here is simply to reinforce what I have asserted earlier: a property rights system lays down the rules, it defines the freedoms and restrictions according to which we evaluate alternatives and make choices, but as such it is conceptually distinct from the alternatives among which we choose.[9]

Although there are some real fundamental confusions in Demsetz-inspired property rights analyses (resulting from the attempt to apply choice–theoretic analytical tools to institutions which by their nature cannot result from consciously evaluated choices), perhaps it is best first to deal with the standard Demsetz proposes to substitute for ethics: economic efficiency.

He provides a number of examples in chapter 5 in which courts have enforced rights in a manner consistent with his view of efficiency (and seems to imply that this is not only what they should do, but even how rights should be defined):

1. "the benefits of assigning rights over noise levels during night time hours to would–be sleepers exceed the costs thereby imposed on would-be nighttime tennis players"
2. "the driver of the second car can avoid such accidents more *cheaply* than the driver of the first car"
3. "the thief who steals an automobile does not necessarily value it more than its original possessor, but the person who purchases it does"
4. "he who has not yet located his business can move his business to another location at less cost than he who has already fixed his assets into a particular location"
5. "competition based on usual notions of private rights is an ill–designed institution by which to foist private costs on consumers even if the collective benefit so obtained is greater than these costs"

Demsetz's decision criterion, determining both what courts do and what they should do to be fair or ethical, requires the judge to compare the amount by which one individual or group is better off with the amount by which another individual or group is worse off. The right is granted to the group with the most to lose: cocktail-party reasoning suggests that the sleepers have more to lose than the maverick nighttime tennis players, so we minimize social disutility by granting them the right, requiring the tennis players to buy it from them at the appropriate price.

But like much cocktail-party conversation this is not reasoning at all. Costs and benefits cannot be compared across individuals, even when monetary sums are involved, because of the impossibility of interpersonal utility comparison. This insight is a straightforward application of the defining principle of the Austrian school: radical subjectivism. Although it is true, as Demsetz (with understandable frustration) points out, that we all rely to some extent on snap introspective interpersonal utility comparisons in our everyday lives, these casual judgments hardly deserve to be elevated to the position of ethical standard. If economics teaches us anything, it should be that the harm imposed upon one individual cannot be compared—even ordinally—with the benefit thereby awarded to another. The scientific basis for Demsetz's "efficiency" argument simply does not exist.

So what meaning can efficiency have? The closest it comes to being meaningful is to identify actions in which the perceived benefits exceed the perceived costs—such as action is efficient—but, of course, to the radical subjectivist who allows the actor to demonstrate his own perceived costs and benefits *every* action is of this nature. Unless we impose some outside, exogenous constraint that allows us to differentiate efficient from inefficient action the term "efficiency" is indeed superfluous. Demsetz suggests that we obtain our standard by scrapping subjectivity, but the subjectivist principle has so much explanatory power throughout economics that to cast it aside is distinctly the wrong way to go. There is another way to develop this exogenous standard and thus to temporarily rescue the term "efficiency," and that's by appeal to *ethical theory*. If we go this route, actions taken within the proper ethical framework are efficient, and those that in some way violate ethical principles are not. But this clearly is not what Demsetz wishes to do: far from the economic concept of efficiency determining what is ethical, we have ethical theory determining what is efficient!

Consider a holdup in which you are ordered at gunpoint to hand over $5,000. As a radical subjectivist, you realize that it is improper to believe that the criminal values the $5,000 either less or more than you do: such comparisons simply cannot be made. You also realize that by most standards the criminal has no ethical right to take money: he, and his gun, impose conditions on your choice framework that conflict with ethical precepts. Nonetheless, you do have options that must be evaluated: hand over the money, fight, run, yell, discuss ethical principles calmly with the robber, and so forth. The concepts of benefit and cost are thus applicable and, within the framework imposed upon your alternatives, you'll choose the most advantageous. Unless we impose exogenous standards such as interpersonal utility comparisons or ethical principles, we must term any action you take "efficient," based as it has been on your own cost–benefit comparison given the circumstances. Clearly, then, if we reject both interpersonal utility comparison *and* ethics, every action (which is, of course, within a particular property rights structure) is efficient. An action taken (and therefore efficient) in one rights system would not be taken (would be inefficient) in another, but this provides nothing we can use to compare and rank systems of rights assignments.

Without an exogenous standard by which to judge either rights or efficiency, we find that all actions taken within any particular rights system are efficient but there is no reason or standard by which to prefer one "efficient action/rights structure" combination over another. Demsetz proposes that we introduce as this exogenous standard the interpersonal comparison of utilities; the alternative is to rely upon the principles of ethics. I am not at all unhappy to note that Demsetz's approach gets us nowhere: this particular example of "economic imperialism" (as Professor Rothbard might term it) deserves to be clipped off at its roots. Ratios of first derivatives of utility functions, and the like, are interesting and important things, but they do not take the place of well–reasoned answers to the problems that have faced philosophers of ethics for centuries.

Demsetz, Hayek, and Natural Rights: An Integrating Perspective

Demsetz is on much firmer ground if his work is interpreted in a different sense. As I have attempted to show, as a concept referring to individual valuation, efficiency simply cannot serve as a replacement for ethics. If, however, we consider his work an analysis of the evolution of common law it becomes much more appealing.

The principal shift in focus is from the realm of conscious individual valuation to the study of "the results of human action but not of human design."[10] Professor Demsetz refers several times to "survival capabilities";[11] this concept is also used by Professor Hayek to describe laws of social order which tend to persist in evolution.[12] Just as Professor Hayek emphasizes that different kinds of societies (for example, tribal, nomadic, industrialized) develop different systems of rights and moral attitudes, so does Professor Demsetz.[13] It is unfortunate that Demsetz failed to distinguish between "the results of human action" and the products of human design or reasoned choice.

The relation between Demsetz and the natural rights philosophers for whom he professes to have little use is less clear. In principle he often comes across as an act or case utilitarian, asserting that only the cost-benefit calculus of the particular situation—and not any fundamental ethical rule—offers us direction. In other places he proposes such criteria only when either of two conceivable "rights assignments . . . seem equally productive of individual freedom."[14]

In this second interpretation Demsetz is on much stronger ground. As both Hayek and Rothbard have emphasized, the principles of social organization consistent with freedom must be grounded in a strong ideological base;[15] as social commentators have been pointing out for years,[16] purely economic defenses of the market system are not convincing in practice and—as we have seen—they can't be supported in theory. If Demsetz would accept the principle that no marginal substitutions involving individual freedom can be tolerated, then he could no longer be considered an act utilitarian and much of the potentially sinister nature of his normative proposals would evaporate.

The goal of the natural rights theorist is and has been for centuries to determine general principles of ethics from the nature of man and the universe. Although the logical presentation of such analyses makes them appear deductive, deducing ethics from the nature of man and reality, writers in this tradition must of course approach their subject with firsthand experiential knowledge of how men behave and which ethical principles seem to result in order, which in chaos. In any case, those seeking the principles on which the free society is founded search, in essence, for general rules from which specific applications consistent with individual freedom follow as special cases. If one follows Hayek's discussion of the evolution of the spontaneous order, one realizes that any general principles lying (logically) behind that order need not have been recognized and articulated; indeed, it could well happen that such a principle could be discovered only after some considerable evolution of a self-generated order provided "data points" by which to deductively test alternative general laws.

To the extent that a society develops in a self-generated manner, is it any wonder to one who appreciates human motivations and the "use of knowledge in society"[17] that material productivity should tend to be large? We should be surprised neither that it coincides with individual freedom nor that principles of natural law (founded as they are in the relation between man and Nature) provide a moral foundation for both (that is, freedom and what people often use it for: material productivity). We might also call it "survival capabilities."

Although Professor Demsetz offers us a number of interesting insights into the evolution of legal principles and the positive behavior of judges, and thus can be interpreted as broadly consistent with the works of both Hayek and the ethical theorists searching for general principles guiding development of the free society, his own interpretation of his work is seriously flawed by his conviction that the economist's concept of efficiency can substitute for ethics. It cannot. Without a firm, reasoned ethical position, even the most witty and technically adept economist can present a case for liberty which is at best unconvincing.

Notes

1. Chapter 5, Harold Demsetz, "Ethics and Efficiency in Property Rights Systems", pp. 97–98.

2. Ibid., pp. 100–101.

3. Ibid., p. 98.

4. Ibid., p. 109.

5. Ibid. *See also* his "Toward a Theory of Property Rights," *American Economic Review* 52, 3 (May 1967): 347–359.

6. Like most or all so–called "schools," however, it is only to the famed casual observer that all recognized or self–proclaimed members of this school look alike; there is probably as much heated argument at the average Austrian get–together as at the average general session of the American Economic Association. So while the assertion probably is futile, I must nonetheless assert that my observations do not necessarily represent the views of any of those others who also believe they are working in the Austrian tradition.

7. For a thoughtful examination of the past and present Austrian school, *see* Lawrence H. White, "The Methodology of the Austrian School," Center for Libertarian Studies, Occasional Paper no. 1 (New York, 1977).

8. *See,* for example, Ludwig von Mises, *Human Action* (Chicago: Regnery, 1966), pp. 654–62, 682–4. Although an outspoken advocate of value-free economics, Murray N. Rothbard in his recent work has often found it necessary to be both economist and theorist of politics and ethics between the same covers; see *Man Economy and State* (Los Angeles: Nash, 1962).

9. It should be clear than when I buy or am given the right to bang the drum outside my neighbor's window I am not buying a change in the rights system. The system still assigns the right to the neighbor; indeed, that's why I must rent it from him.

10. F.A. Hayek, *Studies in Philosophy, Politics and Economics* (Chicago: University of Chicago Press, 1967), pp. 96–105.

11. Chapter 5, pp. 114–115.

12. F.A. Hayek, *Law, Legislation and Liberty,* vol. 1 (Chicago: University of Chicago Press, 1973), p. 39.

13. Compare Demsetz in chapter 5, p. 115 with F.A. Hayek, *Law, Legislation and Liberty,* vol. 2 (Chicago: University of Chicago Press, 1976), pp. 24–7.

14. Chapter 5, p. 101.

15. Hayek, *Law, Legislation and Liberty,* vol. 1, p. 61, vol. 2, pp. 16–17, 54–55. Murray N. Rothbard, *Egalitarianism as a Revolt against Nature* (Washington D.C.: Libertarian Review Press, 1974): 1–13.

16. See almost anything written by Irving Kristol such as "Capitalism, Socialism, and Nihilism." *The Public Interest* 31 (Spring, 1973), pp. 3–16.

17. F.A. Hayek, "The Use of Knowledge in Society," reprinted in *Individualism and Economic Order* (Chicago: University of Chicago Press, 1948), pp. 77–91.

6

The General X – Efficiency Paradigm and the Role of the Entrepreneur

Harvey Leibenstein

The Problem—Ordinary Language and Theory

Words cause problems. Words are not always arranged so that we can use them in the way we mean. One reason for this is clear—words have a history. Some were developed in a simpler age when the contexts in which they were used was more uniform. This is the case with the noun *entrepreneur*. Thus, the ordinary language use of the word was probably much more adequate in earlier periods than it is today. Two characteristics of changes come to mind which suggest why this may be the case: variety and complexity. Since words have a number of nuances and connotations, the nuances and connotations applicable to fairly uniform and simple contexts appear inapplicable and troublesome when the contexts are varied and complex.

Consider a simpler word than *entrepreneur*—say the word *grocer*. There was a time, say half a century ago, when the corner grocer easily identified a specific individual. This is still the case in some small towns and ethnic neighborhoods of large cities. In such circumstances people have a fairly good notion of what the grocer does. But who is the grocer in the world of supermarkets? Does such a person exist, and if he does, what does he do? In a supermarket chain is the grocer a single individual? Is he the manager of the "grocery" department? The answer to the last two questions are not at all clear.

Similar problems arise with the concept of entrepreneur. In a simpler age when the entrepreneur was usually a single individual and the sole owner of the enterprise he organized, ordinary use of the term was fairly simple. The entrepreneur was almost identical to the "boss." One could write a novel about the entrepreneur and think of him (or her—although it was rarely a her) as a fairly well–defined character. One has the feeling that Schumpeter's original entrepreneur was that sort of person. And one can think of him as a person. But who are the entrepreneurs in a world of large multinational corporations, the stock ownership of which is widely distributed? *Who* is the entrepreneur when it is a multi–person venture? What does a multi–person entrepreneur do? How can we recognize the individuals to be included in such a group? Thus in ordinary language, an increase in variety, complexity, and specialization creates difficulties in using a concept precisely.

But our concern is not with respect to ordinary usage. As economists we face a special problem. What do we mean by the entrepreneur, given our economic theories? But ordinary usage is not entirely irrelevant here. There is an imagery that is suggested by words, especially nouns. We cannot help taking at least some of that imagery with us as we shift from ordinary to technical usage. Even in the mathematical models of microeconomics some of the imagery returns as soon as we attempt to interpret our mathematical results.

The special problem facing the economist is to square the concept of the entrepreneur with his microeconomic theory. It is more than just a concept that is involved—it is an amalgam of activities that we believe exists in the real world. Hence a related problem is to find consistency between the behavioral aspects of the real world and our theoretical world. Even ethical considerations enter. Entrepreneurs appear to earn profits. Are these profits justified in some sense? Hence the search for something that the entrepreneur does that is unique and necessary to justify his reward. Are we loath to believe that entrepreneurs are parasites on the economic body? Thus we have to find a connection, not just any connection, but the right connection, between entrepreneurial activities and the theory of profits—or more accurately, the role of profits in our theory.

A related element that is extremely important in this area is the *theoretical* firm in *theoretical* markets. It is well known that over the past century as the neoclassical theory went through successive refinements we ended up with the unalloyed jewel known as the market in general equilibrium. In such a market the firm becomes a trivial and indeterminate entity. If prices of inputs and outputs are known, and if the menu of techniques that translates inputs into outputs is known, then the firm can be presumed to behave quite mechanically. To determine the desirability of entry and exist, or to determine the desirability of expansion or contradiction becomes a simple problem in calculation. There is no special need for the unusual skills we generally associate in ordinary language with the entrepreneur. If we had never heard of the concept our theory would not differ any. The sense of an entrepreneur is unnecessary intellectual furniture in this particular world. The difficulty with Frank Knight's solution of the entrepreneur as a bearer of uncertainty was recognized by Knight himself. In the usual conception of a general equilibrium there would not be any uncertainty.

Some writers in the Austrian tradition changed the game. Instead of addressing the entrepreneurial problem from the viewpoint of a general equilibrium they shifted to the vision of competition as a process. During the competitive *process* there is indeed greater room for entrepreneurship as a factor, especially during the nonequilibrium phase. Even Schumpeter changed the rules by introducing a special type of uncertainty associated with the process of innovation. This is not the place to review the history of doctrine and attempt to see how different writers changed the rules of the puzzle, so to speak, to introduce into their theories reasonably active entrepreneurs worthy of their keep.[1]

The lesson of the previous remarks is clear. If we want to get anywhere to solve the entrepreneurial puzzle, we have to stay away from the neoclassical general equilibrium syndrome. This indeed will also be the approach taken in this paper. In the sections that follow we shall review briefly the main elements of the X-efficiency paradigm, show how it leads to a different picture of the firm and the market, and examine the scope of entrepreneurship from this viewpoint.

A Sketch of the X-Efficiency Theory of the Firm

Normal understanding flows from the familiar to the less familiar, or unfamiliar. Hence it seems desirable to compare the main differences between neoclassical theory and what I have called the X-efficiency paradigm. We now turn to this matter with the aid of table 6-1.

Under X-efficiency theory individuals are, in general, not maximizers; that is, maximizing behavior is not the norm, although there may be some personalities for whom behavior approximates maximization, while for others, maximization behavior is approached only in unusually high-pressured contexts.

We visualize individuals facing a flow of opportunities which, when attended to, yield economic gains. At the same time, there is a flow of related constraints which, if not attended to, yields losses. The concept of degree of constraint concern reflects the extent to which an individual takes advantage of the opportunities and his attention to constraints. A maximizer whose degree of constraint concern would be unity would take care of all such opportunities and always attend adequately to related constraints.

Table 6-1
X-Efficiency Theory and Neoclassical Theory

Components	X-Efficiency Theory	Neoclassical Theory
1. Psychology	1. Selective rationality	1. Maximization or minimization
2. Contracts	2. Incomplete	2. Complete
3. Effort	3. Discretionary variable	3. Assumed given
4. Units	4. Individuals	4. Households and firms
5. Inert areas	5. Important variable	5. None
6. Agent-principal	6. Differential	6. Identity of interests

For normal individuals constraint concern is less than unity. An individual is also willing to trade some degree of less constraint concern for some greater degree of *internal* felt pressure. (For example, we do not all pay our bills on time and can live with some degree of unfulfilled obligation). At the same time we recognize that higher than normal *external* pressure in some economic contexts will induce individuals to behave with a greater degree of constraint concern. In general, (1) contextual pressure and (2) personality (which may be read as "taste for constraint concern") determine the degree of constraint concern; that is, the extent of the deviation from maximizing behavior.

The other elements in our system are much more straightforward than the constraint concern idea. The decision unit is the individual rather than the firm, and we focus special attention on effort decisions. Effort is a major variable. It is also a complex variable, and may be viewed as being made up of the following components: (A) the activities chosen; (P) the pace of carrying out activities; (Q) the quality of the activities; and (T) the time sequence aspect. Assuming that A, P, Q, and T can be assigned values, we can then visualize the vector $APQT$ as an effort point.

Implicit to neoclassical theory is the notion that contracts are complete. Under the X-efficiency viewpoint firm–membership contracts or employer–employee contracts are incomplete. Rather, they are likely to be asymmetrical. The payment part of the contract is frequently well specified, but the work part is not. Thus effort is a discretionary variable. Individuals have to interpret their jobs. There may be some understanding surrounding the bounds of the employer–employee relation, but areas of discretion between understood bounds are still likely to remain. Thus, individuals have to interpret their jobs, so to speak. This last involves the choice of an "effort position"—that is, a subset of effort points that allows the individual to take into account a variety of demands on his effort capacity.

The concept of inert areas in our paradigm is similar to common notion of inertia. Suppose "positions" are related to utility valuations by an individual. We posit the existence of a psychological *inertial cost* of moving from one position to another. Thus an individual who finds himself in one effort position may not move to a superior effort position because the inertial cost is greater than the utility gain. Inertial cost should be viewed as a personality characteristic. An individual who is a maximizer would have zero inertial costs.

An important background idea lies in the possible differential interests between principals and agents. For present purposes it will be best to focus on the case in which decisions are made in a world of agents. This is the case of the multiperson corporation for which stock ownership is widely distributed. Other examples are government–owned corporations, or enterprises run directly by government bureaucracies. Since in these cases the principals are hard to identify, and when identified, hardly likely to speak with a common voice, we can readily speak of possible divergence of interests between agents (say hired managers) and principals. Of course, in other cases, the agent's interests may also diverge from those of the principal, and the agent may be able to act on his own, as it were, to some degree. In the light of the above, where effort discretion exists, it should not be surprising that the effort choices of the agent are not identical to those of the principal.

Given our behavioral postulates one can readily see that the typical firm, outside of a perfectly competitive general equilibrium, will not minimize costs of production. Because of asymmetrical incomplete contract effort discretion exists. To interpret his job an individual exercises his discretion and chooses what we have called an effort position. Now, there exists some set of effort positions that is consistent with cost minimization. But there is no reason why any individual should choose the cost-minimizing effort position. Because of differential principal-agent interests we would normally expect that individuals would choose non-cost-minimizing positions. Even if one individual were to choose a non-cost-minimizing position it would be sufficient to make our case, but there is no reason why most or all individuals would not choose such positions. Also, given the concept of inert areas and positive inertial costs, we should expect some nonminimal cost positions to persist. In view of the assumption of non-maximizing behavior there is no reason why anyone should try to persuade or force others to shift to cost minimizing effort positions.

A final factor we must consider is the concept of organizational entropy. The main idea is simple. Essentially we visualize one of the concerns of management and entrepreneurship to be the struggle against X-inefficiency. The idea of organizational entropy is that if this struggle is not engaged in, things get worse, and X-inefficiency increases, at least up to some point. There are various ways through which we can see this phenomenon. First consider the choice of the effort position. The individual making the choice does so in the light of what he believes are constraining influences. In making his choice he does not do entirely as he pleases. But if he discovers in practice that these constraints do not really exist, he reconsiders his position and has a tendency to move to one more related to his own desires than to his vision of company aims. Thus a gradual attenuation of the coordination of different people's activities takes place as individuals gradually discover that there is an apparent diminishing interest on the part of authorities and peers in efforts toward greater meaningful coordination. It should be kept in mind that we are discussing a potentiality and not an actuality. In describing organizational entropy we are describing one of the forces involved in the absence of the operation of the opposing force. The opposing force is the attempt by management (or entrepreneurship) to counter entropy.

We can summarize and, we hope, clarify many of these ideas with the aid of figure 6-1. In the four quadrants let *P, CC, E,* and *C* represent Pressure (external), Constraint Concern, Effort, and Cost per unit. As we move from quadrant I to IV the following influences are involved. For→read "determines."

$$\begin{array}{ll}
\text{Quadrant} \quad \text{I} & P \longrightarrow CC \\
\text{II} & CC \longrightarrow E \\
\text{III} & E \longrightarrow C \\
\text{IV} & C \longrightarrow P
\end{array}$$

Thus the curve *RR* indicates the degree of selective rationality (that is, constraint concern) as a function of external pressure on the individual. In quadrant II, *EE* indicated effort as a function of constraint concern, while in III, *CC* indicates unit cost as a function of effort, and finally in IV, *CP* shows how the firm sets pressure in response to unit cost. Looking at the figure we can see that the components $P_1 R_1 E_1 C_1$ are all consistent with each

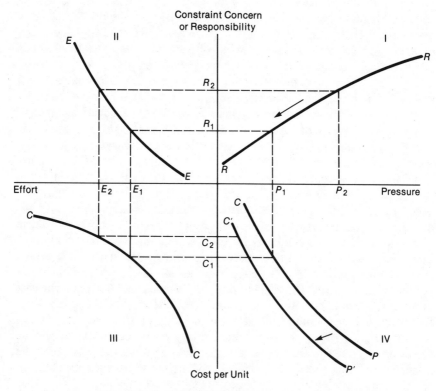

Figure 6-1. General X-Efficiency Paradigm.

other, and hence the point $P_1R_1E_1C_1$ is an equilibrium for the interaction betwen the firm and the individual. However, the components $P_2R_2E_2C_2$ are nonequilibrium components. P_2 leads to gradually lower levels of pressure and may be viewed as a level consistent with the temporary dominance of entropy operating in the system (see arrow). Another possibility is a movement of the function PC in quadrant IV toward $P'C'$. This last would also indicate the operation of entropy in the system.

It is important to note that quadrant IV is very different from the relations depicted in the other three quadrants. In quadrants I, II, and III the relations involved concern *only* the individual in question. In this case they depict the behavior relations of the representative individual. Quadrant IV depicts the *reaction* of the firm to individual behavior. In this case the firm reacts to the imposition of a part of unit cost by the individual on the firm. We ignore for the time being who it is in the firm who perceives the cost imposition and who directly or indirectly imposes the external pressure. We also ignore the possibility that the firm may react differently, depending on how other individuals in the firm behave simultaneously.

The main point is that the entrepreneur may have a role to play with respect to the sort of phenomena depicted or implicit in the cost–pressure reaction relation. On the one hand it represents in some sense a reaction by "the firm" to the individual. That is, it is a reaction by peers and especially authorities to the behavior of the individual. What is not shown, but what is especially important for our purposes, is that such reactions are likely to be influenced by events outside the firm—for example, by degree of competition of other firms, or by prices charged by other firms. We shall argue that of special concern to the entrepreneur are firm–market and firm–other firm relations.

X-Efficiency Theory Implications for the Market

We have argued that what we are likely to think the entrepreneur does will depend very much on our vision of the market. Hence, much of what we have sketched in the previous section represents the building blocks for our vision of the market. Basically, we try to answer the question: If we accept the premises of X-efficiency theory, what does it tell us about the nature of markets? Because of space limitations the previous section cannot be viewed as self-contained, and as a consequence we may be forced to introduce elements not contained above.

We now turn to indicate a number of the implications of X-efficiency theory for firms and markets that may be connected with the essential tasks of entrepreneurship:

1. *Absence of a unique production function:* Because of the existence of effort discretion, it no longer follows that there exists a formula or set of

formulas so that every set of inputs implies a unique quantity of output. In the X-efficiency world the usual production function does not exist. Knowing the price that certain goods are selling for in the market does not enable the entrepreneur to determine uniquely at what cost he can produce the product, and hence easily determine the desirability of entry and exist. The entrepreneur has to be ready to assume the X-inefficiency uncertainty, so to speak. Furthermore, once the firm is organized he has to make sure that the managers are skilled enough to struggle against the organizational entropy forces with the firm.

2. *Holes—lack of filled profit opportunities:* Both the nonmaximization postulate and the theory of inert areas should lead us to expect that there would be holes in the market fabric, so to speak. Nonmaximization and the operation of inertia suggest that not all entrepreneurial opportunities would be undertaken. This implies a lack of complete continuity in the product space of the market. Especially important for our purposes are holes in the input markets.

3. *Technique options:* Nonmaximization and inert areas also imply that many inventions have not been processed sufficiently so that they are available to the business community as technical innovations. Hence, the list of techniques available is in some areas very fuzzy. It is not always a matter of buying a patent-right. There are both empty spaces and fuzzy areas between what is being bought, and what can be done for productive purposes with what is bought.

4. *Market obstacles:* Just as some inputs may be missing other inputs may be available, but not equally available to all. Part of this may be true for some firms or some entrepreneurs, but part may also be due to the political processes in the economy. To retain a monopoly position some firms may not allow access to patents, copyrights, or attempt to protect commercial secrets of one type or another, at the same time governments may require licenses of one type or another. In any event, the X-efficiency theory suggests that there is no reason to expect firms to set themselves up, which would provide equal access to all inputs to all customers (including firms who may want to enter the "equal access" business).

5. *Incomplete cost containment:* In the traditional vision, profits are the ideal signal for entrepreneurial activity. Industries in which profits are high should encourage entry and expansion of scale of operations, and where they are low or negative we should expect contractions and exits. However, this no longer holds under the X-efficiency view. Low profits or even losses may be a consequence of X-inefficiency, or an inability to struggle against organizational entropy. Hence profitable entrepreneurial opportunities may be hidden or be less apparent where X-inefficiency exists. Thus the entrepreneur has the functional of ferreting out opportunities in markets where on the surface no opportunities seem to exist. The converse may

also be true. Opportunities that appear to exist may in fact turn out to be traps for many entrepreneurs, because it may be extremely difficult to create a new organization or expand an existing one, and to operate it at the existing level of unit costs.

6. *Missing inputs and the continuity problem:* One input is always missing in the market, from our viewpoint—motivation. Although motivational advice may be purchasable, the motivational system is not. We view motivation as largely a product of peer group and authority influences. It is a product of the history of the organization, and of the particular individuals that fill organizational slots. Motivation is akin to team spirit. In addition to motivation a variety of other inputs may be missing in the sense of being available, equally to all, in well functioning markets. Another way of looking at this matter is to say that the product space is not continous. It is not so dense everywhere that every variety of product exists. Products come in discontinuous chunks, as it were, and not as individual characteristics or qualities. Hence the entrepreneur has to marshal enough of the missing or difficult to get inputs to produce an integrated collection of qualities.[2]

What Do Entrepreneurs Do?

Once we have spelled out our vision of the market, it seems almost self-evident to determine what it is that the entrepreneur does. Clearly under the X-efficiency vision the market has a great many imperfections. The entrepreneur tries to create new firms or expand existing ones *despite* market imperfections. It is of interest to note that the greater the imperfections, the wider the scope of entrepreneurial activities, and vice versa. This fits the notion that under a perfectly competitive equilibrium the scope for entrepreneurial activities falls to zero, whereas as imperfections increase so does entrepreneurial scope. This is not to imply that there are always entrepreneurs around to meet the challenges of whatever imperfections exist.

On a somewhat more specific level we could break down the categories of entrepreneurial activities into three classes. These are: (1) gap filling and "obstacle overcoming," (2) input completing, and (3) uncertainty bearing of the organization and its environment. Clearly if there are holes in the input market, the entrepreneur has to somehow make up such holes. Where the imperfections are in terms of obstacles to inputs, these have to be overcome. This much is fairly straightforward. However, merely filling gaps in input markets and overcoming obstacles is not sufficient for one to be an entrepreneur. Although anyone who fills some of the holes may be said to *aid* the entrepreneurial function, it does not necessarily add to the supply of entrepreneurship. A necessary and simultaneous responsibility for the entrepreneur is to be an *input completer*. This is critical. That is to say, the entrepreneur must fill enough of the gaps so that *all* necessary inputs can be marshaled in order to produce the commodity in question. The inability to marshal all the requisite inputs leads by definition to ineffectual results.

It is clear from the above that both categories of activities are necessary. The entrepreneur also has to be *concerned* with bearing the uncertainty involved in the firm as an organization. Initially he has to bear the consequences of potential organizational entropy and the related uncertainty of how the organization fares in its economic environment. This is not to suggest that the entrepreneur has to necessarily bear this uncertainty indefinitely, or that he cannot shift it very early in his activities to others who might be willing to bear the uncertainty for a return or potential return. But he has to undertake to bear the uncertainty himself, or to arrange for the transfer of uncertainty bearing to others, whether stockholders, bondholders, or other contributors to the financial assets of the firm.

Two sets of activities which are difficult to determine as belonging to either entrepreneurship or management are the (1) cost containing and (2) market sheltering activities.[3] These are clearly related to the uncertainty-bearing functions mentioned in the previous paragraph. Clearly the uncertainty–bearing function operates as an incentive to introduce measures so that entropy is fought adequately in order for the firm to remain a viable entity. We must bear in mind that substitutes for the cost–containing struggle are those activities that reduce the degree of competitiveness the firm has to face in the market. We will not discuss at this juncture the various options that may be available, including creating imperfections in the product market, which might shelter a firm from the rigors of competition. Clearly this is one of the boundary cases where the activities involved are connected with both the functions of the entrepreneur and the functions of management. Perhaps one way of answering this question in a somewhat determinate fashion is to suggest that the struggle against entropy and market sheltering involves a short run interest of the entrepreneur, but this can be transferred to others so that it can become a long run interest of hired managers. Of course at the same time, we keep in mind that the motivations determining these activities on the part of the entrepreneur may be quite different from the motivations that move hired managers.

What Do Entrepreneurs Get?

The answer to this questions is: whatever they can, or are clever enough to arrange to get. One of the difficulties we have in trying to answer this question is the constraints we normally put on the answer. We have already alluded to the ordinary language versus the theory problem. The problem is essentially a theory problem. There is no point in worrying about the ordinary language problems, or to try to reconcile our theoretical entrepreneur with ordinary language profits.

There is an old tradition in economics that views the entrepreneur (or capitalist, or some such person or group) as receiving the residual that the firm earns after paying wages, rents, and interest. Some unique person (or group) is presumed to be the residual claimant. Under the X-efficiency vision of economic behavior, the firm will normally end up its conventional accounting periods with a positive or negative residual. The firm's accountants may or may not call all of it profits or losses. We are not concerned here with the problems created by accounting convention. What we want to emphasize is that it would be misleading to suggest that the entrepreneur is the claimant to a properly accounted for residual. He may or may not be.

The nub of the matter is that the entrepreneur, as a consequence of his activities as an *input completer,* finds himself to be in a strategic position to work out (usually favorable) contracts, which determine in what form he is to receive his reward. Assume the entrepreneur is in a strong position as a result of his input completing activities—what options may he have? Some possibilities are the following: (1) He can become the residual claimant; or (2) he can be one of a group (for example, common stockholders) who are residual claimants; or (3) he can "forego" or sell his residual claimant reward and take a fixed share immediately of the capitalized value of the enterprise; or (4) he can appoint himself to a strategic managerial role in the enterprise so that he may receive both a wage and a share in the residual claims.

Thus, what the entrepreneur gets depends on a mixture of what he has to offer in order to marshal the "imperfect market" inputs, and what he would like in return. It may be best to offer fixed rewards, or residual claims, or some mixture of the two, depending on circumstances. The other point we must keep in mind is that residual claim rights are frequently saleable. Thus, the entrepreneur who has access to residual claim rights may choose to trade them for cash or some other rights at the very outset. In sum, the reward of the entrepreneur, (be he an individual or group of individuals) lies in the favorable position in which he may find himself in working out contracts that determine the payoff to various individuals including himself (or themselves) as a result of their provision of inputs. However, it would be incorrect to argue that the reward need by in any specific form.

Some Concluding Remarks

Part of the tradition of attempts to explain entrepreneurship is to explain profits; namely, it seems to fill one of the holes in the existing theory attempting to relate all classes of inputs to all classes of returns. However, this function of the theory of entrepreneurship seems to me to be less significant than other possibilities. A more important use, to my mind, is to open up the theory; to use entrepreneurship as a unique category of inputs in order to provide explanations in contexts where such explanations are needed.

The view developed in this chapter is that entrepreneurs are, by the very nature of the theory, far from homogeneous. Entrepreneurs that could fill some gaps and be input completers for some commodities may be unable to fill others. There are types of entrepreneurs, just as there are classes of goods, that may be in excess supply, while at the same time there may be other entrepreneurial groups that are relatively scarce. Perhaps the most important function that a theory could serve is to become a basis of our understanding of degrees of imperfection in the market. Let us assume that most imperfections are caused by two broad influences: those that emanate from the political environment and those that are a consequence of the activities of entrepreneurs. Clearly we have to try to understand much better than we do now in what ways entrepreneurs diminish market imperfections and in what ways and in what contexts they may increase such imperfections.

The main thrust of the Austrian school, apart from a variety of qualifications, is that entrepreneurs work the path toward equilibrium. They make the path, so to speak. They are essentially an influence that decreases the degree of disequilibrium in the market. Whether or not this is the case is impossible to say. X–efficiency theory (as well as older generalizations that go back at least to Adam Smith) suggest that entrepreneurs work in both areas: perfecting markets, and creating barriers. Hence, a next fruitful step might be to study under what circumstances entrepreneurs increase imperfections as against circumstances under which they tend to decrease them; and in what way these activities are related to the relative supplies of different types of entrepreneurial talents.

Notes

1. I am not an expert on the Austrian theory of entrepreneurship. Much of what I have learned recently about that theory comes from two sources: Israel M. Kirzner's *Competition and Entrepreneurship,* (Chicago: University of Chicago Press, 1973) and a senior thesis at Harvard University, written by Susan G. Cole, "The History, Development and Significance of Entrepreneurial Theory" (1977). As I understand the theory, the emphasis is on the *process* of competition rather than on equilibrium. The entrepreneur does his job along the path toward equilibrium, but not in equilibrium. This, I think, is fairly clear from Kirzner's overall thesis in

which the entrepreneur is an arbitrageur par excellence. What is not clear is whether the entrepreneur can also be a disequilibrating influence, on balance. In my own view, using the X-efficiency ideas, entrepreneurs can work toward perfecting markets and hence work toward a competitive equilibrium, but through their sheltering activities they can also create barriers to others, and hence lead to more imperfect markets than before. I see no special reason why, on balance, activities of entrepreneurs should propel markets along the path toward equilibrium.

2. In the well-known paper by A. Alchian and H. Demsetz, "Production, Information Costs, and Economic Organization," *American Economic Review* 62 (December 1972), the firm is viewed as a team that operates a nonadditive production function. That is, the output that results from input X_1 and X_2 is greater than the output obtained from adding the outputs of X_1 and X_2 separately. From this viewpoint also input completing would be a necessary activity.

3. The idea of sheltering seems to me to be consistent with Kirzner's discussion of monopoly. (*See* Kirzner, *Competition and Entrepreneurship,* pp. 131-134, and pp. 205-211). However, our emphasis is quite different. Kirzner emphasizes profits as the inducement for the *alert* entrepreneur, while I emphasize the fact that a sheltered environment reduces the pressure to struggle against organizational entropy.

This last is consistent with Sir John Hicks' famous comment to the effect that the greatest of all monopoly profits may be a quiet life.

Comment:
X – Inefficiency, Error, and the Scope for Entrepreneurship

Israel M. Kirzner

Professor Leibenstein makes a valiant attempt in chapter 6 to rescue the entrepreneurial role from oblivion. In this undertaking, Leibenstein draws heavily on his well-known theory of X–efficiency, discovering that within the paradigm offered by this theory, the entrepreneurial function finds a natural place. At a number of points in the paper, Leibenstein makes brief attempts to relate his approach critically to the work that has, in recent years, proceeded in a similar direction within the Austrian tradition. Leibenstein's paper is necessarily concise in its presentation of the X–efficiency approach. For fuller understanding, one must refer to his recent book, *Beyond Economic Man,* and a series of earlier papers. However, in regard to the implications of the X–efficiency approach for the entrepreneurial role, Leibenstein's book is—somewhat strangely, one might think—virtually silent. Fortunately, a much older paper of Leibenstein's ("Entrepreneurship and Development," *American Economic Review,* May 1968) did tackle the question of the entrepreneurial role. A reading of today's new paper against the background of Leibenstein's more elaborate discussion in his earlier paper, provides a richer understanding, I believe, of Leibenstein's position.

The present discussion will seek to appraise this position from the perspective of the Austrian tradition. In particular, we will attempt to underline the points of contact between Leibenstein's work and the recent discussions within the Austrian approach, while at the same time attempting to clarify and underscore the differences between Leibenstein and the Austrian approach. It is to be hoped that this kind of discussion can make a contribution toward a more sensitive understanding of each other's work among those few economic theorists currently engaged in research on the entrepreneurial function in economic systems.

Entrepreneurship and Disequilibrium

It is now well understood why neoclassical general equilibrium theory cannot find a place for the entrepreneur.[1] No matter which one of the alternative theories of entrepreneurship one wishes to follow, an entrepreneur can emerge only in a world in which he can, at least in principle, hope to discover, or create, or at any rate enjoy, opportunities for pure profit. The state of general equilibrium is simply not consistent with such a world. In general equilibrium each participant is acting successfully to place himself in the best situation available to him. The sets of prices prevailing are such that (1) each and every market participant is able to carry out his planned actions without disappointment and without regret; and (2) there is not a single pair of participants who could both have reached better situations for themselves by trading with each other at prices other than those prevailing in the market. These specifications rule out all opportunities for pure profit, and thus necessarily exclude any possibility for an entrepreneurial role. As Leibenstein has put it in his chapter, "If we want to get anywhere to solve the entrepreneurial puzzle, we have to stay away from the neoclassical general equilibrium syndrome."[2] T.W. Schultz too has recently emphasized that the entrepreneur finds his role in his "ability to deal with disequilibria."[3]

All this has, as Leibenstein recognizes, long been argued by Austrians, who have, moreover, consistently deplored the dominant trends in economic theory to exclude from consideration all but equilibrium states. Both a Schumpeter and a Mises, no matter how sharp their differences on other matters, could agree in rejecting outright the view of capitalism which fails to see it as a dynamic process. From this perspective these new signs of rediscovery of the entrepreneur point encouragingly beyond themselves to a rejuvenated economic theory in which the analysis of equilibrium conditions need no longer dominate the intellectual scene.

Profit Opportunities and the Failure to Maximize

In the world of general equilibrium, all participants are seen as successful maximizers, and, in particular, all firms are viewed as producing efficiently. In the Leibenstein world of possible X-inefficiency, on the other hand, firms do not necessarily maximize, minimum costs are not necessarily achieved. Although Leibenstein is not altogether explicit on the matter in today's paper, it seems clear that a significant explanation for the scope for entrepreneurship arises from this failure of participants to achieve efficiency. As Leibenstein explains, "[non]maximization and the operation of inertia suggest that not all entrepreneurial opportunities would be undertaken."[4] Because of X-inefficiency, "profitable entrepreneurial opportunities may be hidden" and "the entrepreneur has the function of ferreting" them out.[5] As Leibenstein put it in 1968, "[p]ersistent slack implies the existence of entrepreneurial opportunities." Again it is "the difference between actual costs [not minimized as a result of X-inefficiency (I.M.K.)] and true minimum costs" that "offers opportunities for those entrepreneurs who think they can produce at lower costs."[7]

As has been recently emphasized by William Jaffé, Austrians as far back as Carl Menger have refused to view market participants as errorless maximizers, instantaneously selecting the optimum option from the array that confronts them.[8] Where there is room for error, there is surely room for the exercise of the entrepreneurial function. So that here, too, Leibenstein's paradigm might appear to be one that Austrian should find both comfortable and congenial.

A Difference of Emphasis

Despite these highly significant points of agreement joining Leibenstein's position with that of the Austrians, it seems important to identify and discuss several differences that set Leibenstein's views apart from the Austrian approach. Let us begin with what may at first glance appear as no more than a difference of emphasis. For Leibenstein, the role of the entrepreneur seems to be *far less crucial* than it is for the Austrians.

For Leibenstein, the rediscovery of the entrepreneur seems to be quite secondary. Although it is true that, as mentioned earlier, Leibenstein addressed the question of entrepreneurship carefully in his 1968 paper, it is also true that in his book (which bears the significant subtitle *A New Foundation for Microeconomics*), Leibenstein virtually ignores the role of the entrepreneur. In the book, only casual and quite incidental references are made to entrepreneurs (with the exception perhaps of two brief paragraphs on page 206 with a footnote reference to the 1968 paper), and no systematic effort (such as has been presented in the chapter here being commented on, or such as Leibenstein had himself provided in 1968) was made in the book to relate the entrepreneurial role to the X-efficiency paradigm. For an Austrian reading *Beyond Economic Man* this seems an almost extraordinary omission. And, indeed, it appears that this difference in emphasis reflects a deeper difference, between the two approaches, in the significance attached to the entrepreneurial role. For Leibenstein, entrepreneurship is merely one interesting feature of the economic landscape. It is a feature that indeed seems to come into focus when observed through the X-efficiency lens; but the X-efficiency paradigm can be presented without any special reference to entrepreneurs.

For Austrians, however, entrepreneurship is *at the very heart* of the economic process; to attempt to understand economic processes without reference to the entrepreneurial role would, for the Austrians, be a wholly misguided undertaking. This deserves some elaboration.

Entrepreneurship and X-inefficiency

For Leibenstein the matter seems to be as follows. In the X-efficiency paradigm we are presented with a framework for a theory alternative to that of general equilibrium. Both theoretical approaches seek to illuminate the economic world around us. The neoclassical general equilibrium approach does so by assuming that all market participants are successful maximizers. Leibenstein seeks to understand the economic world by viewing market participants as displaying, in varying degrees, X-inefficiency. As Leibenstein demonstrates in his book, his theory lends itself to numerous applications in which phenomena of the real world seem to become understandable when related to specific possibilities for X-inefficiency. In developing this theory, and in drawing implications from it to illuminate our understanding of the real world, the entrepreneurial role is not, in general, referred to. The entrepreneur is not seen as a pivotal figure in a Leibenstein world; such a world can, in Leibenstein's terms, be understood without having to rely upon the entrepreneurial function.

On the other hand, however, the X-inefficiency paradigm, as an alternative to the dominant neoclassical theory, happens to exclude precisely those features of the neoclassical framework that left no room for a neoclassical entrepreneur. Because of this, there is, in the Leibenstein world, once again, a possibility for entrepreneurial activity. In chapter 6, Leibenstein has systematically explored this possibility. In doing this, Leibenstein would presumably consider himself to be further demonstrating the richness of his general theoretical approach. He has given us no reason at all, of course, to believe that he has today revealed the ultimate mainspring—a mainspring kept carefully and successfully concealed throughout his book—for his whole theory. The situation is, for the Austrians, altogether different.

Entrepreneurship and the Austrians

For Austrians, the entrepreneurial role is the key to an understanding of the course of economic phenomena. What is inadequate with an exclusively general equilibrium approach, then, is not merely that it is an approach within which we cannot seem to fit the familiar figure of the entrepreneur. Rather the neoclassical general equilibrium approach suffers most seriously in its inability to address those crucial theoretical tasks for which the notion of entrepreneurship can alone provide the key.

A state of equilibrium is one in which the decisions óf all market participants are, within the given constraints, fully coordinated. Each market participant, making an offer, does so in the correct anticipation that the offer will be accepted. Each action undertaken in anticipation of coordinate actions by others, is in fact able to be successfully carried out; the anticipations are fulfilled. No pair of potential market participants between whom mutually profitable exchange activities might be carried on, fail to exploit such opportunities.

Austrians have long argued that the analysis of such equilibrium states—if not enriched by analyses of possible equilibrating processes—fails to come to grips with the problems of our world. Not only is our world one in which perfect coordination simply never exists (so that equilibrium models can have little direct relevance). In our world, the problem calling for theoretical illumination is precisely that of understanding the course of events generated by an initial *absence* of coordination. For the solution of this problem equilibrium models are distinctly unhelpful. (Moreover, from a *normative* point of view, Austrians following Hayek have consistently emphasized that the relevant task surely is not to understand how efficient an economy may be in the state of equilibrium; rather the relevant task is to evaluate the success with which an economy beset by rampant *absence* of coordination may achieve an approach toward a coordinated state. For all this the analysis of equilibrium states appears as an altogether question-begging enterprise.)

The need for a theory within which entrepreneurial activity can find its place is thus the need for a theory able to embrace the way in which uncoordinated states of affairs possibly change. The economist does, after all, understand that absence of coordination may itself generate systematic attempts to change matters. So that we can hardly avoid recognizing that what renders an uncoordinated state of affairs one of *disequilibrium* is closely related to entrepreneurial reaction to the absence of coordination.

Leibenstein refers critically on more than one occasion in chapter 6 to what he sees as the Austrian view that entrepreneurial activity propels markets strictly in the direction of equilibrium. It should perhaps be pointed out that not all Austrians in fact maintain that all entrepreneurs engage all the time in equilibrating activities. Moreover, and most significantly, what I believe most Austrians believe to be important is not so much that entrepreneurship is equilibrating (if indeed it always is) but that, if there is in fact a tendency towards equilibrium, that tendency can be understood as the result of working out entrepreneurial activity. Or, to put the same idea somewhat differently, the important thing is that the course of events in a disequilibrium setting, *whether or not that course of events converges on equilibrium* can be understood only in terms of entrepreneurial decisions.

This aspect of the difference between Leibenstein and the Austrians may be stated concisely. For Leibenstein only a disequilibrium state provides anything for the entrepreneur to do. For Austrians it is only what entrepreneurs do that enables us to understand what happens in the disequilibrium state.

The Source of X-inefficiency

We have mentioned earlier that one significant point of agreement between Leibenstein and the Austrians consists of the possibility of X-inefficiency. It is this possibility that, for both Leibenstein and the Austrians, provides scope for entrepreneurial activity. The escape that Leibenstein makes from a world of successful maximizers is a move that Austrians cannot but applaud. But, paradoxically enough, the particular escape-hatch through which Leibenstein makes this unorthodox exit is one that Austrians must be inclined to view with a certain coolness. This requires some clarification. Let me try:

Throughout the course of modern economics its critics have attacked some form of its central postulate—the postulate of purposeful individual action. The particular form taken by a particular piece of criticism has depended on the form in which this central postulate has been enunciated. Thus, critics of economics have denounced the notion of economic man; they have derided the postulate of rationality, or of maximizing behavior. Veblen's acid comments on the economist's view of man as a hedonistic "lightning calculator of pleasures and pains" is well known and typifies the kind of criticism to which economists have been constantly subjected.

Economists have defended themselves in one of two ways. One line of defense has been to treat the assumption of rationality as merely a useful first approximation. The alternative defense has been to argue that what seem to be examples of nonrational, nonmaximizing behavior (for example, impulsive behavior, or behavior governed strictly by adherence to custom) seem to be such only because certain important kinds of utilities or sacrifices have not been taken into account. On the first of these two lines of defense, non-efficient action is indeed possible, but is deliberately assumed away in economic theory for purposes of analytical simplicity. On the second of these lines of defense, nonefficient action *appears* possible only because the observer has—illegitimately—ignored some satisfactions that have in fact entered into the calculations of the agent.

Professor Stigler has recently taken Leibenstein sharply to task for treating X-inefficiency as inefficiency at all from the viewpoint of economics.[9] Prominent among the sources of X-inefficiency are inadequate motivation and effort. "The simple fact is that neither individuals nor firms work as hard, nor do they search for information as effectively as they could."[10] But, as Stigler points out, if individuals are not sufficiently motivated to work harder, then this presumably reflects, deliberately and correctly, their preference for leisure. If, again, firms have not succeeded in organizing production so as to enhance worker motivation, this constitutes the firm's choice of one "technology" of production, as against the possibility of alternative (more "productivity"-conscious) technologies. But choice of one technology, yielding lower physical output per week than another available technology does not, without our knowing all the relevant costs, warrant our asserting the presence of inefficiency in the choice of technologies.

Now Leibenstein has in his book already, perhaps, anticipated this line of criticism. He has explained that "the problem may be partially semantic . . . One can interpret utility in such a way that *all* behavior is subsumed under some version of utility maximization. But this would rob the concepts of utility and maximization of real meaning."[11] In other words, Leibenstein, in joining the century-old line of critics of mainstream economic theory is rejecting *both* of the above-mentioned possible defenses employed by economists. He is not prepared to broaden the notion of utility so as to render *all* action efficient. And he believes that the use of the maximizing model as a first approximation blinds us from understanding many economic phenomena, which come into focus only when we "loosen the psychological assumptions behind normal economic behavior in such a way so that rationality [does] not necessarily imply maximizing utility"—that is, only if we admit the possibility of X-inefficiency.[12] The Austrian reaction to this is somewhat complex.

Austrians and X-inefficiency

William Jaffé has recently argued that the early Austrians, or at least Menger, were not really vulnerable to Veblen's attacks on neoclassical theory. Jaffé argues that "[m]an, as Menger saw him, far from being a 'lightning calculator' is a bumbling, erring, ill-informed creature, plagued with uncertainty, forever hovering between alluring hopes and haunting fears, and congenitally incapable of making finely calibrated decisions in pursuit of satisfactions."[13]

At the same time it has been the Austrians, in particular, Mises, who have most staunchly maintained the universal rationality of human action. Man always acts purposefully; more accurately: the very concept of human action is altogether inseparable from its purposefulness.[14] Because men pursue purposes, their actions are governed by their reason; because of this the economist, by using his own reasoning powers, can understand actions taken in the light of relevant goals postulated. Two points emerge from our consideration of Mises. First, it is clear that unless we are prepared to cut Mises off from his intellectual forbears, some effort at reconciliation with Jaffé's reading of Menger is urgently called for. Second, Mises' extensive discussions of the universality of the action-postulate and of the nature of economic reasoning, make it very clear how he (and hence modern Austrians) view Veblen-type critiques of economics. Austrians will emphatically not accept the purposefulness of human action merely as a useful first approximation. They will (as does the other of the two alternative lines of defense mentioned earlier) insist on the full validity of the postulate of purposefulness, accounting for apparent real world counterexamples by simply arguing that some significant purposes have evidently not been understood by the observing economist.

All this must seem to intensify Austrian disagreement with X-inefficiency. Surely Stigler is correct in pointing out that the cases of X-inefficiency that Leibenstein explains in terms of motivational deficiency and insufficient effort, do not qualify as aberrations from the universal purposefulness of human action. These cases can be seen as examples of inefficiency only by choosing to ignore certain purposes of which the firms and the individuals in the market take significant account.[15] Leibenstein may legitimately choose to concern himself with certain utilities to the exclusion of others. But for Austrians this does not successfully demonstrate the possibility of actions being taken that do not seek to pursue chosen goals with complete purposefulness.

On the other hand, however, Austrians do emphasize the scope for entrepreneurship. And, as stated earlier, this certainly does call for accepting the possibility of non-efficient actions. How can we reconcile the Austrian insistence on the universal purposefulness of action with the Austrian emphasis on entrepreneurship and, in particular, with Menger's recognition of *error* in human action? It is here that the possibility of a sympathetic reinterpretation of the concept of X-inefficiency becomes appealing to Austrians (if not, perhaps, to Leibenstein).

Choice, Allocation, and Action

Ever since Lord Robbins' *Nature and Significance of Economic Science* in 1932, economists have seen their discipline as concerned with the efficient disposition of means to achieve given ends. Economizing activity is that which seeks to impose upon the utilization of means, that pattern which is alone faithfully consistent with the adopted ranking of ends. Modern microeconomics is conducted very much *within* such a postulated means-ends framework. In contemporary parlance the task of *economizing* is identified with that of *allocating* scarce resources among competing uses to maximize utility, or profit, or something. And this task of allocation—itself essentially a computational task—is often described as *choice*. The selection of an optimal program of resource use with respect to a given ranking of goals is described as *choice*.

On the other hand, some contemporary economists, including not only the Austrians proper but also such critics such as Shackle, have emphasized that to describe as choice the task of optimal allocation, with ends already ranked in advance, is to do violence to the nature of human decision making. True choice, or decision making, true human action, it is pointed out, must embody also the very selection and ranking of ends. More, it is argued in particular by Austrians, true choice must embrace not only the task of allocation but, at the same time, the *very perception of what ends and what means are to be relevant for allocation.* To commence an analysis of choice *after* a particular ends–means framework has been declared known and relevant, is to deal with choice in a manner that renders it completely mechanical. The *creativity* of choice, the element that makes action human, has been left out.

For Austrians, then, the role of purposefulness in human affairs goes far beyond ensuring that all actions will be efficient, with respect to adopted ends–means frameworks. Purposefulness becomes of overriding importance in inspiring man's alertness to the desirability of hitherto unknown means. For Austrians action may be genuinely in error, not in the sense of failing to optimize within an adopted ends–means context, but in the sense of having overlooked the desirability of possible ends, and the availability of ready-at-hand means. Universal purposefulness and the omnipresence of error are by no means inconsistent in the Austrian view; on the contrary they go hand in hand.

Notice that error means something other than lack of information. Information may, of course, be deliberately ignored because its acquisition is too costly. "Mistakes" made as the result of such ignorance are not true errors. They are the consequences deliberately accepted in the calculated gamble taken in not buying the costly information. But men also make mistakes in that they ignore possibly attractive opportunities not on account of deliberately avoided costs but on account of sheer failure to see what is there to be seen. Men do fail to maximize in this sense. And the notion of X-inefficiency does provide a tempting filing cabinet in which to pigeonhole this kind of error–laden action. In drawing attention to the broader notion of choice, transcending as it does the narrower concept of allocation and of economizing, the Austrian may well feel that he is roaming "beyond economic man."

Error and the Entrepreneurial Role

Scope for entrepreneurial activity is created in the market whenever (1) the same item is sold at different prices in different parts of the same market (or, as a special case, when the sum of prices of an input bundle is lower than the corresponding output revenue); or (2) two market participants, between whom a mutually beneficial exchange might have taken place, failed to enter into the trade. Each of these opportunities for profit cannot be imagined to emerge except as a result of error. It is thus *error* that is both responsible for absence of full coordination and to be credited with providing the incentive for its own discovery and correction.

Entrepreneurial alertness sparks the discovery of profit opportunities (and thus the elimination of discoordination). The market *process* then becomes visible as a series of innumerable changes in plans, each set in motion by the discovery of hitherto overlooked opportunities, or by the discovery of the *non*existence of opportunities previously believed to be available.

The concrete form in which a hitherto overlooked opportunity may present itself and thus the concrete tasks that an entrepreneur will undertake are of no particular consequence at this level of generality. What is of importance is that as the result both of the ignorance existing in the market at any given point in time, and of the circumstance that spontaneous and continual changes (in human tastes, resource availabilities and technological knowledge) generate a ceaseless flow of fresh ignorance, as it were, into the market—that as a result of this there is continual scope for the discovery by alert entrepreneurs of newly created opportunities.

The market offers incentives for the discovery of errors, in the profit opportunities that errors engender. Such opportunities for profit rest, in the last analysis, on the circumstance that, due to error, it may be the case that the current utilization of a unit of a resource or commodity fails to exploit its full productive or value potential. Error has generated inefficiency and thus an opportunity for entrepreneurial alertness to win profits through wiping out the inefficiency. Such inefficiency, it should be emphasized again, consists not in anyone's failure to seek allocative optimality—that is ruled out by the universal purposefulness of action; it consists in sheer unawareness of the available opportunities. Hence, the temptation (of course, only if its author so permits) to apply the term X-inefficiency (as distinct from allocative inefficiency) to these error-generated wastes in the elimination of which the entrepreneurial role consists.

At one point in his chapter,[16] Leibenstein appears to fear that X-inefficiency, by bringing about low profits or even losses, may in fact *inhibit* the entry of entrepreneurs. "In the traditional vision," Leibenstein remarks, "profits are the ideal signal" to attract entrepreneurial activity. But, because of low profit X-inefficiency, we are given to understand, "profit opportunities may be . . . less apparent. Thus the entrepreneur has the function of ferreting out opportunities in markets where on the surface no opportunities seem to exist." I would submit that the entrepreneurial function must necessarily always be that of sniffing out opportunities that on the surface *do not* appear to exist. Once a profit opportunity has become *obvious,* it no longer retains its character of a pure profit opportunity. The market will have at once taken note of the opportunity by appropriate price changes, squeezing out the margin of pure profit. When we say that in the traditional view entrepreneurial entry is triggered by the discovery of pure profit opportunities, we must mean not so much the discovery of pure profits already made by others, as the discovery by alert, daring and far-sighted entrepreneurs, of profit opportunities in the future, as yet unnoticed and unexplored by others.

Entrepreneurship, Market Processes, and the Current Scene in Economics

The neoclassical general equilibrium paradigm has long reigned, virtually unchallenged, at the core of economic theory. We are witnessing in our time a rather widespread dissatisfaction and disenchantment with that paradigm. It is beginning to become clear that the various proposals being made to enrich or improve or revise that paradigm cannot escape the task of grappling with the contribution that an understanding of the entrepreneurial function can provide. Austrians view these developments with very great interest indeed. It has been a pleasure to comment on one of the more imaginative proposals in this regard—the X-efficiency approach developed by Professor Leibenstein.

Notes

1. W.J. Baumol, "Entrepreneurship in Economic Theory," *American Economic Review* 58 (May 1968): 72.
2. Chapter 6, Harvey Leibenstein, "The General X-efficiency Paradigm and the Role of the Entrepreneur," p. 129.
3. T.W. Schultz, "The Value of the Ability to Deal with Disequilibria," *Journal of Economic Literature* 13 (September 1975).
4. Chapter 6, p. 134.
5. Ibid.
6. Harvey Leibenstein, "Entrepreneurship and Development," *American Economic Review* 58 (May 1968): 75.
7. Ibid., p. 77.
8. William Jaffé, "Menger, Jevons and Walras De-Homogenized," *Economic Inquiry* 14 (December 1976).
9. G.J. Stigler, "The Xistence of X-efficiency," *American Economic Review* 66 (March 1976).
10. Harvey Leibenstein, "Allocative Efficiency vs. 'X-efficiency'," *American Economic Review* 56 (June 1966): 407.

11. Harvey Leibenstein, *Beyond Economic Man* (Cambridge: Harvard University Press, 1976), p. 8.

12. Ibid.

13. Jaffé, "Menger, Jevons and Walras De-Homogenized," p. 521.

14. On this, *see* I.M. Kirzner, *The Economic Point of View* (Princeton, New Jersey: Van Nostrand, 1960), pp. 163-172.

15. *See also* B.J. Loasby, *Choice, Complexity and Ignorance* (Cambridge: Cambridge University Press, 1976), p. 119.

16. Chapter 6, p. 134.

7

Rational Expectations, Politics, and Stagflation

Gerald P. O'Driscoll, Jr.

Economic Fluctuations and Economic Theory

Professor Robert Lucas has reminded us of the business cycle theorists of the interwar years, who saw the problem of trade cycle theory as "the incorporation of cyclical phenomena into the system of economic equilibrium theory, with which they are in apparent contradiction."[1] Professor F. A. Hayek, prominent among these earlier theorists, clearly posed the theoretical issue:

> There is a fundamental difficulty inherent in all Trade Cycle theories which take as their starting point an empirically ascertained disturbance of the equilibrium of the various branches of production. This difficulty arises because, in stating the effects of that disturbance, they have to make use of the logic of equilibrium theory. Yet this logic, properly followed through, can do no more than demonstrate that such disturbances of equilibrium can come only from outside—i.e. that they represent a change in the economic data—and that the economic system always reacts to such changes by its well–known methods of adaptation, i.e. by the formation of a new equilibrium.[2]

Lucas predicted that "the most rapid progress toward a coherent and useful aggregate economic theory will result from accepting the problem statement as advanced by the business cycle theorists, and not from further attempts to refine the jerrybuilt structures to which Keynesian macroeconomics has led us."[3] Viewed from Lucas' framework, Rational Expectations (RE) theory represents a rediscovery of the problem statement of the business cycle theorists, and a renewed attempt to rationalize economic fluctuations in a general equilibrium framework. In this attempt, RE theorists have constructed models overtly "classical."

Simultaneously with the development of RE theory, other theorists have formulated a view of the business cycle as a political rather than an economic phenomenon. Political Business Cycle (PBC) theory is, however,

The helpful comments on earlier drafts of James M. Buchanan, John Egger, Roman Frydman, Roger Garrison, Axel Leijonhufvud, Richard E. Wagner, and Leland Yeager are gratefully acknowledged. Comments by various participants in the New York University Conference on Issues in Economic Theory (January, 1978) are also acknowledged.

Research for this paper was partially funded by the Fred C. Koch Foundation and the Liberty Fund. This support is gratefully acknowledged.

seemingly inconsistent with RE theory. The purpose of this essay is to offer a perspective on these two developments, a perspective distilling essential features of each. In so doing, I try to demonstrate that each approach makes elementary though nontrivial points. In this chapter I also argue the general consistency of the two approaches, though I note undeniable points of disagreement. Though research in these areas has been virtually isolated from that in the other, it has recently been argued that the two theories are inconsistent.[4] I believe it is worthwhile to demonstrate consistency, for each development has produced important insights, though each has produced fundamental errors.

The literature in the two areas is vast, and is continually growing. It is thus impossible to consider explicitly every or even most contributions. Among RE theorists, I concentrate on the pioneering and authoritative work of Professors Lucas, Sargent, and Wallace. I believe this concentration is fruitful; in any case, concentration was necessary.

Rational Expectations

The RE literature is noteworthy for the complexity of the mathematics and the sophistication of the arguments employed. Nonetheless, its major conclusions can be stated very simply. Macroeconometric models assume that the parameters of estimated reduced form equations are invariant (that is, truly parametric) with respect to policy rules. Economic theory does not support this assumption and econometric evidence casts doubt on it. To the extent that RE theory is correct in its criticisms of standard macroeconometric models, most of these are of doubtful value for policy simulation purposes. These models overlook the fact that estimations capture transactor responses to expectations of *particular* policies.[5] Such responses and the expectations on which they are based will not ordinarily be invariant to the policies adopted and expected in the future. Thus simulations of the effects of alternative policies will not accurately portray the effects of such policies insofar as these policies are expected. In its strongest form, RE theory suggests that any systematic macroeconomic policy will be anticipated.[6] Thus, if policymakers respond to transactors' behavioral responses to prior policy changes, then macroeconomic policy becomes both ineffective and endogenous. Acceptance of these conclusions has lent support to fixed monetary rules, since the latter minimize disturbances generated by unsystematic or initially unanticipated actions by policymakers. In other words, macro policy can only create more "noise"; it cannot stabilize or eliminate the irreducible "noise" in an economy. The goal of macroeconomic policy therefore becomes minimization of its disturbing impact on otherwise stable economic environments.[7]

It is not that standard macroeconometric models have identified the wrong independent variables or estimated coefficients of these variables incorrectly. Rather, in any macro model consistent with general economic theory, there are no truly independent variables, save perhaps the weather. In a real sense, there is no "right-hand side" of macroeconometric equations. Where relationships between "dependent" and "independent" variables have seemingly been discovered, macrotheorists have generally not demonstrated consistency with rational economic behavior. Professor Neil Wallace has observed that:

> [T]he main problem confronting macroeconomists is the explanation of observed positive correlations between aggregate demand variables, on [the] one hand, and output and employment, on the other hand. More directly, why do not shifts in aggregate demand impact only on prices as is implied by what might be called the "classical" full employment flexible wage and price macroeconomic model?[8]

He noted further that the "currently used macroeconometric models simply include versions of the paradoxical correlations and treat them as invariant (structural) relationships, invariant in the face of alternative policy rules."[9] In so doing, macroeconomists have taken for granted what needs to be explained.

Wallace's point is echoed in Lucas' statement of the task of macrotheory: "The first theoretical task—indeed, the central theoretical problem of macroeconomics—is to find an analytical context in which [output fluctuations] can occur and which does not at the same time imply the existence of persistent, recurrent, unexploited profit opportunities."[10]

The dominant post-Keynesian macrotheories are susceptible to RE critiques, which restated somewhat loosely, argue that policymakers cannot fool all the people all the time, certainly not with the same policy. In these critiques, RE theorists follow Professor Muth's formulation of RE. Given a stochastic structure or objective probability distribution, rational economic agents' anticipated value of a variable X will equal the statistically expected value; rational expectations are statistically unbiased expectations.'[11] RE theorists contend—correctly, I believe—that standard macromodels incorporate transactor irrationalities of various types.[12]

Though RE critiques have centered on Keynesian macromodels, monetarist models are also susceptible to these criticisms.[13] An example using early formulations of the Natural Rate hypothesis illustrates both the general nature of the problem and its universality. In the past, Professor Milton Friedman and others have pictured economic agents as forming expectations adaptively, for example, forming expectations of future inflation rates on the basis of averages of past rates. As is now well known, this behavior would result in underestimation of the inflation rate when it is accelerating and overestimation when it is decelerating. Agents are thus being treated as biased or irrational in their expectations, as has been explained by Wallace:

> [I]t could be the case that the structure during the sample period (including government policy) was such that the best forecast of the future price level is the current price level—often called static expectations. But such a scheme would not be best if for whatever reason, possibly a different government policy, the price level turns out to increase at, say, 7 percent per year. A model that implicitly assumes that people forecast as if the price level takes a random walk around a zero trend when, in fact, it has a nonzero trend is a disequilibrium model.[14]

To extend Wallace's argument, the greater the macroeconomic disturbance and potential disequilibrium, the less acceptable is the criticized assumption. Although we can imagine transactors anticipating a zero rate of inflation in the face of 1 percent inflation for a moderate period of time, we cannot do so in the fact of seven percent inflation for an extended period of time. The magnitude of the disturbance is too great to permit the assumption to go unchallenged.[15]

One is nonetheless left with the feeling that "irrationalities" in macro models capture some real world phenomena. Moreover, certain of the conclusions of RE theory are counterintuitive, as, for example, the Sargent-Wallace "policy conundrum":

> [I]nvoking this kind of complete rationality seems to rule out normative economics completely by, in effect, ruling out freedom for the policy maker. For in a model with completely rational expectations including a rich enough description of policy, it seems impossible to define a sense in which there is any scope for discussing the optimal design of policy rules. This is because the equilibrium values of the endogenous variables already reflect, in the proper way, the parameters describing the authorities' prospective subsequent behavior, including the probability that this or that proposal for reforming policy will be adopted.[16]

In the next section, I consider criticisms of RE theory both to assess the above-mentioned reaction to RE theory and to bring the essential truths of RE theory into sharper focus. This, in turn, facilitates consideration of the older, business cycle theory tradition whose research program Lucas perceives RE theory to be implementing. As I argue that this program is indeed worthy of implementaton, it is necessary to understand the relation between that tradition and RE theory.

Rational Expectations: Criticism

A number of critiques of RE theory have now appeared. One of the most potentially serious ones contend that "rational forecasting requires that forecast errors be serially uncorrelated.[17] This criticism is, however, erroneous, as explained by Milton Friedman in a counterexample:

> For about five years, the futures prices of the Mexican peso was decidedly below the current price. And every year, while the Mexican government maintained the price of the peso at 8¢ a peso, the people operating in the futures market made an error in the same direction. Anybody who sold the peso short was bound to lose money. Did that mean that expectations were not rational? Not at all. What it meant was that every single year there was one chance in four that the peso was going to go down 50 percent; and that meant that it was appropriate for the future price to be 12½ percent below the current price. And that continued for 4 or 5 years.[18]

A basic tenet of RE theory is that transactors make the *best use* of available data, so that subjective estimates of the data correspond to the objective probability distribution.[19] As Friedman's example illustrates, this use is consistent with error; but rational expectations when incorrect will be *correctly incorrect*. Speculators choose correctly given the probabilities and, as in Friedman's example, this can lead to serially correlated errors.[20] A more interesting and more general problem is suggested by this case—the amount of error allowable in a RE model:

> [There is] an interesting analytical tension which must arise in any cycle theory based on incomplete information. On the one hand, it is easy to postulate agents and market institutions which ignore or foolishly waste information: the result is a theory which seriously understates agents' abilities to vary their decision rules with change in the environment (such as, for example, the theory underlying the major econometric forecasting models). It is equally easy to postulate "efficient" securities markets which rapidly transmit *all* information to all traders: the result is a static general equilibrium model. To observe that one must avoid both extremes to understand the business cycle does not take one very far in discovering the correct "centrist" model, but it seems nonetheless an essential point of departure.[21]

Lucas' statement raises what I see as the central problem confronting RE theorists and one that must be considered at length. It would be ironic if the outcome of a decade and a half of concern with the economics of (imperfect) knowledge resulted in the renewed dominance of models incorporating perfect knowledge assumptions. There is a real danger of this happening. Thus Professor Poole observed that "rational-expectations theory might be regarded, in principle, as only slightly amending perfect-certainty models. One need only substitute the assumption of perfect knowledge of probability distributions for the assumption of perfect knowledge of outcomes."[22]

Professor Benjamin Friedman has argued that RE models are both classical and long-run in nature, protestations of their short-run character to the contrary notwithstanding. First, let us consider again the Sargent-Wallace "policy conundrum":

> In this system, there is no sense in which the authority has the option to conduct countercyclical policy. To exploit the Phillips curve, it must somehow trick the public. But by virtue of the assumption that expectations are rational, there is no feedback rule that the authority can employ and expect to be able systematically to fool the public. *This means that the authority cannot expect to exploit the Phillips curve even for one period.* [23]

One is immediately struck by the undefined "period," the length of which matters in assessing the relevance of the Sargent-Wallace economic policy model.[24] Benjamin Friedman argued that as a matter of economic logic, their model incorporates a purely long-run theory:

> Models which assume that economic agents form their expectations rationally on the basis of knowledge of the "true" economic model must implicitly assume, therefore, either that no changes ever occur in the variables omitted in economic agents' approximate specification, or that the most recent such change has occurred so far in the past that economic agents' current model has fully converged to the new situation. In either case, *the context is one familiarly associated with some form of long-run equilibrium.* [25]

One must carefully distinguish theories yielding the properties of equilibrium states from theories of the approach to these states. In equilibrium, all the available information will have been processed at the least known cost, relevant knowledge (of outcomes or of probability distributions) will be complete, and no unexploited profit opportunities will exist. This is all true because the absence of any of these conditions signals the absence of equilibrium. But observations about the completeness of knowledge in equilibrium do not constitute explanations, much less theories, of how that knowledge is acquired and processed. Nor do these observations demonstrate the ability of economic actors to process information and establish new equilibrium relationships in response to disturbances. RE models lack a theory of the learning process by which information is acquired.[26] By Lucas' methodological structures, Sargent-Wallace and other have failed to produce a coherent cycle model, having instead developed a static equilibrium model.

Another aspect of this criticism is revealed when one considers an assumption prevelent in the RE literature: monetary authorities possess no informational advantage. Though it is generally not specified, it is implicit that *no* agent possesses any informational advantage.[27] This is a very curious and very stringent assumption, far more stringent than is required even for general equilibrium analysis. Moreover, this is an assumption that renders the use of prices unintelligible.

A decentralized ("market") economy operates with an economy of information. Prices convey a substantial part of the necessary information for individuals' planning. Under specified conditions, these plans result in *coordinated behavior*, behavior that moves individuals closer to equilibrium relationships. Dependence on prices for information conveyance can only be rationalized by assuming that information is initially decentralized, or in Hayek's words, there is a "division of knowledge."[28] It may be true that "useful information has a habit of becoming available";[29] but this claim recalls Benjamin Friedman's observation: to be convincing, the claim must be coupled either with an assumption of no further changes or the complete absorption of previous information. In either case, the long-run equilibrium character of the model is again revealed.

Moreover, it is unnecessary to assume that agents possess the identical information set or that these sets include knowledge of the economy's structure. The price system enables individuals to plan *without knowing* the underlying data generating those prices.[30] If these data were known, then prices, which are signals relecting changes in the data, would be unnecessary and their existence unintelligible.

In this instance, it is unacceptable to argue that RE theory is merely an "as if" theory. ("It is 'as if' individuals acquired perfect knowledge of probability distributions.") For this "as if" assumption is fundamentally inconsistent both with the phenomena (markets) being studied and the short-run nature of the specific policy problem, that is, economic fluctuations, discussed in the literature. Bluntly put, RE models suggest that it is "as if" there are no informational problems involved. Yet in the context of the short-run monetary problems observed in these models, the informational problem is as essential to what is being studied as is the scarcity constraint. One could equally well develop models in which it is "as if" there were no scarcity.

Professor Leijonhufvud confronted some of the issues in treating wealth effects in macro theory. Aggregate real balance and real financial effects represent an apparent analytical difficulty. In general equilibrium theory, resources and technology, assumed constant in macro models, determine real wealth. This assumption avoids the question of whether perceived wealth is necessarily equivalent to actual wealth:

> Clearly, the postulate that perceived and potential wealth are the same involves more than just the assumption of individual "rationality." It assumes *full information* and (by all means) "rational" appraisal of that information. To assume that the "wealth positions" of individuals as determined by their subjectively perceived opportunities "add up to" the potential wealth of the system as a whole, in or out of equilibrium, is to presuppose a consistency of individual views that *under certain conditions* may be brought about by the interaction of individuals in markets. "Absence of illusions" arguments merely fudge the question of whether these conditions will be fulfilled for the problem under study.[31]

Essentially the same issue is at stake in arguing that transactors' expectations are consistent with the process generating the data as is true in Leijonhufvud's case. The whole coordinating market process, including learning behavior, is pushed aside by the full information assumption being criticized here. To be more concrete and to anticipate later discussion, it is not obvious that a system in which individuals must form expectations concerning other individuals' expectations will always generate consistent expectations in the aggregate.

One additional facet of this criticism should be noted before considering a possible resolution. RE theory is most persuasive for situations in which the relative fequency of occurrences is at least ascertainable in principle. It is not persuasive for situations of genuine or Knightian uncertainty.[32] One of the important differences between situations of risk and of uncertainty has recently been noted by Professor Loasby:

> [Uncertainty] like risk . . . requires a complete listing of all possible courses of action. In general, such listings are not available. When someone says he is uncertain, what he usually means is not just that he doesn't know the chances of various outcomes, but that he doesn't know what outcomes are possible. [33]

Business cycles are characterized in part by uncertainties (and not mere risk). This realization adds to one's uneasiness concerning the handling of information in RE theory.

Rational Expectations: Reconstruction

In the previous section, I argued that RE theory lacks a needed theory of learning, indicated the similarity between the assumption of knowledge of outcomes and knowledge of distributions, and suggested that RE models conflate risk and uncertainty. Nonetheless, certain features of RE theory are compelling, especially Lucas' original strictures against the use of macroeconometric models for policy simulation. One need not assume that ordinary economic actors have the same information sets as monetary authorities to conclude that over time the former will acquire *some* information about the actions of the latter. This is sufficient to result in apparent parametric shifts in forecasting models.[34] With transactors learning more about policymaking, policies no longer work the way they used to work. The effects of policy become more unpredictable the more they are used. This is not difficult to believe today.

Lucas concluded "that the features which lead to success in short-term forecasting are unrelated to quantitative policy evaluation, that the major econometric models are (well) designed to perform the former task only, and that simulations using these models can, in principle, provide *no* useful information as to the actual consequences of alternative policies."[35] His argument has apparently been accepted by some critics of RE theory.[36] This acceptance is significant, for the critique is an attack that goes further than Milton Friedman's arguments against stabilization policies.

Poole has noted that "rational-expectations theory has provided much more insight into the failures of empirical macro models than into the construction of successful ones."[37] This statement partly reflects the fact that RE models must be different than traditional ones, and hence, not "successful" by conventional criteria. And the degree to which all macro theorists are heeding some of the strictures of Lucas, Sargent, Wallace, and others is silent testimony to the insights of their analyses.

Not being identical, RE models do not all raise the same questions. In the Sargent-Wallace model, we see classical long-run theory with no learning behavior. Lucas' model has more scope for error and specifically short-run phenomena, but it raises new questions. Having first constructed and solved a neoclassical growth model, Lucas developed a model of a purely monetary cycle. Two limitations characterize this latter analysis: first, there is zero elasticity of investment with respect to expected yield and second, monetary shocks are "one shot," stochastic, and unevenly distributed across all markets. Lucas noted the results:

> One notes that the effects of an initial shock in the purely monetary model, will *persist* but can never *cumulate*: the largest effect must come in the first period. To account for the observed gradual upswing, it appears that one must introduce systematic patterns in the shocks or modify the internal structure of the model.[38]

He modified the structure so as to generate a monetary overinvestment cycle. His monetary overinvestment model is characterized by a unitary period of production; transitory demand shifts produce an accelerator effect. Capital goods production is first stimulated in markets experiencing the shocks; since capital stocks must return to normal after demand returns to normal, investment in these markets for a time makes a negative contribution to employment.[39] In this way, Lucas captured some of the essential features of business cycles absent in his purely monetary model. The nature of his assumptions must, however, be examined. First he adopted Professor Phelps' technique of assuming that trade occurs in *isolated* markets. Second, he excluded any economy–wide market for capital funds. Third, he continued to assume random and unsystematic monetary shocks.

Poole criticized the first assumption: "The distinction between knowledge of the past and present on the one hand and knowledge of the future on the other . . . seems . . . to be a much more solid basis for building a theory of the cycle than is the distinction relied upon by Lucas—that between known and unknown current data."[40] This assumption does lead to certain realistic features of the model: "Since traders follow different paths, each will have different information in hand, so that in general one would need to describe the informational state of the economy by a distribution of agents by information held. . . . This informational state will influence prices and will then itself be an obejct of speculation—*agents will form expectations about the expectations of others.*"[41] This characterization approximates the informational realities of market economies, realities absent in other RE models. Yet Lucas did not consider any of the more radical implications of individuals' forming expectations about others' expectations. It is no longer simply a matter of specifying an actual or objective state of the economy and a given state of opinions about this state. For the possibility of "self–confirming" expectations, perhaps unrelated to the "data," is now logically admitted; such expectations are a feature of genuinely classical theories notably absent from RE models.[42] Although one need not develop the analysis as did Keynes, his "dark forces of time and ignorance" must be addressed. Once having opened the floodgates, one must analyze the effects.

Poole's criticism is thus on the mark. Time is brought in, but only in a limited way. Capital investment takes time, but the period of production is technologically limited. By not permitting the period of production to vary, Lucas was virtually compelled to rely on ignorance of *currently available* data; he had severely constrained the amount of intertemporal informational and allocational effects of monetary disturbances. As will be explained later, this latter limitation is yet more significant because of the *unsystematic* nature of the monetary shocks in his model.

Lucas saw the exclusion of an economy–wide capital market as necessary to preserve the logic of his model. The market clearing interest rate would convey information to isolated traders about aggregate state variables "uncontaminated by local disturbances."[43] He averred that "with an accelerator effect present, it seems likly that the existence of an economy-wide bond market would dampen cyclical movements but not eliminate them or alter their qualitative character. Without further analysis, however, the question remains open and, clearly, crucial.''[44] This question is crucial both for Lucas' model and because it involves very general questions first raised in the business cycle literature to which Lucas has referred.

The Business Cycle Theorists

Having accepted the problem statement of the cycle theorists, Lucas departed from their solution. As a result, important features of their theories—notably Hayek's—are absent from his model. Incorporation of these features would obviate the criticism leveled against Lucas' and other RE theorists' models. To illustration, I briefly outline Hayek's solution.

Hayek saw the medium of exchange function for money as the basis for a solution. This function breaks the demand and supply nexus of barter, general equilibrium constructions in which goods offered for sale logically must constitute demands for other goods.[45] He also focused on the micro-allocational or relative price effects, deemphasizing the classical general price effects.[46] He argued that monetary disturbances are systematic and not random in their impact on particular markets, specifically intertemporal markets. In doing so, he did *not* rely on ad hoc isolation of these markets but on the fact that information about others' plans is conveyed largely through relative prices and interest rates. Perhaps most importantly in this regard, he developed a theory of how these prices and interest rates could transmit misinformation, thus exaccerbating the effects of exogenous shocks. Finally, Hayek emphasized the *variability* of the period of production.

There are subtle though important differences separating Lucas and Hayek. Lucas desired a mechanism to keep market participants partially ignorant of the economy's state; he isolated markets geographically. Hayek saw partial ignorance as inherent in workings of markets; he did not further isolate economic actors nor did he deny them access to existing economy-wide markets. While Lucas suggested that these markets would dampen errors and misallocations, Hayek saw them as the mechanism for transmitting monetary into real disturbances. He focused on intertemporal ignorance and error in allocation, rather than nonuse of currently available data.

So long as saving and investment occur through a medium of exchange, then so long can one vary ex ante without the other's varying in the same way. This process can be illustrated as in figure 7-1.

The discrepancy between n and i_t can be caused in one of two ways:

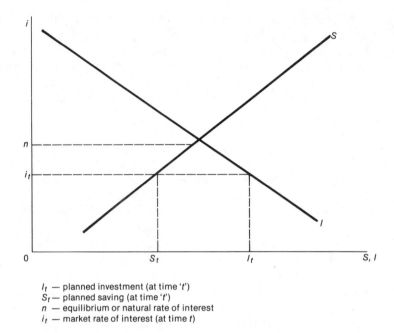

I_t — planned investment (at time 't')
S_t — planned saving (at time 't')
n — equilibrium or natural rate of interest
i_t — market rate of interest (at time t)

Figure 7–1. Saving and Investment.

either an activist central bank can generate or permit an expansion of loans by the commercial banking system that autonomously lowers the market rate of interest; or the central bank can passively accommodate shifts in the investment demand function, the explanation of such shifts being unspecified here. At this point, it does not matter which is the cause of the monetary expansion. While planned saving (S_t) is less than planned investment (I_t), the increased money, being made available as credit, enables borrowers—primarily but not exclusively entrepreneurs—to command a larger quantity of society's real resource and use them for investment projects. In other words, ex post saving equals planned investment of I_t at the interest rate i_t.

All magnitudes are in nominal terms, so the increased quantity of money in the system will eventually cause the schedules to shift; as will be explained, these shifts do not restore equilibrium. What is important now is that the medium of exchange has disturbed the equilibrium relationships whose existence is inevitable in barter, general equilibrium constructions, but only in those constructions.[47]

So long as the monetary disturbance persists, equilibrium will not be restored either by "income effects" from rising prices or "price expecta-

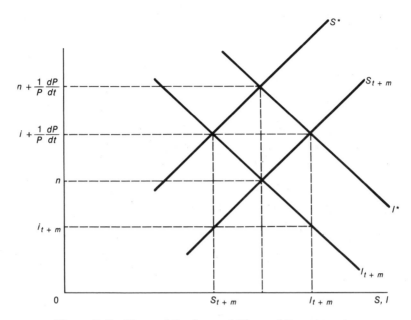

Figure 7–2. Planned Saving and Planned Investment.

tions effects.'' So long as the monetary disturbance persists, market interest rates lie below the hypothetical nominal rate that would equate planned saving and planned investment [see figure 7–2].[48]

At the end of m periods of proportional increase in the stock of money, S_{t+m} and I_{t+m} are respectively planned saving and planned investment in real terms. With inflation now anticipated, these functions shift upwards, reflecting an equilibrium inflation premium. The old market rate of interest plus this premium ($\frac{1}{P}\frac{dP^e}{dt}$) remains below the natural rate plus this premium.[49] Indeed, in terms of the model and its transmission mechanism, this conclusion follows by necessity. For if there were no such discrepancy there would be no further monetary or price inflation. But without continued inflation, no inflation premium could exist. The Wicksellian cumulative process continues so long as the assumed monetary policy creates a discrepancy between equilibrium and market interest rates; and so long as the process continues, there is no intertemporal equilibrium.

The nonneutralities in Hayek's model stem from the effects on real variables of purely nominal disturbances that affect interest rates and economy-wide credit markets. Interest rates are ratios of relative prices; changes in interest rates accordingly represent changes in relative prices and concomitant changes in the goods produced. Hayek concluded that the changes would be systematic and their general form predictable. Stated briefly, his analysis predicted overproduction of capital goods with relatively long periods of production and underproduction of consumer goods and capital goods with relatively short periods of production. Moreover, the effects of monetary disturbances persist even after the cessation of the disturbance because the excess capital goods must be "worked off" while the supply of other goods is increased.[50]

Like other business cycle theorists, Hayek attempted an integration of value and business cycle theory. Unlike modern RE theorists, he viewed monetary disturbances as causing changes in the demand and supply functions, and thus in relative prices, consumption, investment, and so forth. These changes do not represent new equilibria, because they are unsustainable changes (an infinite rate of credit expansion being necessary in the long run to sustain the changes). To repeat, the credit expansion transfers real resources among productive sectors and individuals.

Granting Hayek's assumptions, one notes several characteristic features of business cycle thereby explicated: the greater variability of measured investment relative to measured consumption over the cycle, the diffusion of price changes, variations in unemployment and even stagflation.[51] In the context of this chapter, however, I will focus on the rationality of expectations in Hayek's analysis and his emphasis on the nonrandomness of monetary shocks.

The crucial question devolves around the source of errors in cyclical episodes. In Hayek's analysis, misallocations and errors occur as economic actors respond to genuine price signals. It is *not* necessary that they mistake general for relative price changes as is generally the case in RE models.[52] *Relative prices do change;* these changes reflect the nonneutralities in the theory. Entrepreneurs are being offered a larger command over the real resources in society; the concomitant changes in relative prices make investing these real resources genuinely profitable. There is surely nothing "irrational" in entrepreneurs grasping real profit opportunities.

At some time in the future, the profits will turn to losses as the unsustainable credit expansion slows or ends entirely. Nonetheless, the profits accrued due to actual changes in demand and supply relationships, changes wrought by the monetary and credit expansion. Individuals may even avoid the eventual losses on these investments by effecting trades at opportune times. Someone will, however, bear the losses that accrue after the misallocations—viewed ex post and from a long-run perspective—are revealed. The self-reversing character of monetary disturbance is a conclusion of Hayek's neo-Wicksellian "natural rate" theory, just as it is a conclusion of the modern "Natural Rate hypothesis."[53]

If prices transmit the (limited) amount of available information in the economy, then monetary disturbances occurring as postulated will alter transactors' perceptions and expectations, as well as relative prices. Whether these expectations are "rational" depends on how much is packed into that concept. Strictly interpreted, rationality implies transactors' knowledge of the economy's structure. Likewise, strictly interpreted (a la Sargent and Wallace), rationality implies that nonpolicymakers possess as much information about the probability of a given policy's being implemented as do policymakers themselves.

What has been termed the "privacy of information" argues against that conclusion. Put simply, either I have better information on what I am going to do in the future, or the concept "I" (as distinct from "you") has no operational (or cognitive) meaning. If, however, rationality is so strictly interpreted, then expectational rationality is absent from business cycle theories such as Hayek's. I would argue, however, that the existence of "irrational" (and divergent) expectations is an essential feature of monetary economies. In any case, to repeat the argument presented already, many of the changes Hayek analyzed were real, though temporary ones.

If, on the other hand, rationality of expectations is taken more loosely to mean that transactors make the best use of available information, then Hayek's transactors have rational expectations.

It is sometimes argued that monetary disturbances can only temporarily affect market values, real factors alone determining equilibrium prices. The assumption that "real factors alone" determine resource allocation is a full information assumption. Inconsistency of perceptions and expectations with these data insures that reallocations will be necessary; but proof that economic events depend on this inconsistency does not demonstrate its impossibility. (Indeed, the reallocations preserve any long-run neutrality of money properties in our models.) Investigations with models possessing neutrality properties even in the shortest of runs are investigations "of 'possible worlds' in which the occupation of monetary theorist would serve no useful social function."[54]

Making the best use of available information will *not* normally involve transactors possessing full information about the economy's structure, the probability of given policies being implemented, and the economic effects of given policies. Indeed, on the latter issue, economists possessing technical training lacked by businessmen and other transactors by no means agree on macroeconomic theories. To hypothesize that entrepreneurs make unambiguous judgments about the distribution of interest rates, prices, and so forth, after the beginning of a monetary expansion, involves postulating that those who lack such training can adjudicate scientific issues still in dispute.[55]

Moreover, even if entrepreneurs knew the expected course of a business cycle, they would not necessarily alter their behavior; they would not necessarily do otherwise if convinced of the temporary nature of the demand shifts. Here Hayek and Lucas differ. In Hayek's analysis, responding to the demand shifts can be profitable so long as they persist. Failure to respond would involve foregone profits. Efficient use of the assumed information would lead entrepreneurs to form rational expectations about the duration and intensity of cyclical demand changes. Variance around expected values will result in "error," as entrepreneurs fail to "bail out" in time (or "bail out" too soon). No irrationality is evidenced in this process. Although I continue to question the world view of RE theorists (interpreted strictly), the Austrian model is innocent of RE criticisms and avoids the problems associated with RE models.[56]

One other of Hayek's assumptions is open to legitimate questioning: the systematic nature of monetary shock leading to variations in the process of production. This I take up in the last section. But I would point out that the one recurring theme in this criticism of RE theory is the importance of information acquisition in market economies. This importance focuses our attention on the entrepreneur, the forgotten figure in the RE literature, no less than in neoclassical economics generally. The degree to which policy-makers can fool the public depends crucially on its ability to generate entre-preneurial error, that is, to interfere with the equilibrating function of the entrepreneur. The failure of RE theorists satisfactorily to specify the mone-tary institutions and policies consistent with the most efficient performance of this equilibrating entrepreneurial function reflects their failure either to assimilate a theory of the entrepreneur or to develop their own. Professor Israel Kirzner has produced a coherent entrepreneurial theory.[57] His theory has not been generally accepted or integrated into general economic theory, nor has the need for such an integration received widespread acceptance.[58] Still less have monetary economists recognized a need to integrate monetary and entrepreneurial theory.[59]

The Political Business Cycle

We have seen that RE theory partly involves a return to the older business cycle tradition; some of the issues raised by the former were analyzed in detail in this older tradition. One heretofore unnoted difference between the two is the almost total absence of institutional considerations in the RE literature, as compared to the central place accorded such considerations in the business cycle literature. I find almost no suggestions in RE models that the kinds of monetary and fiscal institutions that we have might affect either the information possessed by transactors (bank or nonbank) or the frequency and magnitude of disturbances generated. (Endorsement of a monetary rule comes closest to such a realization.) This absence confirms the affinity between RE theory and perfect-knowledge, institutionless neo-classical economic theory.

As a business cycle theorist, Hayek emphasized the importance of institutions. For him the most obvious aspect of money creation in modern economies is that it takes place in credit markets, a process that disturbs relative prices in particular and generally predictable ways. In this section, what I defend is not Hayek's specification of the systematic features of monetary disturbances, but the contention that they will be systematic. Monetary (and fiscal) policy is employed by policymakers to attain specific ends. These ends are not usually served either by attention to aggregate economic goals, or by consistent or predictable policy such as monetary rule. The ends are certainly not served by *random* shocks to particular markets.

R.J. Gordon has observed that modern monetary theories of economic fluctuations leave much unexplained.[60] It is now generally agreed that sustained price inflation cannot continue without sustained monetary expansion. Theories such as monetarism (or its outgrowth, RE theory) do not explain why monetary expansions occur. I conjecture that RE theorists would find this a particularly vexing question so long as they remain convinced that no systematic policy can predictably affect real variables. In this view, the money creation process as we know it is unintelligible. Perhaps policymakers and only policymakers are irrational; this hypothesis is not, however, in the RE spirit.

Political Business Cycle (PBC) theorists have suggested that *"the government . . . chooses economic policies during its incumbency which maximizes its plurality at the next election.''*[61] We can agree that what kinds of policies succeed are not readily identifiable, a realization reflected in the high returns to successful vote getters. Economists have not been particularly successful in identifying the political-economic determinants of successful vote garnering.[62] And PBC theorists are certainly open to criticism for their sometimes naive approach to expectations, as when Professor Nordhous asserted that "unemployment is a control or policy variable of the economic system which the policymakers can set at any level they wish.''[63] One scarcely need believe in extreme rationality to have doubts about this characterization. With the aid of an apt metaphor, Professor Wagner, a prominent believer in fiscal illusion and other "irrationalities," identified the central weakness of conventional PBC models:

> The injection of new changes in policy is . . . .like adjusting one particular link in [an] erector set. . . . Readjustments will disturb a whole set of anticipations and plans, with the consequences of these readjustments extending over various periods of time.[64]

Despite formulations of PBC theory that render them unacceptable to RE theorists, these are complementary rather than mutually exclusive. PBC models rationalize monetary and fiscal actions by governments, elected officials and bureaucrats alike.[65] I devoted considerable attention to Hayek's analysis in part because of its emphasis on the nonrandomness of monetary disturbances and their effects. PBC models, especially when formulated along lines suggested by Wagner, help explain why policies are nonrandom.

Wagner observed that "it has been tacitly assumed either that politicians will act selflessly to promote economic stability or that their interests in their own political survival will require them to act to promote such stability."[66] PBC theorists like Wagner have replaced the standard macroeconomic paradigm with a public choice paradigm. Wagner criticized the literature for continuing to focus on aggregate variables as the policy targets of policymakers:

> Simple coalition theory would suggest that a policy of attempting truly to act on aggregate variables would be dominated by a policy of attempting to act on individual variables. A policy of affecting all prices equally would be dominated by a policy of affecting particular prices. It is quite possible, of course, that the latter course of policy would bring about macroeconomic consequences, but the story that would be told would be quite different one. In either case, the conduct of democratic politics may contribute to business cycles. But in one case it is the intent of political action to influence the state of the aggregate variables, while in the other case it is the intent of political action to influence the state of variables affecting particular individuals, with the aggregate consequences emerging merely as a by-product. In the former case, politics aims to influence the volume of aggregate spending; in the latter case politics aims to influence the structure of relative prices, with changes in aggregate spending themselves but a consequence.[67]

Wagner's reformulation of PBC theory provides an insight into Hayek's basic conclusion: monetary disturbances are nonneutral and hence affect (relative) prices and production. The modern PBC theorists asked the question, "Why do governments generate monetary disturbances that lead to economic fluctuations?" Wagner, adopting a public choice rather than a macroeconomic perspective, developed an analysis in which the main thrust of Hayek's analysis of business fluctuations is supported by modern public choice reasoning. The ramifications of Wagner's public choice macroeconomics—a blending of Austrian monetary theory and public choice theory—are numerous and important. Four implications are especially noteworthy.

First, in Wagner's reformulated PBC theory, policymakers may neither realize the macroeconomic consequences of their overtly distributional monetary and fiscal policies, nor be capable of acting directly on macroeconomic variables in a predictable way. The reformulated PBC theory is neutral with respect to whether policymakers could control macroeconomic vairables if they so desired.

Second, this new approach suggests macroeconomic ills are an inevitable by-product of the mixture of democratic politics *and* a central government sizable enough to produce macroeconomic consequences in pursuing political power.[68] The pessimistic diagnosis is made worse by the realization that even if consensus is reached on the bad consequences of economic policy no remedies will be taken solely on conventional macroeconomic grounds. This is true for the same reason that the demonstrated bad consequences of tariffs and minimum wages do not lead to their repeal, *at least not for the general good.* Coalitions whose particular interest in the hypothesized policies is relatively great devote more resources to continuation of these policies than the diffuse "public" to their cessation.

Third, the new approach directs our attention to the fact that there are effects on real variables due to monetary and fiscal policy actions, actions which through they employ aggregate policy tools (conventionally defined) are not primarily for macroeconomic reasons. This realization both supports and contradicts RE theory. It supports RE theory to the extent that the analysis lessens dependence on illusions. In Wagner's version at least, the beneficiaries are certainly not being fooled. One need not assume that the public's illusion extends beyond what is optimal and inevitable: the public does not have the incentive to invest in the requisite economic knowledge or political action.

RE theory is weakened by the findings of the new approach to the extent that the former continues to operate with categories and concepts inherited from macroeconomics; in general, RE theory explains macroeconomic phenomena in terms of falsified expectations about price levels, distributions of random disturbances, etc. This observation leads me to the fourth ramification of the new approach.

Both RE and PBC theory, albeit from different perspectives, are ultimately attacking the traditional concept of macroeconomics. Lucas and Wagner are surely doing this, each suggesting that macroeconomics poses questions erroneously, analyzes the problems incorrectly and generates false conclusions. Each is calling for a new macroeconomic paradigm. In so doing, each supports Hayek's call of forty years ago for a microeconomic approach to monetary problems. Hayek's vision can perhaps finally be implemented by a critical reformulation of Rational Expectations Theory and by the analysis of the *political* nature of business cycles.

Notes

1. Lucas quoted Professor F.A. Hayek here, the latter characterizing the position of A. Lowe in *Monetary Theory and the Trade Cycle*, translated by N. Kaldor and H.M. Croome (1933; reprint ed., New York: Augustus M. Kelley, 1966), p. 33n; *see* Robert E. Lucas, Jr., "Understand-

ing Business Cycles'' (paper prepared for the Kiel Conference on Growth Without Inflation (Chicago, June 1976), p. 1.

2. Hayek, *Monetary Theory and the Trade Cycle*, pp. 43–43.

3. Lucas, "Understanding Business Cycles," p. 2.

4. *See* Bennett T. McCallum, "The Political Business Cycle: An Empirical Test," *Southern Economic Journal* 44 (January 1978): 504–15.

5. The best single source here is Lucas, "Econometric Policy Evaluation: A Critique," in *The Phillips Curve and Labor Markets* ed. Karl Brunner and Allan H. Meltzer (New York: North–Holland Publishing Co., 1976), pp. 19–46.

6. *See* Thomas J. Sargent and Neil Wallace, *Rational Expectations and the Theory of Economic Policy* (Minneapolis: Research Department, Federal Reserve Bank of Minneapolis, 1975), pp. 7–9.

7. This conclusion has been forcefully restated in McCallum, "Price-Level Stickiness and the Feasibility of Monetary Stabilization Policy with Rational Expectations," *Journal of Political Economy* 85 (June 1977): 631–32.

An earlier statement of this basic position was made by Professor Milton Friedman: "The first and most important lesson that history teaches about what monetary policy can do . . . is that monetary policy can prevent money itself from being a major source of economic disturbance." Milton Friedman, "The Role of Monetary Policy," in *The Optimum Quantity of Money and Other Essays* (Chicago: Aldine Publishing Co., 1969), p. 106; this essay was his A.E.A. Presidential Address (1967).

8. Neil Wallace, "Microeconomic Theories of Macroeconomic Phenomena and Their Implications for Monetary Policy," in *Rational Expectations and the Theory of Economic Policy, Part II: Arguments and Evidence,* Thomas J. Sargent and Neil Wallace (Minneapolis: Research Department, Federal Reserve Bank of Minneapolis, 1976), p. 24.

9. Ibid., p. 25.

10. Lucas, "An Equilibrium Model of the Business Cycle," *Journal of Political Economy* 83 (November/December 1975): 1114.

11. See John F. Muth, "Rational Expectations and the Theory of Price Movements," *Econometrica* 29 (July 1961): 315–35. For more recent statements of this formulation, *see* Robert J. Gordon, "Recent Developments in the Theory of Inflation and Unemployment," *Journal of Monetary Economics* 2 (April 1976): 199–200; and William Poole, "Rational Expectations in the Macro Model," *Brookings Papers on Economic Activity* 2 (1976): 464–65. A caveat for asymmetries appears in McCallum, "Price-Level Stickiness," pp. 632–633.

12. Detailed consideration of irrationalities in various macro models would be beyond the scope of this paper. The reader is referred to the cited works and additional references contained in these works.

13. "In the past several years, in our Workshop on Money and Bank-

ing at the University of Chicago, my major problem has been battling with the proponents of Box–Jenkins on the one hand, and rational expectations on the other.'' Milton Friedman, ''The Monetarist Controversy: Discussions by Milton Friedman and Franco Modigliani,'' *Federal Reserve Bank of San Francisco Economic Review Supplement* (Spring 1977): 13.

14. Wallace, ''Microeconomic Theories,'' p. 26. Friedman made a similar point in his invited address to the 1974 Southern Economic Association meetings.

15. Cf. Gordon, ''Recent Developments in the Theory of Inflation and Unemployment,'' 193, for a discussion of the ''threshold hypothesis.'' Lucas found a favorable short–run output–inflation tradeoff for moderate but not for high and volatile inflation rates. Lucas, ''Some International Evidence on Output–Inflation Tradeoffs,'' *American Economic Review* 63 (June 1973): 326–334.

16. Sargent and Wallace, *Rational Expectations and the Theory of Economic Policy,* p. 7.

17. Poole, Rational Expectations in the Macro Model,'' p. 465.

18. Friedman, ''The Monetarist Controversy,'' p. 14; *see also* Edmund S. Phelps, ''Comments and Discussion'' of Poole, Rational Expectations, pp. 506–507; and Poole's response, p. 511.

19. The connection between the Rational Expectations and Efficient Market hypothese is most obvious here. Poole developed this connection in Poole, ''Rational Expectations in the Macro Model,'' pp. 467–479.

20. Professor J. Huston McCulloch argued in private that this is not a case of serial correlation.

21. Lucas, ''An Equilibrium Model of the Business Cycle,'' p. 1138.

22. Poole, ''Rational Extectations in the Macro Model,'' p. 504.

23. Sargent and Wallace, *Rational Expectations and the Theory of Economic Policy*, p. 6, emphasis added.

24. ''The length of the period is not specified, but for the result to be interesting, one supposes that it is a year or less.'' Stanly Fischer, ''Long–Term Contracts, Rational Expectations, and the Optimal Money Supply Rule,'' *Journal of Political Economy* 85 (February 1977): 194.

25. Benjamin Friedman, ''Rational Expectations Are Really Adaptive After All,'' Harvard Institute of Economic Research Discussion Paper Number 430 (Cambridge, Mass. 1975), pp. 27–28; emphasis added.

26. Ibid., p. 24.

27. No distinction is made among noncentral bank agents, for instance; *see* Fischer, ''Long–Term Contracts,'' pp. 193–194. Differences among RE theorists do become significant here. In Lucas' ''Equilibrium Model of the Business Cycle,'' market participants possess different information sets.

28. F.A. Hayek, ''Economics and Knowledge,'' in *Individualism and Economic Order* (Chicago: University of Chicago Press, 1948), p. 50.

29. Fischer, "Long–Term Contracts," p. 194.

30. Hayek developed this argument in "The Use of Knowledge in Society," in *Individualism and Economic Order,* pp. 77–91, especially pp. 86–91.

31. Axel Leijonhufvud, *On Keynesian Economics and the Economics of Keynes* (New York: Oxford University Press, 1968), p. 271; footnote reference to Hayek's "Meaning of Competition" omitted.

32. Cf. Lucas, "Understanding Business Cycles," pp. 13–14.

33. Brian J. Loasby, *Choice, Complexity and Ignorance* (New York: Cambridge University Press, 1976), p. 9. Cf. Mario J. Rizzo, "Knight's Theory of Uncertainty: A Reconsideration" (Paper prepared for the American Economic Association Annual Meetings, Chicago, 1978).

34. This is Lucas' stochastic parameter drift. "Econometric Policy Evaluation: A Critique," pp. 24–26.

For a recent analysis of transactors having incomplete knowledge of future policy decisions, see Finn E. Kydland and Edward C. Prescott, "Rules Rather than Discretion: The Inconsistency of Optimal Plans," *Journal of Political Economy* 85 (June 1977): 473–91.

35. Lucas, "Economic Policy Evaluation: A Critique," p. 20. Lucas quoted Franklin Fisher as saying that "the notion that one cannot fool all of the people all of the time [need not] imply that one cannot fool all the people even some of the time." Ibid., p. 29. As Lucas observed, Fisher is correct, but when we fool people we do not know how they will be fooled, or that they will be fooled in the same way by the same policy implemented in different periods.

36. *See* Poole, "Rational Expectations in the Macro Model," pp. 501–503.

37. Ibid., p. 505.

38. Lucas, "An Equilibrium Model of the Business Cycle," p. 1135.

39. Ibid., 1137.

40. Poole, "Rational Expectations in the Macro Model," p. 483.

41. Lucas, "An Equilibrium Model of the Business Cycle," p. 1123; emphasis added.

42. For example, *see* John Stuart Mill, *Principles of Political Economy,* ed. Sir William Ashley (Clifton, N.J.: Augustus M. Kelley, 1973), p. 526.

43. Lucas, "An Equilibrium Model of the Business Cycle," p. 1137.

44. Ibid., 1138

45. See Hayek, *Monetary Theory and the Trade Cycle,* pp. 41–46. Hayek has demonstrable intellectual priority over Keynes in this matter.

46. Cf. Gerald P. O'Driscoll, Jr. *Economics as a Coordination Problem: The Contributions of Friedrich A. Hayek* (Kansas City: Sheed, Andrews and McMeel, 1977), pp. 37–43.

47. This observation raises an analytical problem that cannot be

resolved here. Although the existence of a medium of exchange is necessary for the attainment of equilibrium, its existence both alters the nature of the equilibrium and makes possible movements away from equilibrium. Cf. F.A. Hayek, *The Pure Theory of Capital* (Chicago: University of Chicago Press, 1941), pp. 29–40.

48. This analysis is taken from William P. Yohe and Denis S. Karnosky, "Interest Rates and Price Level Changes, 1952–69." *Federal Reserve Bank of St. Louis Review* (December 1969): 31–34; they borrowed it from Thomas J. Sargent, "Commodity Price Expectations and the Interest Rate," *Quarterly Journal of Economics* 83 (February 1969): 127–140.

49. I am not committing myself to the proposition that correct inflation premiums will ever develop; I only wish to show that even if correct inflation premiums emerged, these would not restore equilibrium in capital markets.

50. For an explanation of why Hayek's is *not* an accelerator model in the conventional sense, see his essay, "Profits, Interest and Investment," in F.A. Hayek, *Profits, Interest and Investment* (1939; reprinted New York: Augustus M. Kelley, 1970), pp. 3–71.

51. On diffusion of price changes, see Geoffrey H. Moore, "The Cyclical Behavior of Prices," *The Business Cycle Today,* ed. Victor Zarnowitz (New York: Columbia University Press for the National Bureau of Economic Research, 1972), pp. 137–166. The applicability of Hayek's analysis to stagflation is explicated in Gerald P. O'Driscoll, Jr., and Sudha R. Shenoy, "Inflation, Recession and Stagflation," in *Foundations of Modern Austrian Economics,* ed. Edwin G. Dolan (Kansas City: Sheed and Ward, 1976), pp. 185–211.

52. Lucas and Sargent-Wallace adopted the Lucas-Rapping aggregate supply funcion, in which transactors can mistake general for relative price movements. Cf. Lucas, "Some Intertemporal Evidence on Ouput-Inflation Tradeoffs"; and Sargent and Wallace, "'Rational' Expectations, the Optimal Monetary Instrument, and the Optimal Money Supply Rule," *Journal of Political Economy* 83 (March/April 1975): 241–254. Other RE theorists have followed their lead here.

53. On the self-reversing character of montary disturbances, see Hayek, *The Pure Theory of Capital,* pp. 33–34.

54. Leijonhufvud, *On Keynesian Economics,* p. 261.

55. Cf. James M. Buchanan and Richard E. Wagner, *Democracy in Deficit: The Political Legacy of Lord Keynes* (New York: Academic Press, 1977), p. 63; and P.T. Bauer and A.A. Walters, "The State of Economics," *Journal of Law and Economics* 18 (April 1975): 6.

56. The very issue of expectations in the Austrian model of economic fluctuations was debated in surprisingly modern terms over thirty years ago. Cf. L.M. Lachmann, "The Role of Expectations in Economics as a Social

Science," *Economica,* N.S. 10 (February 1943): 12–23; and L. von Mises, "'Elastic Expectations' and the Austrian Theory of the Trade Cycle," *Economica,* N.S. 10 (August 1943): 251–52.

57. Israel Kirzner, *Competition and Entrepreneurship* (Chicago: University of Chicago Press, 1973).

58. But *see* Theodore W. Schultz, "The Value of the Ability to Deal with Disequilibria," *The Journal of Economic Literature* 13 (September 1975): 827–846.

59. Cf. Gerald P. O'Driscoll, Jr., "Rational Expectations and Entrepreneurship" (Paper delivered to the August 1978 Meetings of the American Economic Association, Chicago.)

60. See Gordon, "Recent Developments in Theory of Inflation and Unemployment," pp. 197–199, and 213–215.

61. William D. Nordhaus, "The Political Business Cycle," *The Review of Economic Studies* 42 (April 1975): 174; footnote reference omitted. A restatement of the PBC approach with references to the literature appears in C. Duncan MacRae, "A Political Model of the Business Cycle," *Journal of Political Economy* 85 (April 1977): 239–63.

62. Cf. George J. Stigler, "General Economic Conditions and National Elections," *American Economic Review* 63 (May 1973): 160–67; also, cf. the comments and discussion of this paper, ibid., pp. 168–180.

63. Nordhaus, "The Political Business Cycle," p. 170. In a footnote to this passage. Nordhaus observed that "the assumption that unemployment is a control variable is unrealistic in a decentralized, capitalist economy. It is generally agreed, however, that through judicious choice of fiscal and monetary policy the government can (within a margin of error) set unemployment rates at any desired level."

64. Richard E. Wagner, "Economic Manipulation for Political Profit: Macroeconomic Consequences and Constitutional Implications," *Kyklos* 30 (Fall 1977): 395–410.

65. I am simplifying the analysis by ignoring the semiindependence of monetary authorities in the United States. For an argument that independence is lacking, see Buchanan and Wagner, *Democracy in Deficit,* pp. 114–121.

66. Wagner, 396.

67. Wagner, p. 14 of original draft; cf. Wagner, "Economic Manipulation for Political Profit," pp. 401–402.

68. Cf. Buchanan and Wagner, *Democracy in Deficit* p. 5 and *passim.* As they observed, this realization does not constitute an argument for altering one or the other element in the mixture.

Comment: Politics, Monetary Control, and Economic Performance

Richard E. Wagner

The chapter to be commented on is another illustration of the careful scholarship we have come to expect from Professor O'Driscoll. The puzzle he explores is why an economy should be subject to episodes of macroeconomic disequilibrium or discoordination. This question is obviously an important one. It is also a vexing one, for economic fluctuations are irreconcilable with notions of general equilibrium. In addressing his central question, O'Driscoll surveys the recent literature on rational expectations, the Austrian literature on business cycles, and the recent literature on political business cycles to assess their insights.

O'Driscoll portrays nicely the analytical tension created by rational expectations. Fluctuations could be explained in ways that imply the existence of unexploited profit opportunities and other inefficient uses of information, but this route is inconsistent with reasonable notions about rationality. In avoiding this task, it is easy to end up assuming the efficient use of all information. But doing this brings us back to general equilibrium, in which fluctuations cannot occur. Among the ways this tension might be resolved are to allow people to differ in their information states, and to consider the possibility that the economy operates somewhat differently than suggested by this literature. These two means of resolution are where the other two bodies of literature O'Driscoll describes are pertinent, for they quite naturally allow for differences in information among people and they adopt a different perspective toward the economic order. The approach to the business cycle developed by Hayek builds upon the nonneutral character of monetary change to show how monetary disturbances can induce economic fluctuations. The literature on the political business cycle, at least as reformulated along the lines favored by O'Driscoll, reinforces Hayek's approach to economic fluctuations. Monetary disturbances are treated as arising naturally from differences in knowledge and incentive possessed by participants in the economic process. Governments can pursue monetary expansion despite the cyclical outcome because of the anticipated gains to those in a position to make such a choice. Macroeconomic ills thus become, as O'Driscoll notes, by–products of the mixture of democratic politics and a central government that is large enough to produce macroeconomic consequences in pursuing political ends.

In discussing chapter 7, I shall not develop a line–by–line commentary. O'Driscoll and I are too much in agreement to make this approach interesting or valuable. Rather than presenting a "commentary" as such, I shall present some "reflections" on O'Driscoll's chapter. What I shall do in my alloted space is to explain how some recent literature, particularly on property rights and public choice, reinforces the main thrust of O'Driscoll's chapter by providing insight into how existing monetary institutions tend to promote macroeconomic discoordination as an outcome of the rational pursuit of political self–interest, at least within an institutional framework that confounds government finance and monetary control.

Government Monopoly over Money: Rationalization vs. Explanation

Existing monetary institutions create a link between politics and monetary control. It is well recognized that economic instruments are employed by government to advance the purpose of those in control of the apparatus of the state. Government monopoly over money is simply one such instrument. The state's monopoly over money will certainly be used when suitable in the pursuit of political gain. As O'Driscoll noted, however, the consequence of monetary monopoly combined with the pursuit of political self–interest can be macroeconomic discoordination. The resulting monetary expansion brings about, because of the nonneutral character of the expansion, the discoordination which O'Driscoll discusses.

Government monopoly over money is not, of course, advocated because of its harmful consequences. Rather, such monopoly typically has been rationalized in terms of hypothetical gains in economic efficiency. As compared with a commodity standard, a purely fiduciary or fiat system of money holds out the promise of a potential social saving. This saving is possible because the commodities that otherwise would have been tied up in money stocks could be used for other purposes under a fiduciary standard. The inventories of gold that would have been held as media of exchange can now be put into jewelry, mouths, and other uses. The adoption of a fiduciary standard instituted by government fiat offers, in other words, the potential of an outward shift in the economy's production set. The services formerly supplied by the money commodity, and which require the dedication of stocks of the commodity to that use, can now be supplied costlessly through government fiat, at least in principle.

Rationalization, however, should never be confused with explanation. Although one can develop a rationalization for government monopoly to institute a fiduciary standard to replace a commodity standard, this act of rationalization does not guarantee that government monopoly will actually yield the potential social saving. Wishing doesn't make it so; we have all learned this many times over. This lesson applies to government monopoly over money as well. It is contrary to reason and to history to expect that a monopoly position will fail to be exploited for the benefit of those in a position to practice such an exploitation.

It is the costlessness with which fiduciary money can be created, the very source of its rationalization, that creates difficulties of monetary control with government monopoly. One must sweat to produce gold, but a push of the button will print currency almost effortlessly. A fiduciary standard, in other words, makes it possible to produce claims to real resources at nearly zero cost. One could mine an ounce of gold and exchange this for a television set. Alternatively, one could simply print up $200 worth of currency to trade for the television. A fiduciary system is obviously subject to strong forces of corruption. Counterfeiting is quite natural; whether currency is printed by private citizens or by government, the end result is the same, and the pressures and temptations leading to printing are identical. A private citizen might print because he did not want to work to gain the desired purchasing power. A government might print because it did not want to tax to gain the desired purchasing power.

There are strong analytical grounds for understanding both the temptation by government to resort to money creation and the resulting harm of such monetary debasement. O'Driscoll applies a "public choice" ascription to support these consequences of government monopoly over money. Before considering these consequences in more detail, I should note that only a part, though an increasing part, of this literature supports this position. The majority of the literature would suggest that government monopoly will tend to work as the rationalization describes. This segment of the literature is captivated by the superficial similarities between government and the market. Politicians compete for the support of citizens just as firms compete for the patronage of customers. Although differences are duly noted, the analytical focus is on the essential similarities between the two institutional forms. A person gets some services from a public goods store as it were, while getting others from a private goods store. Just as the propelling force in a market economy is consumer needs, with firms scurrying about to service those needs, so the propelling force in the public sector is viewed as citizen demands, with politicians doing their best to service those demands.

There are strong grounds, however, for suggesting that the differences between government and the market are more pronounced than the similarities, particularly as governments get larger, both in terms of area and in terms of the range of services undertaken. In the public sector there is no *choice* and there are no *prices,* and all the discussion about theories of *public–choice* based on *tax-prices* cannot offset the crucial differences that exist. Individual incentives are generally weaker in government. Knowledge and the scope for entrepreneurship are also more limited, for reasons that should be clear to readers of Mises' work on socialism and Kirzner's work on knowledge and entrepreneurship.[2] Furthermore, and in relation to some of the points discussed by O'Driscoll, prices generally provide sufficient information for rational economic action. Rational economic action does not require people to know the underlying economic structure that generated the price signals, as Hayek pointed out so clearly.[3] It is different, however, for rational political action. Not only are prices absent, but also some presumption about causation is necessary. Whereas the economizing property of the market is that it allows people to act rationally in response to observations on "what," rationality in political choice requires judgments about "why." It is one thing to adapt privately to changes in anticipated rates of inflation. It is quite a different, far more complex matter to determine the cause of that inflation. Yet, the choice among political programs requires essentially a choice among competing views of causation. That part of the public choice literature I have in mind, which stresses the difference between the public sector and the private, strongly lends support to O'Driscoll's suggestion that considerations of rational political action support insights developed from the Hayekian approach to business cycles.

Rational Politics and Monetary Expansion

Although governments will use the instruments at their disposal in the pursuit of political gain, the particular manifestations as well as the consequences of such usage will depend upon the existing institutional framework. Within a commodity standard, for instance, an increase in the benefits promised to one set of citizens necessarily requires a decrease in the benefits promised to another set of citizens, for this is how the increased benefits must be paid for. Government monopoly over a fiduciary standard, however, severs this link between positive and negative benefits, and it now becomes possible to make inconsistent or excessive promises of benefits. In consequence, a program designed to benefit one set of citizens may be enacted without having either to curtail a program designed to benefit another set or to increase taxes. Positive promises can be made without negative offsets, for the excess of desires to spend over the means to pay for such spending can be bridged through money creation. The creation of government monopoly over money, it thus seems clear, alters the constraints within which government conducts its activities, and alters them systematically by creating a bias toward monetary expansion.[4]

What is especially relevant for our purposes is recognition that political action focuses on the *structure of relative prices,* not on something called the level of absolute prices. Discrimination among citizens is the very essence of majoritarian politics, and such discrimination becomes intensified as such institutions as government monopoly over money arise to facilitate such discrimination. A simple illustration should suffice to make the general point. Suppose an electorate consists of three persons, and consider two alternative programs for potential political action. One program would provide equal benefits to all, say $1.00 per person. The other program would concentrate benefits by giving $1.50 to each of two persons. Within a majoritarian political setting, the latter, discriminatory, program would dominate the former, nondiscriminatory program.

What is referred to as macroeconomic policies always works through affecting the structure of relative prices. Particular patterns of tax reductions are advocated, and other particular patterns of tax reduction of the same aggregate magnitude are rejected. *Particular* programs of public expenditure are advocated, while other programs of equal magnitude are rejected. In all these instances, particular produce and factor prices are affected. Although the level of absolute prices may increase, this increase is simply incidental to the change in the structure of relative prices. In the operation of the process of money expansion, the money balances of particular persons are increased. Where lies the support for a nondiscriminatory drop of money from a helicopter in Patinkinesque fashion? Why not adopt an institution in which everyone's checkbook balances are increased proportionately? Why not adopt any of numerous other forms of money expansion that would operate approximately in a neutral, nondiscriminatory fashion? Because to do so would require government to refrain from using one of its instruments—its monopoly over money—in its most effective fashion. To fail to use its money monopoly for political or discriminatory purposes is to turn politicians into statesmen. It was Harry Truman, I believe, who put it so well: "A statesman is a defeated politician," and is in a position generally aspired to only in the memoir–writing stage of life.

Many people seem prone to ask: "What causes inflation?" It might seem as though a reasonably correct answer is "Money creation." Obviously, a sustained rise in prices must be accompanied by sustained money expansion, practically everyone will agree. But to attribute the rising prices to money creation does not provide any understanding as to why we find ourselves living within such an inflationary experience. The standard response gives no explanation as to why the money creation takes place. One may well observe a child lying in a street beside a car, and describe an association between the two. This description, however, would simply be the starting point of an investigation, not the end. With the child, one would want to understand the process by which the child came to lie in the street. With the expanding supply of money, it would seem as though we should be interested in understanding why it has expanded in the manner it has.

Under existing institutional arrangements it is profitable for those in control to keep the printing presses turning. Looked at from this perspective, different monetary institutions can be looked upon as creating different patterns of ownership over the printing presses. Accordingly, the pattern of monetary expansion that results depends upon the particular structure of ownership, along with the anticipated pattern of costs and gains to the owners from their printing activities. Different monetary institutions can influence both the pattern of ownership and the pattern of costs and gains. Different frameworks for central banking within a system of government money monopoly could be explored from this perspective. More significantly, forms of government monopoly over money could be compared with different ways of allowing competition in the provision of money. The treatment of monetary arrangements within this property rights framework is, I realize, a topic appropriately treated as a paper of its own rather than as an element in a discussion of someone else's chapter, but a brief mention at this time seems helpful in clarifying the political nature of the pattern of monetary disturbance under existing institutions.

Rational political action will strongly favor discriminatory policies over nondiscriminatory policies. Actions that alter the structure of relative prices will tend to dominate actions that leave the structure of prices unchanged and operate instead merely to alter all prices by some equal percentage. Actions that increase some people's cash balances more than others will tend to dominate actions that increase all money balances by the same rate. (I might note at this point that rational expectations does not really leave the process of money expansion unintelligible, as O'Driscoll states it does. Even if money expansion were neutral, expansion would still redistribute wealth to those whose money balances were increased.) This focus on politics as rationally focusing on the structure of relative prices fits in nicely with the Austrian emphasis on the nonneutral character of monetary change. This Hayekian emphasis is on how monetary change brings about systematic changes in the structure of relative prices; rational political action similarly will aim at achieving systematic alterations in the structure of relative prices.

Economic Discoordination Resulting from Government Monopoly over Money

Government monopoly over money has operated with an expansionary bias historically, and this bias is easily understandable theoretically. If monetary disturbance were neutral, such disturbance would affect the distribution of wealth, but not the allocation of resources. Some people would be wealthier and others poorer as a result of monetary expansion, but no macroeconomic discoordination would result from this expansion. Rational political action with government monopoly over money would bring about transfers of wealth to early recipients of the newly created money from the remainder of the populace. Although some may question the ethics of the state's monopoly over money being used to transfer wealth through this process of legally sanctioned counterfeiting, no sources of economic discoordination would arise to plague us.

But monetary disturbance does bring about economic discoordination, and this nonneutral character of monetary change is where the other element of O'Driscoll's paper comes in—namely, the Austrian or Hayekian theory of economic fluctuations. As originally formulated by Hakey, cycles resulted from the process set in motion by credit expansion. As a result of the market rate of interest falling below the natural rate, the economic process leads to a lengthening of the structure of production. A period of inflation–induced boom results. This lengthening, however, is inconsistent with the data of equilibrium because this lengthening does not result from a reduction in the rate of time preference. Consequently, the expansion is reversed with the passage of time.

In terms of the specific historical experience when Hayek wrote, this particular process of expansion and cyclical reaction seems reasonable. In our present institutional setting, however, this process may operate somewhat differently, as O'Driscoll suggests. For this reason, it is possible to accept the essential point of Hayek's emphasis without accepting his specific description of that process. When Hayek wrote, government was small, and the source of difficulty seemed to reside primarily in money expansion as a result of an elastic currency. Today, however, government is large, and its actions are a prime source of money expansion. The specific relation between the treasury and the banking system differs among nations, of course, but in most cases it is generally recognized that a failure by government to meet all of its expenditure promises by tax extractions will be validated to some extent by money creation. Monetary expansion will be used to finance public spending beyond what is covered by taxation. In our present context, money creation is used in large measure to finance transfer payments. In consequence, the expansion will lead initially not to an artificial lengthening of the structure of production, but to a shortening. Although the particular description of the discoordination will thus be different, macroeconomic discoordination will arise all the same.

Why, however, should concern over the discoordinative properties of government monopoly over money be limited to cyclical fluctuations in such aggregate variables as unemployment rates and price levels? Does not this very limited focus itself illustrate the erroneous conceptual foundations of macroeconomics that O'Driscoll mentioned? To illustrate in concrete terms, consider a typical Hayekian–type cycle caused by credit expansion. The structure of production at first lengthens and subsequently shrinks again. Specifically, this might entail initially a shift of resources from raising chickens to growing timber, with a subsequent shift back to raising chickens again.

It certainly causes an economist no difficulty to postulate a set of circumstances under which the necessary shifts in labor will take place without affecting the unemployment rate. It is no trouble to conceive of labor engaged in raising chickens and producing the required capital goods to move instantaneously to raising timber and the required capital goods, and then to move back, again instantaneously, to raising chickens. To the extent that such instantaneous shifts in employment take place, the rate of unemployment will *not* be affected by this monetary disturbance. But this constancy of the rate of unemployment should not be taken as a sign of a smoothly working economy. The chickens that initially were raised with the intention of producing eggs, then subsequently destroyed to make room for trees, along with the myriad other plans that were altered in the switch from raising chickens to raising timber, a switch due to the monetary expansion, are all wasted. A similar waste results when the structure of production changes again, this time from growing timber to raising chickens. Mistakes cannot be corrected costlessly, even though labor may be fully employed in the process of correcting those mistakes. All those plans that are revised in response to the changing structure of relative prices entail waste, for what could have been produced had the disruption of plans not taken place is lost forever. All of this wastage of what could have been produced to satisfy human needs had the monetary expansion not taken place to discoordinate individual plans is also a cost of that expansion, even though the rate of unemployment may have remained unchanged.

A different illustration may solidify the point, at least for professors. Suppose a professor had in a fit of extraordinary excitement worked around the clock to write a paper. Upon completing the last sentence of the manuscript twenty–four hours after starting, he knocks over the pot of coffee setting on his desk. Because he has used a felt–tipped pen, the manuscript smears so much it cannot be submitted to a typist without first being rewritten. Looked at in terms of labor supplied in preparing the manuscript for typing, the professor was fully employed for forty–eight hours. Only twenty–four hours labor was engaged in truly worthwhile production. The other twenty–four hours were devoted to correcting a mistake. What could have been produced in those twenty–four hours had the coffee not been spilt is lost forever.

Monetary manipulation for political gain inherently involves alterations in the structure of relative prices. The resulting adaptations in the structure of production involve economic waste, even if unemployment is unaffected. And even if unemployment does occur, an assessment of the extent of economic discoordination by looking at the rate of unemployment will understate the amount of loss from such discoordination. Moreover, it seems to me a reasonable conjecture that the loss due to such shifts in the structure of employment exceeds considerably any losses due to unemployment. Measures of the economic success of political programs in terms of measures of the rate of unemployment are, in other words, fraudulent, for they misrepresent what is at stake in choosing among different courses of political action.

Concluding Thoughts

State monopoly over money was not supposed to contribute to macroeconomic discoordination, but a growing body of literature suggests that it does and explains why it does. Although rationalizations can be advanced for anything imaginable, a chasm separates rationalization from explanation. Although one may concoct rationalizations for government monopoly over money, macroeconomic discoordination can be explained quite sensibly as a product of such monopoly. The pursuit of political gain in conjunction with an institutional setting of state monopoly over money leads to politically induced disturbances in the organization of economic activity. What I have tried to do in these reflections is to point out supporting lines of analysis that reinforce the direction taken by O'Driscoll's chapter. The kinds of monetary and fiscal institutions in existence can affect both the information possessed by transactors and the frequency and magnitude of economic disturbances, as O'Driscoll noted. Recognition of the nonneutral character of monetary disturbance combined with an awareness of the patterns of rational political action allows one to understand more clearly how existing institutional arrangements contribute to macroeconomic discoordination. O'Driscoll notes quite clearly that both the rational expectations literature and the political business cycle literature contribute to our understanding of why this is so, and both thereby reinforced in different ways and in contemporary settings the essential perspectives developed earlier by Hayek in his analysis of economic fluctuations. O'Driscoll's chapter, along with my supporting comments, strongly support Professor Hayek's call to separate public finance from monetary control. As he put it in *Denationalisation of Money:* "If we are to preserve a functioning market economy (and with it individual freedom), *nothing can be more urgent than that we dissolve the unholy marriage between monetary and fiscal policy,* long clandestine but formally consecrated with the victory of Keynesian economics."[5]

Notes

1. For a survey of these perspectives, see Richard E. Wagner, "Advertising and the Public Economy: Some Preliminary Ruminations," in *The*

Political Economy of Advertising, ed. David G. Tuerck (Washington: American Enterprise, forthcoming).

2. *See* Ludwig von Mises, "Economic Calculation in the Socialist Commonwealth," in *Collectivist Economic Planning* ed. Friedrich A. Hayek (London: Routledge and Kegan Paul, 1935); and Israel M. Kirzner, *Competition and Entrepreneurship* (Chicago: University of Chicago Press, 1973.).

3. Friedrich A. Hayek, "The Use of Knowledge in Society," *American Economic Review* 35 (September 1945): 519–30.

4. *See,* for instance, James M. Buchanan and Richard E. Wagner, *Democracy in Deficit: The Political Legacy of Lord Keynes* (New York: Academic Press, 1977).

5. F.A. Hayek, *Denationalisation of Money* (London: Institute of Economic Affairs, 1976), p. 89.

8 Capital Paradoxes and the Concept of Waiting

Leland B. Yeager

This chapter argues for regarding *waiting* as a factor of production whose price is the interest rate. Doing so helps clear up certain paradoxes. It displays parallels between determination of the interest rate and determination of other factor prices, bringing capital and interest theory comfortably into line with general microeconomic theory. It reconciles nicely, I think, with Austrian theory, although the paper does close with just a little preaching at the Austrians.

Reswitching and Capital Reversal

Professor Rizzo asked me to take off from my paper of 1976 on capital paradoxes.[1] Certain critics of orthodox economic theory take particular aim at the notion that the rate of interest (or profit, as they sometimes say) corresponds to the marginal productivity of "capital" in any sense of that word. Abstract examples supposedly discredit that notion.

Paul Samuelson has offered an example which, though simple, exhibits the crucial features. Either of two techniques can produce a definite amount of champagne. Technique *A* requires employing 7 units of labor two periods before the final product is ready, and no further input. Technique *B* requires 2 units of labor three periods before and 6 more units of labor one period before the output emerges. In each technique, while ripening into final product, labor is presumably embodied in incomplete champagne and perhaps in machinery also. (That particular distinction is unessential: inventories and capital goods alike represent intermediate stages in the time–consuming transformation of ultimate factors of production into goods ready for consumption.) In each technique, compound interest accrues, so to speak, on the value of invested labor. Straightforward arithmetic shows that technique *A* is the cheaper at interest rates above 100 percent per period, *B* is cheaper at rates between 50 and 100 percent, and *A* is cheaper again at rates below 50 percent. This is the paradox known as reswitching.

If a decline of the interest rate through one of its two critical levels brings a switch from the less to the more capital–intensive of the two techniques, which seems normal enough, then the switch to the other technique as the interest rate declines through the other switch point is paradoxical. If we view the latter switch in the other direction, an increased interest rate prompts a more intensive use of capital. This perverse response of capital intensity to the interest rate is known as capital reversal.

Examples of perversity or reversal seem not to depend on trickery in measuring the stock of capital. A technique is defined by its ratios of inputs to each other and to output, by the timing of inputs and output, and by everything else that physically characterizes it, including its stock of capital goods and other intermediate goods existing at each of its time stages. These physical specifications stay the same regardless of the interest rate and regardless of whether the technique is actually in use. If technique A has physically more capital per man than B at one switch point, then it still has more at any other interest rate. This remains true by any physical index of capital, even for measurement in tons of steel, provided only that one does not change measurement conventions in mid–example. If the capital/labor ratios of A and B are such that the switch between those techniques at one critical interest rate is nonparadoxical, then the switch at the other must be a paradoxical change of capital intensity in the *same* direction as the interest rate. We cannot, with consistency, deny perversity at both switch points— unless we abandon a purely physical conception of capital.

One can concoct examples in which capital reversal occurs without reswitching. Suppose that some third technique C happens to be cheaper than both A and B in a range in interest rates including the rate at which the nonparadoxical switch between those two would otherwise occur. In the interest–rate range where the paradoxical switch between A and B occurs, however, technique C happens to be economically out of the running. Since C dominates both A and B at what would be their nonparadoxical switch point in C's absence, no actual *re*switching occurs. Yet with C out of the running at the paradoxical switch point between A and B, capital reversal does occur.

This perversity is the really bothersome phenomenon. The chief role of reswitching in the whole discussion is to provide the simplest sort of example in which capital reversal occurs. Reswitching cannot occur with production functions having the neoclassical properties of constant returns to scale, diminishing marginal returns, and smooth, continuous substitutability among factors.[2] Even so, such production functions can exhibit the capital reversal just described.[3]

With emotions ranging from glee to gloom, numerous economists have viewed reswitching and especially capital reversal as an embarrassment for neoclassical capital and interest theory and even for the whole marginalist theory of production and functional income distribution. The thus embarrassed modern orthodoxy sees the prices of factors of production as determined basically by supply and demand, with demand mainly reflecting how use of a bit more or less of a factor would change the total value of output in each line of production or business firm employing that factor. In brief, factors of production tend to be paid in line with their marginal contributions to the value of output. (The theory is concerned with explaining, not justifying, the incomes of factor owners.)

Economists gleeful at the supposed embarrassment of orthodoxy include, notably, some neo-Recardians or neo-Marxians at Cambridge University in England. They seem enamored of paradox for almost purely destructive purposes. The resulting controversy would be terribly important if the capital paradoxes referred to the real world. Actually, and whether or not the controversialists realize it, they refer to problems spawned by inappropriate theoretical concepts; they refer to paper and pencil exercises. Economic theory has become its own subject matter. Something is happening in economics analogous to what passes for scholarship in departments of English. Academic narcissism reigns.

The Root of Paradox

Saying this does not, of course, dispose of the paradoxes. Unfortunately, most would-be defenders of orthodoxy have not pinpointed the source of error. The trouble lies in a purely physical conception of capital, or whatever it is whose yield or price is the rate of interest. The paradoxes dissolve when we recognize that the amount of that factor required in a physically specified production process does indeed depend on its own price.[4]

Reswitching turns out to be closely akin to multiple internal rates of return in an investment option, which Irving Fisher showed long ago to be hardly mysterious at all. As is well known in connection with the criterion of maximizing the present value of a project, or of one's options, a low interest rate tends to favor projects or techniques whose revenues occur relatively remote in time in relation to outlays, while a high interest rate tends to tilt choices toward projects whose revenues occur relatively early in relation to outlays. In examples of reswitching, neither of the two (or more) options considered has revenues that are unequivocally more remote in relation to outlays than the other option has. In Samuelson's example, technique B employs some of its labor earlier and some of it later than A. Which technique employs its labor earlier on the whole? The answer depends on the weights accorded to amounts of labor employed at different times; and this is a matter of time-discounting, that is, of the interest rate.

We can illuminate this ambiguous relation between the two techniques by subtracting A's outlays and revenues from B's to construct a fictitious project. The "champagne" produced at the same time and in the same amount by both techniques subtracts itself out of the picture. The subtractions for the earlier time periods yield a stream, valued in labor units, of -2, $+7$, and -6 in three successive time periods. (The negative and positive signs indicate outlay and revenue, respectively.) We might interpret this series of figures as referring to a strip–mining project. The coal is ready for sale in the middle period, an outlay to repair the damaged landscape being required afterwards. The present value of this mining option at the start and at each interest rate can be calculated by a familiar formula. The option has a positive present value only at interest rates between 50 and 100 percent, has a negative present value at both lower and higher rates, and has *two* internal rates of return (that is, rates at which the present value is zero).

Our project's crucial feature is that its outlays occur neither unequivocally earlier nor unequivocally later than its revenues. A clearcut outlay–before–revenue project has a lower present value the higher the interest rate, for its remote revenues are more exposed to discounting than its early outlays. A clearcut revenue–before–outlay project, conversely, has a higher present value the higher the interest rate; for discounting affects its remote outlays more strongly than its early revenues. Whether, in some overall sense, our strip–mining project is of the outlay–before–revenue or revenue–before–outlay type itself depends on the interest rate. At very high rates the project is of the outlay–before–revenue type; and as with any such project, its present value falls as the interest rate rises. Very high interest rates not only have their normal effect of diminishing the present value of an outlay–before–revenue project but themselves intensify that outlay–before–revenue character. At the other extreme of very low interest rates, the revenue of the coal–mining project falls short of its total outlay quite straightforwardly. Furthermore, the fact that its revenue comes before most of its outlay (discounting being too slight to upset this comparison) means that the project is of the type whose present value suffers from lowness of the interest rate. Its relative timing of outlay and revenue is particularly ambiguous in the intermediate range of interest rates. There, neither discounting at a high interest rate of revenue coming effectively after outlay nor discounting at a low rate of outlay coming effectively after revenue makes the project's present value negative. A single shift between effective outlay–before–revenue and revenue–before–outlay characters occurs in this intermediate range, at 71.429 percent, where present value is a maximum.

Constructed as it is by subtracting *A* figures from *B* figures, the strip–mining example serves to compare techniques *A* and *B* with regard to their *relative* outlay–and–revenue–timing characters. The comparison shows that technique *B* possesses a lower degree of time–remoteness of revenue relative to outlay than *A* at interest rates below 71.429 percent and that the reverse is true above this figure. Since the effect of the interest rate on the relative present values of the two techniques depends on their relative remotenesses in the sense just indicated, and since these relative remotenesses do change with the interest rate itself, the reswitching that occurs with regard to which technique has the greater present value is hardly surprising.

The capital-intensities or roundaboutnesses[5] of alternative techniques or options cannot, then, always be compared in purely physical terms.[6] We have to recognize waiting as a factor of production—the tying-up of value over time. In a physically specified production process, a reduced interest rate not only cheapens the waiting that must be done but also reduces its required value-amount. It reduces the interest element in the notional prices of semifinished and capital goods for whose ripening into final consumer goods and services still more waiting must be done. Increased thrift is productive not only because it supplies more of the waiting required for the use of capital and intermediate goods but also because, by lowering the interest rate, it reduces the amount of waiting required by any physically specified technique. The amounts of waiting required by alternative physically specified techniques will in general decline in different degrees, which gives rise to the possibility of reswitching.

This same line of reasoning also clears up the puzzle of supposed capital reversal even in the absence of reswitching. When a decline in the interest rate brings an apparently perverse switch to a technique which is less capital-intensive by some physical criterion, the explanation is that the decline in the interest rate, although reducing the waiting-intensities of both techniques, reduces them differentially in such a way as to bring a larger reduction in the overall cost of producing by the adopted technique.

When increased thrift lowers the interest rate, the associated decline in the waiting requirements of a physically specified process is not so merely arithmetical as it might seem. Production of various goods by various techniques may ultimately expand not only because of the increased total supply of waiting but also because of a genuine economy in the waiting required per unit of output. A decline in thrift and rise in the interest rate, conversely, intensifies the status of waiting as a scarce factor to be economized on. It becomes scarcer not only because of its reduced supply but also because of increased requirements per unit of output produced in any physically specified way. The double-barreled advantages of thrift appear in reverse.

Preconceived insistence on measuring all factor quantities and factor-intensities in purely physical terms clashes with the fact of reality—or arithmetic—that the amount of waiting required in accomplishing a physically specified purpose does depend on its own price. Not only the waiting-intensity of a physically specified process but also the relative waiting-intensities of alternative processes really are affected by the interest rate. The seeming paradoxicality of reswitching and capital reversal depends on overlooking this truth. When a switch of technique occurs, the technique adopted really is the more economical on the whole, the inputs, waiting included, being valued at their prices. When one technique displaces another upon a rise in the interest rate, the displaced one has become relatively too waiting-intensive to remain economically viable. It is irrelevant as a criticism of economic theory, that *by some other criterion* the displaced technique counts as less capital-intensive.

It is particularly useful in clearing up supposed mysteries to recognize waiting for value over time as a scarce factor of production whose rationing by the interest rate is quite in accord with the logic of a price system. Waiting cannot be measured in purely physical terms, and the amount of it required in a physically specified production process does depend partly on its own price. If these truths run counter to familiar prejudices about capital theory, so much the worse for those prejudices.

The Consumption Paradox

One paradox not cleared up to my full satisfaction concerns consumption. With the interest rate above 100 percent and technique A in use in Samuelson's example, a given output is obtained with 7 units of labor. Now a decline in the interest rate below 100 percent cheapens production by both techniques but cheapens it more by B, which is adopted. The same output now requires 8 units of labor (2 plus 6); output per man falls. An increase in thrift, if that is what has reduced the interest rate, has apparently proved counterproductive. If the example is interpreted as describing the entire economy rather than only one line of production, furthermore, one wonders how the technique yielding less output per man could ever be preferable, regardless of the interest rate. It seems inadequate to reply that labor is not the only factor of production and that the higher output per man in technique A does not, at all interest rates, mean higher output in relation to labor and waiting together. It is people, not abstractions, whose welfare interests us; and more output does, after all, make more consumption possible. Since this consumption paradox is a direct arithmetical implication of paradoxes already cleared up, and in particular of capital reversal or perversity, one might contend that no paradox remains. Yet this remark is not wholly satisfying.

The lower output per man of technique B than of technique A must have some physical interpretation: it must trace to labor's having a smaller aggregate physical amount of intermediate goods, including capital goods, to work with.[7] The shift from technique A to technique B as the interest rate falls below 100 percent involves a transitional rundown in this stock of goods and a corresponding spurt in consumption. This spurt in current consumption at the cost of a cut in future consumption hardly suggests an increase in thrift after all. If increased thrift is not the cause of the decline in the interest rate that prompts the switch of techniques, the example casts no discredit on traditional ideas about the productivity of thrift. What, then, did cause the interest rate to drop? Perhaps the supply and demand curves of waiting had been intersecting at an unstable equilibrium, so that

decreased thrift, represented by a leftward shift of the supply curve of waiting, makes the new and also unstable intersection occur at a lower rate. We
may well ask, of course, whether interest rates in the real world would ever
settle at *unstable* equilibria.

Actually, the literature on capital paradoxes is silent or vague on the
question of what determines the interest rate and changes in it. Strictly
speaking, the literature deals with comparison of alternative steady states
("on separate planets") rather than with processes of change. How these
steady states come to be goes unexplained. References to changes in the
interest rate and switches of techniques serve stylistic convenience only.

A further question concerns whether it is legitimate to aggregate, as just
plain labor, labor performed at different time stages of the production process, even though at the same calendar time in the steady state. As mentioned in footnote 3, labor performed three periods before and labor performed one period before emergence of final product in technique *B* are in a
sense different factors of production. Can we simply add their amounts
together and compare their total to the single amount of labor performed
two periods before emergence of output in technique *A*? Doing so, not distinguishing between the time stages when labor is performed, ignores the
role of time in production; and that is at the root of the paradoxes being
examined.

A related question starts from recognition that a steady state with technique *A* in use is preferable to a steady state with technique *B* because of the
greater output per man. How, however, could an economy in state *B* make
the transition to state *A*? Doing so would require accumulating the larger
physical stock of capital and intermediate goods characteristic of state *A;* it
would require a transition period of exceptional frugality in consumption.
Do the long-run gains adequately reward the transitional sacrifice? The
answer is not obvious; it depends on time preference.

People who insist on crying paradox over examples of the kind we have
reviewed have an obligation, it seems to me, to spell out what they suppose
to be happening in enough detail to disclose crucial assumptions and to permit comparison of their story with the real world. Standard theory need not
be embarrassed by stories that do not even say how the interest rate is determined and changed, why one economy might be in a steady state employing
one technique and an otherwise similar economy in a steady state employing
another, or how an economy might make a transition between such states.

Advantages of the Recommended View

As I hope to have shown, interpreting capital abstractly, as waiting, helps to
clear up bothersome paradoxes. That view of waiting as a factor of production has further advantages. It gives intelligible meaning to such familiar

phrases as "interest on capital," "the cost of capital," "the capital market," "shortage of capital," and "international capital movements." It facilitates bypassing certain distracting questions and the supposed necessity of making certain distinctions, as between types of goods that do and do not count as physical capital. It aids in demolishing certain fallacies, such as that technical progress or economic growth is necessary for a positive rate of interest. It permits a straightforward treatment of the odd but conceivable case of a negative rate of interest. It brings the interest rate within the purview of ordinary theories of supply and demand and of functional income distribution. It shows how the principle of derived demand figures in the determination of the interest rate, as of other factor prices; and it even figures in explaining how international trade in goods can tend to equalize interest rates internationally, like other factor prices. It helps show what sort of opportunity cost the interest rate measures. More generally, the concept exploits parallelisms between waiting and other factors of production, and it provides deeper understanding of the logic of a price system by applying that logic to a particularly challenging phenomenon.

A.R.J. Turgot noted over two centuries ago that the interest rate is "the price given for the use of a certain quantity of value during a certain time." He put this use on a par with other factors of production.[8] This use of value over time enables a borrower to devote wealth or productive resources to his own purposes sooner or on a larger scale than he would without the loan. The lender receives interest for postponing the use for his own purposes of wealth or productive resources over which he could have exercised current command. Borrowing and lending money, however, is by no means the only way in which the use of value over time is transferred and is priced.

In some respects "waiting" is an unfortunate label for the factor whose price is the interest rate. It does not describe the service bought and sold equally well from both points of view. The seller (lender) is indeed waiting; he is postponing the exercise of command over resources that he could have currently devoted to consumption or other purposes of his own. The buyer of the service (the borrower), however, is not acquiring waiting but *avoiding* it; he is paying someone else to do waiting for him. He is buying advanced availability of resources—early command over them.[9] In short, the lender is postponing and the borrower is advancing or anticipating command over resources.

Another disadvantage of the term "waiting," especially when identified with Nassau Senior's "abstinence," is that it conveys to many people the idea of irksomeness or sacrifice, so inviting misunderstandings and quibbles.[10] Actually, waiting may be the opposite of a sacrifice for some people and in some circumstances; and even when irksome at the margin, it may not be so on the whole.

It would indeed be useful to have a neutral or appraisal–free term designating equally well what the lender is supplying and the borrower is demanding. We might avoid the unwanted connotations of a familiar word used as a technical term by imitating the natural sciences and coining a term from Greek roots, perhaps coming up with *chronaxia* or *anamoni* for value-over-time or waiting. I am afraid, though, that the Greek solution would not catch on.

If we cannot find or devise a suitable term, we may as well *force* the neutral and symmetrical meaning we want onto "waiting." A number of precedents recommend this solution after all.

The factor waiting, so interpreted, can be supplied or performed and demanded or avoided in many ways besides granting and obtaining loans of money. Competition, substitution, and arbitrage tend to make waiting performed by lending money, performed by holding an investment in capital goods or in land, and performed in other ways all bear the same price or net rate of return—with obvious qualifications about risk, liquidity, and the like. Consider business firms deciding whether to buy automobiles or rent them. The higher the interest rate in relation to the rental charge, the less will firms borrow money to buy cars and the more will they rent them. Their doing so will tend to reduce money interest rates and increase rates of return in the car-rental business. Conversely, the lower the interest rate in relation to rental charges, the greater the borrowing to buy cars and the less the volume of renting, again tending to bring the interest rate of loans and rental charges in relation to the values of cars into an equilibrium relation.

Whether capital interpreted as waiting is "really" a distinct factor of production, on a par with labor and land-use, is not a genuine issue. The issue, if any exists, is not one of fact but of convenience in presenting and organizing facts and deriving implications from them.[11] In some contexts, admittedly, it is convenient to regard machines, buildings, and other capital goods, or their services, as factors of production and not to probe more deeply or theorize more abstractly. In other contexts, particularly those concerned with the interest rate, the service for which it is a payment, and its functions and logic, it is convenient to regard that rate as the price of a factor and to probe into the nature of that factor. Treating waiting as a factor makes a number of facts fall into convenient patterns. It exploits analogies, displays several apparently distinct principles as instances of more general principles, and provides a convenient framework for contemplating the consequences of changes in wants, resources, and technology.

Why it is idle to argue over what is or is not really a factor is related to why it is idle to argue over the "real" nature of a production function. What to count as inputs into a production function is a matter of convenience in each particular context. In investigating an individual factory making a particular product, we would probably find it most convenient to count purchased parts and materials among the inputs; in investigating the whole industry making that product, we would probably find it more enlightening to count as inputs not the parts and materials traded between firms but rather the labor and other more ultimate factors embodied in those parts and materials. Particularly when we are concerned with the role of prices in coordination of the economic system as a whole, it is convenient to resolve parts and materials and capital goods into the waiting (as well as labor and land-use) necessary for their existence. Admittedly we cannot draw the isoquants of a production function with waiting counted as an input because such diagrams presuppose measurement in purely physical units; but this limit to how far the analogy with other factors can be pushed is no problem for economic actors in the real world, and economists can describe the productivity of waiting in other ways.

We need not claim *exclusive* validity for the view that waiting is a factor and that interest is its price. Others, including the Austrian view, can also be valid. We have here an example of Niels Bohr's Principle of Complementarity.[12] In some branches of theory it is useful to have different but reconcilable conceptual frameworks available (or even to work with different frameworks that we do not yet know how to reconcile). In some contexts it is legitimate to focus on the wave nature of light, in others, on its particle nature. In some contexts, it is fruitful to view human beings as exercising free will; in others, it is fruitful to view human behavior as causally determined. In economics, we have both the income-expenditure and quantity-velocity or money-supply-and-demand approaches to analysis of total spending; we have the elasticities, absorption, and monetary approaches to balance-of-payments analysis; we have both stock and flow theories of exchange rates and both interest-parity and expectations theories of the relation between spot and forward exchange rates; and we have the general-equilibrium emphasis and the Austrian market-process emphasis in micro-economic theory. Similarly, the suggested view of waiting and its price does not clash with seeing the interest rate as expressing a price relation between present and future goods or between consumption goods and factors of production. Present goods are future goods coupled with avoidance of waiting for them; future goods bear a lower explicit price than present goods because part of their total price takes the nonpecuniary form of the waiting that must also be performed to obtain them.

Bypassing Unnecessary Distinctions

Now I shall try to show how the concept of waiting fulfills some of the claims made for it earlier. First, it permits bypassing some distracting and often essentially irrelevant questions associated with a physical conception of capital, such as the question of what types of goods—producers' plant and equipment, inventories of consumer goods and other goods in the hands of producers, durable and nondurable goods in the hands of consumers, and improved and unimproved land—should and should not count as capital. Because of such puzzles about classification and for other reasons, the concept of an aggregate of physical capital is inherently fuzzy. Some capital goods are always being worn out and scrapped, and new ones are always being constructed. Whether the aggregate is growing or shrinking or staying unchanged may be hard to say, especially since unforeseen changes in technology and tastes are always occurring and raising or lowering the market values and the genuine usefulness of particular capital goods.[13] Nobody conducts transactions in the aggregate of capital goods, and the prices of the individual capital goods that are bought and sold are quite distinct from the interest rate. Waiting for value over time is something more nearly homogeneous than physical capital. It commands a price of essentially the same nature whether it is devoted to the fresh accumulation or to the mere maintenance of physical capital. In a number of contexts, then, the concept of waiting spares us from trying to distinguish between gross and net production, maintenance and accumulation, and gross and net saving and investment.

A person can be performing waiting and so promoting the maintenance or accumulation of physical capital even by just continuing to own a capital good or other resource instead of selling it and spending the money on current consumption.[14] The interest rate he receives is expressed by the relation between the value of the services of the resource, net of depreciation and the like, and the value of the resource itself. One might object that the resource will continue to exist whether or not its current owner sells it and spends the proceeds on consumption. How, then, does his continuing to own it promote maintenance or accumulation of physical capital? Most obviously, he is not engaging in consumption that he might have engaged in and is thereby not bidding resources away from capital maintenance or accumulation as he might have done. If he were to sell the resource, furthermore, his doing so would tend to depress it and competing resources in price, leading people desiring such resources to acquire them by purchase rather than by fresh construction. Another way of looking at the matter is to realize that sale of the resource and depression of its price would tend to raise its net percentage yield and, through substitution and arbitrage, raise the general rate of interest in the economy, thereby deterring real investment.

The recommended view in no way entails slipping into the sort of mysticism criticized by Hayek.[15] We need not conceive of waiting as a sort of abstract homogeneous quantity or fund enduring through time and embodying itself in a changing assortment of physical capital goods. Persons supply waiting by refraining from current consumption out of their incomes and wealth and instead make loans, own capital goods, and do other quite unmysterious things. So doing, they are contributing, by and large, to the maintenance or accumulation of physical capital.

We should not overemphasize physical capital formation, however, and it is a further merit of the concept of waiting that it helps us avoid this overemphasis. Waiting can be productively employed in largely nonmaterial ways, as in the training of human beings and in research. Like other factors, too, some waiting is devoted directly to consumption: consumer loans are analogous to labor in domestic service and to land maintained for pleasure as gardens or wilderness.

Negative Interest

The concept of waiting enters straightforwardly into an explanation of the conceivable phenomenon of a negative interest rate. (That possibility shows, by the way, that waiting need not imply sacrifice and that time preference need not necessarily be positive.) Consider an isolated community where all goods produced are perishable, where no money and no equity securities exist, where land is either superabundant and free or else not subject to private ownership, and where there is no collectively organized or family-centered social-security system. How could anyone provide for his old age? Retired people could not live by borrowing because they would be in no position to promise repayment. With accumulation of wealth in other forms ruled out, the only way to store up command over goods to be consumed in one's old age is to acquire claims on borrowers. (In the absence of money, loans are expressed in particular commodities or in composite baskets of commodities.) Retired persons can live on repayments to them of loans they previously made only if younger persons do in fact borrow. If people of all generations are to accomplish their purposes, then, the typical person must borrow goods in his early working years, both repay this borrowing and lend goods in his later working years, and receive repayment when retired. In his early working years, he must consume in excess of his current income; and in his later working years, he must consume an amount that falls short of his current income by more than his earlier excess consumption. In retirement he consumes only the repayments of loans he made in his late working years. (For simplicity we are assuming a stable population of uniform age distribution and are abstracting from any differences in people's tastes, including time preferences, at corresponding periods of their lives; people differ only in belonging to different generations. Each person's total production and earnings are the same, furthermore, in both working periods of his life.)

Since the marginal utility of consumption diminishes with its volume in a given period,[16] the typical person would want a more nearly even distribution of consumption over his lifetime than the one just described. He would want to borrow less in his early working years and receive more repayments in retirement, which implies making both smaller repayments and larger loans in his late working years. This, anyway, is what he would desire at a zero rate of interest. With all persons having preferences of this sort, however, desired lending would exceed desired borrowing. Only a negative rate of interest can clear the loan market. The rate has to be negative to persuade people to depart from the otherwise preferred equal distribution of consumption over their adult lifetimes. Only a reward for borrowing would persuade people to consume especially heavily in their early working years. Similarly, people in their late working years are willing to pay young people to take loans from them so that they can live on the repayments in retirement.[17]

All this is easy to say in terms of waiting. Prospects of old age make people want to postpone consumption of part of their current incomes; yet they are able to wait only if younger people accommodate them by doing the opposite, anticipating consumption out of incomes to be earned later. The desired performance of waiting exceeds the volume accommodated at a zero rate of interest. Clearing the market requires that waiting be penalized and accommodating it rewarded.

Considering the odd conditions necessary for a negative interest rate helps us see, by contrast, why the interest rate must almost certainly be positive in the real world. Among its other features, our imaginary economy lacked storable goods, money, and scarce privately ownable land.

Both a negative price of waiting and a negative wage rate are farfetched but conceivable. At a zero wage, the supply of labor to a particular occupation might exceed the demand, perhaps because the job afforded valuable training or experience or was enjoyable for more than enough people with independent incomes. But does a negative equilibrium interest or wage rate imply a negative marginal productivity? The question might seem inapplicable to our imaginary economy, where all loans are consumption loans and waiting has no productivity. (Even here, though, we could speak of negative productivity, since investment in inventories of perishable goods is lost entirely.)[18] As for labor of a particular type, employing more of it could indeed conceivably reduce net revenues—unless employees paid for the privilege of working. If cooking were an immensely attractive kind of work, cooks, while spoiling the broth at the margin, might subsidize restaurants to permit selling meals cheap enough to provide a market–clearing number of jobs in the kitchen. My purpose is not to dwell on these odd cases but only to point out how supply and demand theories of the prices of waiting and of labor apply *even* to them, and in parallel ways.

The Interest Rate and International Movements of Capital and Goods

International capital movements pose another test of alternative conceptualizations of what the interest rate is a payment for. Capital movements are not shipments of capital goods in particular. People in the lending country are giving up and people in the borrowing country are acquiring something more abstract—current command over goods or resources in general. Through the processes of overall balance-of-payments adjustment (for example, through movement of freely floating exchange rates), imbalance on capital account tends to be matched by opposite imbalance on current account. The financial side of the capital movement thus develops its real counterpart in the form of net shipments of goods and services out of the lending country and into the borrowing country. (These net shipments need not take place entirely or even at all between the lending and borrowing countries directly; in general, trade with third countries also adjusts.) While, in general, the borrowing country both increases its imports and reduces its exports, with opposite changes occurring in the trade of the lending country, this is not necessary. In an extreme case, the borrowing country might develop a net inflow of goods and services entirely by reduction of its exports. The real transfer could take place, furthermore, even if not only no capital goods but no tangible goods at all were traded internationally; the borrowing country could experience a rise in imports or fall in exports of services. In all such cases, nevertheless, the lenders are waiting to exercise command over real resources, and the borrowers are obtaining advanced command over them.

The conception of capital as waiting also integrates smoothly with the theory of how, under certain conditions, international trade tends to equalize the prices in different countries of the factors of production "embodied" in the goods traded. Consider new wine and matured wine, produced with relatively little and relatively much waiting. If waiting is relatively scarce and the interest rate relatively high in the home country, matured wine commands a correspondingly large price premium over new wine in the absence of trade. Abroad, where waiting is relatively abundant and cheap, matured wine commands only a relatively small price premium. Now trade opens up. The home country imports high-waiting-content matured wine and exports low-waiting-content new wine (or vodka or other low-waiting-content goods). Trade tends to equalize product prices, reducing the price premium of matured over new wine in the home country and shrinking production of matured wine there. Trade lessens the effective scarcity of waiting and so reduces the interest rate.[19] Waiting formerly devoted to the maturing of wine is freed for other uses.

The interest-equalization tendency does not depend on whether waiting enters "directly" or only "indirectly" into production functions of goods.[20] Perhaps waiting enters "directly" into the production of widgets, which, like wine, require time to mature. Alternatively, widgets are manufactured with machines that embody much waiting. Still another possibility is that widgets are made by specialists who must undergo years of expensive training. What difference does any of this make for the interest-equalization tendency? Widgets are expensive, since their costs include high salaries corresponding to the expensive waiting invested in training technicians.[21] Now international trade brings imports of cheap foreign widgets. The domestic industry shrinks. Waiting formerly devoted to training technicians becomes free for other purposes; and, as in the wine example, the interest rate falls.

Derived Demand and Productivity

A more general argument for the concept of waiting is that it enlists supply and demand analysis. In considering what determines the price of waiting, we can explore, as we do for other factors of production, what accounts for the supply and for the demand. On the demand side we explore why people will pay to avoid waiting and gain advanced availability of command over resources; and on the supply side we explore why, in general and at the margin, waiting will not be performed free. Except for consumption loans, the demand for waiting (-avoidance) is a derived demand. The demand for waiting, as for labor and land-use, derives from the factor's capacity to contribute to output—ultimately, output of consumer goods and services— and from consumers' demand for that output. The relative strengths of consumer demands for goods embodying relatively large amounts of particular factors affect producer demands for those factors and so affect their prices. A decline in consumer demand for a highly waiting-intensive good tends to lower the rate of interest. This point was illustrated in the example of matured wine, whose importation from abroad reduces the demand for its domestically produced counterpart. A shift of consumers' demand away from low-waiting-content vodka toward high-waiting-content wine would tend to raise the interest rate. The principle is the same as the one suggesting that a shift of tastes away from land-use-intensive wheat toward labor-intensive watches would tend to raise wages relative to land rents.

Particularly for an audience of "subjectivist" economists, a few paragraphs may be in order on the productivity of waiting or roundaboutness. Böhm-Bawerk, with his familiar examples of fishing with and without a net, quarrying with and without a crowbar, and bringing water from a spring in buckets or by a log pipeline, makes the point quite well (and he goes on to more sophisticated analysis). Waiting is substitutable for other productive factors at the margin. Consider a house of definite specifications to be delivered to the buyer on a definite date. The sooner (within limits) construction can begin and so the more time it can take, the smaller is the quantity of inputs other than waiting required.[22] The house probably could be built in only five days as a stunt, but imagine the attendant inefficiencies and expense. Morris Adelman notes an example of substitutability in the oil industry: "The productivity of a pool is less than proportional to the number of wells because past a certain point there is well 'interference.' The area over which oil migrates through permeable sands is very wide, so that one well could ultimately drain a very large reservoir. If time—meaning the value of money—were no object, that would indeed be the best because it would be the cheapest way. . . . If time were no object, with zero rate of return or cost of capital, one well would drain a whole reservoir at lowest cost."[23] These examples of substitutability at the margin between waiting and other factors show that waiting can indeed "enter into the production function."

Walter Eucken has offered additional insights into the productivity of roundaboutness. The opportunity to wait for results widens the ranges of economically relevant natural resources and human skills, making a finer division of labor advantageous. Without a stock of consumer goods, Robinson Crusoe must adopt quick-yielding production methods; and many resources are worthless to him. Starting with or somehow borrowing a stock of consumer goods, however, he can take time to make tools and weapons; and otherwise useless wildlife, arable land, offshore fishing banks, trees, and fibers become valuable to him. He may find it worthwhile to develop skills as a butcher, tanner, and shoemaker. In a complex modern economy, skills that are relevant thanks only to time-consuming production methods include those of rolling-mill workers, tool-and-die makers, and scientists and research workers of all kinds.[24]

Although resting on extremely familiar and pervasive facts, the proposition about the greater productivity of roundabout production methods is an empirical generalization and cannot be proved by abstract logic alone.[25] The same is true of propositions about the productivity of labor or fertilizer. Supposed refutations occasionally cite examples of how a more roundabout method could be less productive than a quicker or more direct one; a Rube Goldberg machine is an extreme case. The valid proposition postulates that more time-consuming methods are intelligently adopted. Böhm-Bawerk spoke of "well-chosen roundabout capitalist methods," of "skillfully chosen circuitous methods," and of "a wisely selected extension of the roundabout way of production."[26] Of course a roundabout method arbitrarily imposed on a producer might be less efficient than a more direct method freely chosen, just as the arbitrarily imposed use of additional labor or fertilizer might reduce output. The opportunity to wait for results is productive because it broadens the range of production processes among which intelligent choice can be made.[27]

Businessmen will pay for such productive opportunities. Most obviously, they will pay for loans enabling them to adopt more time-consuming production methods or to install plant and equipment already embodying waiting along with other factors. Businessmen's demands for waiting (-avoidance) derive, then, from the productivity of waiting and from consumers' demands for goods produced with its aid. This view fits in nicely with the Austrian theory of imputation, which traces the values of capital and intermediate goods and factors of production to the subjectively appraised utilities of the final consumer goods and services into whose production they directly or indirectly enter. Counting interest among the factor prices does not challenge the Austrian position but extends it.

To insist on the productivity of waiting is not necessarily anti-Austrian. Böhm-Bawerk emphasized this element in interest-rate determination. Hayek emphasized it throughout his *Pure Theory of Capital* and in one passage (pp. 420-421) even criticized Irving Fisher for according it too small a role in relation to time preference. It is rejected in favor of a pure time-preference theory only by an extreme subjectivist wing of contemporary Austrianism. Even Frank A. Fetter, whose recently reprinted writings are currently in vogue with the subjectivists, does recognize, if in a backhanded way, the influence of objective reality, including "productivity," on the interest rate.[28]

With reference to derived demand, I have been arguing for a broadened view of the subjective factors that can affect the interest rate. This is already at least implicit, I think, in Austrian theory. For one more example, suppose that tastes shift away from poetry readings toward science-fiction movies, presumably a form of entertainment whose production is more roundabout or waiting-intensive. The tastes that influence the interest rate are not confined to direct time preferences between present and future consumption. The pattern of tastes for different goods and services all demanded at the same time also plays a role.

Waiting expresses itself in many ways. Consumers perform it by buying houses and durable goods and then waiting for their services over time. If they become less willing to wait and decide to become renters, paying for the services of houses and other durables only as they consume them, and if they do not manifest an offsetting increase in their willingness to wait through ownership of other assets and claims, then the rate of interest tends to rise.

The Pervasiveness of Interest

As these examples suggest, interest is a pervasive phenomenon. It appears not only in the explicit price of money loans but also in price relations among final goods, intermediate and capital goods of higher and lower "orders," and factors of production.[29] It even lurks in the price relations between consumer goods embodying relatively large and relatively small amounts of waiting. All these relations exemplify general economic interdependence.

One methodological point is worth mention. How changes in wants, resources, or technology affect these price relations should be explainable in terms of the explicit interest rate determined on the loan market and of substitution and arbitrage between loans and other forms in which people supply and demand waiting. This precept warns against forgetting the literal and narrow definition of interest as the price of money loans.

No doubt only small portions of total supplies of and demands for waiting confront each other directly on the money loan market. This fact, together with the tendency for percentage rates of net return on bonds, equities, land, and all sorts of capital goods to become equal—subject to standard qualifications—has tempted many economists to describe the interest rate as fundamentally the ratio of income to capital. Other expressions for broadly the same idea are the relation between the value of services and the value of their sources (in short, the services/assets ratio), the reciprocal of the price of a permanent income stream (for example, the yield on a perpetual bond), and the pure hire value of assets.[30] Such formulations have a praiseworthy motive. They serve to emphasize, by contrast, the hopeless superficiality of interest theories that consider only the loan market, money, and liquidity preference. They emphasize the pervasiveness and fundamentally "real" character of the interest rate and related rates of return.

Unfortunately, an economist does not make people understand these truths by broadening the coverage of the term "interest rate." It is a mistake conceptually to identify the interest rate on loans and other rates of return with the marginal rate of time preference or the marginal rate of transformation of potential present goods into future goods by way of investment. Those various rates do, after all, only tend to become equal. It is a serious error to suggest that magnitudes whose equality at the margin is a condition of equilibrium are conceptually identical. Doing so risks suppressing questions of how markets for various claims, assets, and services intertwine and how changes in thrift and technology affect even the interest rate in the strict sense of the term. It suppresses consideration of how arbitrage operates. Suppressing questions by definition is no adequate substitute for facing and answering them. Furthermore, insistence on terms like "services to sources ratio" or, alternatively, "agio of present goods over future goods" obscures the parallelism between the interest rate as the clearest manifestation of the price of waiting and the prices of other productive factors. It obscures the sometimes convenient distinction between demand price and supply price, which are equal when the market clears but not conceptually identical.

The Function of Interest

The view I have been proposing fits in nicely with the view of the price system as a means of transmitting information and incentives. Like other prices, the interest rate is a signaling and rationing device. In view of its price, each businessman restrains his use of waiting; he restricts the amount of value that he ties up over time in uncompleted processes of transforming primary productive factors into final consumer goods and services. Prices similarly restrain his employment of labor and land. But *why* should he restrain himself if he could use additional waiting, labor, or land *productively*? The answer appeals to the very logic of a price system. Their prices indicate that factors of production are scarce. Employing units of them in any particular line of production has an opportunity cost: it costs the loss of what they could have contributed to output in some other line. The prices of factors and products force each businessman to act as if he were considering not merely whether additional factor units would add *something* to his output but also whether they would add *enough* to the value of his output to warrant the necessary sacrifice of valuable output elsewhere in the economy.[32] Prices enable him, in effect, to compare consumers' evaluations of the additional output he could offer and its cost as measured by consumers' evaluations of other goods necessarily forgone.

When the interest rate restrains a businessman from adopting a still more roundabout or waiting–intensive process, the reason is that his doing so would have blocked a more valuable employment of waiting elsewhere. At least this is true of an economy functioning in accordance with the logic of a price system. The rationing function of the interest rate is on all fours with that of other factor prices. Constructing apartment buildings that will serve with little maintenance for many years is a more waiting–intensive method of providing housing services than constructing buildings with shorter lives or requiring more current maintenance. Even though the more durable buildings require more labor and other inputs in the first place, their services over their entire lives will be greater in relation to inputs of factors with which waiting is substitutable. This does not mean that constructing the more durable buildings is unequivocally advantageous; for the longer average interval between inputs of resources and outputs of services, as well as the fact that the economies in maintenance accrue not all at once but only over time, imply an opportunity cost. That cost pertains to other projects and products ruled out because the scarce capacity to wait has been devoted to the durable apartments. The market brings this cost to the attention of businessmen in the form of interest.

The market brings to the attention of consumers, also, the opportunity costs of the waiting (and other factors) embodied in the goods and services from which they have to choose. It leads them to consult their preferences in the light of the terms of choice posed, in part, by objective reality.

Monetary factors can temporarily distort the interest–rate signal, just as various interventions can distort the signals that other factor prices convey. The terms of choice among goods as well as among factors are then misrepresented. The Austrian theory of the business cycle would enter the discussion here, were reviewing it not peripheral to the particular purpose of this chapter.

An Eclectic Theory

The physical productivity of waiting or roundaboutness is an objective element in interest–rate determination. Objective and subjective factors interact. The rate of time preference, or the subjectively appraised agio of present over future goods, is a marginal concept;[33] and where the margin occurs depends largely on how extensively people have made provision for present and future consumption. This in turn depends partly on the transformability through investment of present goods into future goods.

Austrian theory as I understand it, and its extreme subjectivist strand in particular, explains the relative prices of goods by their relative marginal utilities. A television set is worth a great many pins because its marginal utility is so much higher than that of a pin. But why, for consumers of both goods, are their marginal utilities so different? Pins are much more abundant in relation to desires for them than television sets are; people can essentially satiate their desires for pins but not for televisions. This difference in relative abundances has much to do with objective reality: a pin can be produced at much smaller sacrifice of other things than the opportunity cost of a TV. There is no *one*-directional determination of relative prices from relative marginal utilities. Nor is there any one–directional determination of the interest rate from the marginal rate of time preference. The relative marginal utilities of different goods and the marginal rate of time preference are determined by subjective elements in interaction with objective elements, notably opportunity costs and intertemporal transformability.

The view that stresses this point could be called "eclectic," but so what? Applied to price theory, "eclectic" is not properly a term of reproach. No single causal factor explains any price; the principle of general economic interdependence, as well as everyday observation of specific cases, tells us this. Any monistic theory to the contrary is simply wrong. Every price is determined by many circumstances classifiable under the headings of "wants" and "resources and technology" (or, almost equivalently, "subjective factors" and "objective factors") or, alternatively and not equivalently, "supply" and "demand."[34] The supply and demand theory of interest as the price of waiting is eclectic, but no more so than the theory of the price of any other productive factor or of any good.

The productivity and time–preference concepts of interest theory have analogues in the productivity and disutility concepts of wage theory. In equilibrium, under appropriate simplifying assumptions, the marginal value productivity of labor = the wage rate = the monetary measure of the marginal disutility or the subjectively appraised opportunity cost of labor. Neither the marginal productivity nor the marginal disutility of labor determines the wage rate. All three equilibrium magnitudes emerge from a system of general interdependence in which the *schedules* of marginal productivity and marginal disutility (or subjective opportunity cost) largely (though not exclusively) account for the schedules of demand for and supply of labor. A similar tendency operates in the market for waiting: the marginal productivity of waiting (that is, the marginal rate of return in transforming forgone present goods into future goods) = the interest rate = the marginal rate of time preference.[35] Neither the productivity element nor the time–preference element determines the interest rate. All three equilibrium magnitudes emerge from a system of general interdependence in which schedules of marginal returns and marginal time preference largely account for the demand for and supply of waiting.

One final parallel between the interest rate and other factor prices deserves mention. To speak of "the" interest rate is a simplification; many rates exist. Waiting is not actually homogeneous; waiting from 1979 to 1980 is not the same as waiting from 1978 to 1979. Different assets and securities bear different yields because of differences in risk, liquidity, and so forth. Quite similarly, labor is not homogeneous, and "compensating differences" exist between the wage rates on jobs requiring similarly qualified labor. It is a mere matter of convenience in each individual context whether we treat land, labor, and waiting as three factors only or regard the different varieties of each of these as many separate factors.

A Concluding Sermon

To view waiting as a factor of production helps dissolve nihilistic paradoxes. It exploits parallels and contributes to uniformity in price theory.

(After all, it is generally counted as progress in a scientific field to show links and parallels between formerly separate explanations of superficially distinct phenomena.) Still, I am not insisting that we view the interest rate as a factor price to the exclusion of other conceptualizations of capital and interest; for these can be complementary.

I cannot believe that the Austrians have a *pure* time-preference theory of interest (despite, for example, the praise that extreme subjectivists accord to Frank A. Fetter and Ludwig von Mises for supposedly having worked such a theory out). I ask them to imagine the invention of a machine, very cheap to produce, which has the following property: Whatever objects one sticks into the machine, 50 percent more objects of the same type emerge one year later. Can anyone doubt that this invention would tend to raise the rate of interest, and with it the marginal rate of time preference, from the levels of well below 50 percent that had been prevailing? Or, to phrase the same question in a more general and less fantastic way, can anyone doubt that if the state of technology and other aspects of objective reality were much different from what they now are in fact, then the interest rate and the marginal rate of time preference would also be different from what they now are?

Subjectivist Austrians may contend that objective, physical reality can influence the interest rate and other prices only *through* people's subjective perceptions of it and the valuations they make in accord with it. I will not quarrel with that contention. It does not banish the influence of objective reality. Businessmen (and consumers) who perceive reality correctly will thrive better on the market than those who misperceive it. A kind of natural selection sees to it that physical reality does get duly taken into account. This notion of selection of entrepreneurs by the market process surely accords well with Austrian theory.

The subjectivist Austrians cannot really mean what their slogan about a pure time-preference theory, taken literally, conveys. I suggest they drop that slogan, as well as the one about a purely subjective theory of value. Such slogans mislead people outside the inner circle; they impair communication. The goal of the Austrians is presumably not to recite slogans that reinforce comfortable feelings of camaraderie among members of an in-group. Instead, their goal, shared with other libertarian economists, is presumably to gain and communicate understanding of economic (and political) processes in the real world as it is, has been, and potentially could be. They want to extend and communicate that knowledge so as to increase whatever chance there may be that man's deepest values will ultimately prevail. Respect for the straightforward meanings of words will aid in that endeavor.

Notes

1. Leland B. Yeager, "Toward Understanding Some Paradoxes in Capital Theory," *Economic Inquiry* 14 (September 1976): 313–346. Here I forgo repeating many of the citations, technicalities, and bits of arithmetic to be found there.

So far as I am aware, my thinking on capital and interest traces mainly to Eugen von Böhm-Bawerk, *Capital and Interest,* trans. George D. Huncke and Hans F. Sennholz, 3 vols. (South Holland, Ill.: Libertarian Press, 1959); Irving Fisher, *The Theory of Interest* (1930; reprint ed., New York: Augustus M. Kelley, 1955); Walter Eucken, *Kapitaltheoretische Untersuchungen,* 2nd ed. (Tübingen: Mohr, Zürich: Polygraphischer Verlag, 1954); Maurice Allais, *Économie et Intérêt,* 2 vols. (Paris: Imprimerie Nationale, 1947); and Gustav Cassel, *The Nature and Necessity of Interest* (1903; reprint ed., New York: Augustus M. Kelley, 1956).

2. Edwin Burmeister and Rodney A. Dobell, *Mathematical Theories of Economic Growth* (New York: Macmillan, 1970), p. 279, theorem 5. For a nonmathematical sketch of the proof, see Leland B. Yeager and Edwin Burmeister, "Reply," *Economic Inquiry* 16, no. 1 (January 1978).

3. Tatsuo Hatta, "The Paradox in Capital Theory and Complementarity of Inputs," *Review of Economic Studies* 43 (1), no. 133 (February 1976): 127–142. Hatta regards the two techniques of Samuelson's example as together constituting a production function (not a neoclassical function, of course). He regards units of labor employed at different time stages of production as distinct factors. The labor units employed three periods and one period before output emerges in technique *B* are complementary factors, since the production function requires employing both those time-stage types of labor if either is employed. Hatta traces capital reversal to such complementarity, which can appear in sufficient degree even in neoclassical production functions.

4. Writing before appearance of the literature on capital paradoxes, Friedrich A. Hayek noted that it is not always possible to say, on purely technical grounds, which of two different investment structures involves more waiting or is longer in time. (He did not, however, endorse the conception of waiting as a productive factor.) Once one knows what one is looking for, one can find passages in Hayek's book that suggest the key to dissolving the paradoxes. See *The Pure Theory of Capital* (Chicago: University of Chicago Press, 1941), especially pp. 76–77, 140–145, 191–192. I am indebted to Roger Garrison for this reference.

5. I do not imply that "capital-intensity" or "waiting-intensity", on the one hand, and "roundaboutness," on the other hand, are fully synony-

mous terms. Waiting, as I shall argue below, has the two dimensions of time and value units, whereas roundaboutness, conceived of as some sort of average period of production or investment, has the single dimension of time units. This chapter uses the term "roundaboutness" loosely and heuristically.

6. Measurement of an average production or investment period in time units appears, superficially, to be a purely physical measurement. Yet with waiting and compound interest given due recognition, the calculated length of such an average period itself depends on the interest rate.

7. An index–number problem concerning the aggregation of heterogeneous capital and intermediate goods is not crucial here. What could explain the lower output other than that labor has a smaller real amount, in a meaningful sense, of these produced inputs to work with?

The response of the price–weighted average of changes in equilibrium per capita stocks of capital and intermediate goods to a change in the interest rate—briefly, the response of real capital per man—is known as the "real Wicksell effect." It is said to be "normal" if negative—if real capital per man changes in the opposite direction from the interest rate—; a positive effect is perverse. The consumption paradox depends on a perverse real Wicksell effect and is precluded by a normal one. The appeal to intuition that I have been making suggests this relation; for proof, see Edwin Burmeister, "Real Wicksell Effects and Regular Economies," in *Essays in Modern Capital Theory,* ed. Murray Brown, Kazuo Sato, and Paul Zarembka (Amsterdam: North–Holland Publishing Company, 1976), pp. 145–164.

Actually, a positive and apparently abnormal real Wicksell effect need not be truly perverse after all, as one realizes on abandoning a purely physical conception of what it is that is rationed by the interest rate.

8. *Sur la formation et la distribution des richesses* (1766), §78, quoted in Cassel, *The Nature and Necessity of Interest,* pp. 20–21. Turgot's formulation, says Cassel, has "never afterwards [been] surpassed in clearness and definiteness."

9. Compare Armen A. Alchian and William R. Allen, *University Economics,* 2nd ed. (Belmont, Calif.: Wadsworth, 1967), p. 203: "the rate of interest is the price of earlier rather than later *availability* . . . . Rigorously speaking, interest is the price of earlier availability of rights to use goods rather than later availability."

10. For examples of these and of sheer clowning around with questions about what it is that the supposed waiters are waiting for, see Böhm-Bawerk, *Capital and Interest,* especially I, 379, 388ff., and some of the attached footnotes. Böhm-Bawerk attributes the term to S.M. MacVane and treats it as essentially a synonym of "abstinence."

11. Nevertheless, numerous economists have taken a position on it. Gustav Cassel regarded it as settled, "once and for all, that interest is the

price paid for an *independent and elementary factor of production* which may be called either waiting or use of capital, according to the point of view from which it is looked at. . . . It is . . . an independent or primary factor in this sense, that it cannot be reduced to more elementary factors." *Nature and Necessity of Interest,* pp. 67, 89. More recently, Robert Dorfman "reaffirmed the reality of waiting as one of the primary factors of production, co-ordinate with labor, land, etc. . . . waiting is a genuine scarce factor of production. . . . The unit of waiting [may be taken as] one unit of consumption deferred for one unit of time." "Waiting and the Period of Production," *Quarterly Journal of Economics* 73 (August 1959): 367, 370. Compare Mark Blaug, *Economic Theory in Retrospect* (Homewood, Ill.: Irwin, 1962), pp. 471–475.

For examples of denial that waiting is a distinct productive factor, see Friedrich A. Hayek, "The Mythology of Capital," *Quarterly Journal of Economics* (February 1936), reprinted in American Economic Association, *Readings in the Theory of Income Distribution* (Philadelphia: Blakiston, 1946), pp. 355–383, esp. p. 377; *The Pure Theory of Capital,* e.g., pp. 5, 93–94, 266–267, and *passim,* where Hayek again criticizes "mystical" notions of free capital or a capital fund but softens his criticisms of the concept of waiting; Böhm-Bawerk, *Capital and Interest,* I, chapters 8 and 9, II, 97ff., 117, 341, III, 194ff.; Fisher, *The Theory of Interest,* pp. 485–487, 534–541; and Joseph Conard, *An Introduction to the Theory of Interest* (Berkeley and Los Angeles: University of California Press, 1959), p. 32.

12. Bohr himself noted that the principle applies outside the area of physics in which he introduced it. See Otto H. Theimer, *A Gentleman's Guide to Modern Physics* (Belmont, Cal.: Wadsworth, 1973), pp. 143, 245–246, 248, 274.

13. Hayek urges points like these in *The Pure Theory of Capital,* pp. 296–297, 335–336, and *passim.* The fuzziness of the concept of aggregate physical capital is not a problem, of course, for economic actors in the real world but only a problem for theorists and econometricians trying to work with aggregate production functions.

14. The resource in question could be land, and the present paragraph affords some insight into the nature of the service that the landowner is performing. It would be off my subject to discuss the special problems regarding land (as well as holdings of money) that Maurice Allais asserts in widely scattered sections of his *Économie et Intérêt.*

15. Recall the references in footnote 11.

16. To avoid the implication of measurable and diminishing marginal utility, this and related propositions could be restated in terms of marginal rates of substitution between entitlements to consumption at different dates.

17. These paragraphs draw on a discussion among Paul A. Samuelson, Abba P. Lerner, W.H. Meckling, and David Cass and Menahem E. Yaari

in *Journal of Political Economy* 66 (December 1958): 467–482; 67 (October 1959): 512–525; 68 (February 1960): 72–84; and 74 (August 1966): 353–367.

Earlier, Maurice Allais had published an essentially similar description of an economy with a negative interest rate, *Économie et Intérêt*, I, 48ff.

18. Fisher's parable of the rotting figs illustrates a lesser degree of negative productivity. *The Theory of Interest*, pp. 191–192.

19. Paul Samuelson reaches a similar conclusion, though without using the concept of waiting and so by a less straightforward route, in "Equalization by Trade of the Interest Rate along with the Real Wage," in Robert E. Baldwin et al., *Money, Growth, and the Balance of Payments* (Chicago: Rand McNally, 1965), pp. 35–52.

20. Recall the argument of a few pages earlier that how to conceive of a production function is a matter not of right or wrong but simply of convenience in each particular piece of analysis. For a contrary view, emphasizing the supposed direct/indirect distinction, see Peter B. Kenen, "Nature, Capital, and Trade," *Journal of Political Economy* 73 (October 1965): 437–460.

21. This remark does not betray any cost theory of value. High costs restrain supply, with the result that widgets have correspondingly high marginal utility.

22. Cf. Armen Alchian, "Costs and Outputs," in Moses Abramovitz et al., *The Allocation of Economic Resources* (Stanford: Stanford University Press, 1959), especially pp. 31–35, 39.

23. Morris Adelman, *The World Petroleum Market* (Baltimore: Johns Hopkins University Press, 1972), pp. 19, 63.

24. Eucken, *Kapitaltheoretische Untersuchungen*, pp. 75–76, 89–90.

25. Eucken, *Kapitaltheoretische Untersuchungen*, p. 214; Böhm-Bawerk, *Capital and Interest*, II, 12.

26. Böhm-Bawerk, *Capital and Interest*, II, 82–84; cf. III, 45–56.

27. In general, knowledge always exists of roundabout productive processes being used less extensively than they would be if the supply of waiting were greater and the interest rate lower than they are in fact. The productivity of roundaboutness that enters into interest–rate determination does not hinge on continuing growth of technological knowledge, despite the contrary assertions of, for example, Donald Dewey in *Modern Capital Theory* (New York: Columbia University Press, 1965), pp. 8–9, 43–45, 47–48, 50.

28. Frank A. Fetter, *Capital, Interest, and Rent* (Kansas City: Sheed Andrews and McMeel, 1977), pp. 242, 247, 312. To forestall misunderstanding, I want to agree that Fetter's analyses are on the whole excellent.

29. This, of course, is an old theme of the Austrians. The real rate of interest, Hayek writes, "is not a price paid for any particular thing, but a rate of differences between prices which pervades the whole price structure." Hayek, *The Pure Theory of Capital*, p. 353. I would disagree only in

maintaining that it is indeed useful to regard the interest rate as the price of a "particular thing." The wage rate also, if not in just the same way, "pervades the whole price structure."

30. Leon Walras, *Elements of Pure Economics,* trans. William Jaffé, (Homewood Ill.: Irwin, 1954), esp. pp. 274–276; Fisher, *The Theory of Interest,* esp. pp. 32, 332; Milton Friedman, *Price Theory* (Chicago: Aldine, 1976), chapter 17; W.H. Hutt, *Keynesianism—Retrospect and Prospect* (Chicago: Regnery, 1963, p. 211); and discussions with and unpublished memoranda by Professor Hutt.

31. "Within a single economy . . . there may at one and the same moment be a hundred different agios on present goods and hence a hundred different rates of interest. But those hundreds and thousands of partial markets are not hermetically sealed off from each other. There is intercommunication among them through lively and incessant arbitrage." Böhm-Bawerk, *Capital and Interest*, II, 379. Böhm-Bawerk goes on to elaborate.

32. It is perhaps an additional recommendation of the concept of waiting that without it Irving Fisher blundered, astonishingly, into denying that interest measures any genuine cost. *The Theory of Interest,* pp. 485–487, 534–541.

33. Even most Austrians seem to recognize this point. See, for example, Böhm-Bawerk, *Capital and Interest*, I, 393–397, II, 287–288; Hayek, *The Pure Theory of Capital*, pp. 413ff.; Murray N. Rothbard, *Man, Economy, and State*, 2 vols. (Princeton: Van Nostrand, 1962), I, 323ff., 329–330; Murray N. Rothbard, "Introduction" to Frank A. Fetter, *Capital, Interest, and Rent,* esp. p. 4; and Frank S. Arnold, "Issues in Interest" (unpublished paper, Menlo Park: Institute for Humane Studies, Summer 1977), pp. 2ff. Arnold explicitly rejects the contrary view of time preference urged by Ludwig von Mises.

34. One might be tempted to identify subjective factors with demand and objective factors with supply on the markets for goods and to make the reverse identification on the markets for productive factors, including waiting; but these identifications would be wrong. The supply schedule for a particular good largely reflects the schedule of costs of production; these costs reflect not only technology but also factor prices; and factor prices are influenced by consumers' demands—tastes—for all goods in whose production the factors are employed. Similar considerations tell against putting all objective factors on the demand side and all subjective factors on the supply side of the market for waiting.

On the interplay of objective and subjective factors and the absurdity of a purely objective or a purely subjective theory of value, see Gustav Cassel, *The Theory of Social Economy,* trans. S.L. Barron, new revised edition (1932; reprint ed., New York: Augustus M. Kelley, 1967), chapter IV, esp. pp. 146–148, 155–164.

It is not objectionable and can be convenient to have two or more ways available for classifying the influences that work themselves out on the market.

35. This statement requires some qualification when we recognize that waiting cannot, after all, be rationed by the interest rate alone. This is a fact of reality and not a market "imperfection." It is most obvious with regard to loans. Because of uncertainty about whether borrowers will repay, lenders must practice nonprice rationing to some extent and cannot grant loans in whatever amounts requested to all borrowers promising to pay the going rate of interest. Tibor Scitovsky insist on the implications of this fact in *Welfare and Competition,* rev. ed. (Homewood, Ill.: Irwin, 1971), pp. 205–208.

Comment: Waiting in Vienna

Roger Garrison

Introduction

Professor Yeager is eager for his fellow economists to adopt the term *waiting* as the name of the thing whose price is the rate of interest. He claims advantages of two kinds. By using the concept of waiting, certain paradoxes in capital theory can be dissolved, and certain parallels between the determination of the interest rate and the determination of other factor prices can be exploited. His chapter, taken as a whole, is a demonstration of another more general advantage of the concept. Thinking in terms of the supply and demand for waiting, Yeager was able to digest and interpret many technical and mathematical formulations of capital theory without allowing himself to get embroiled in the mathematics. In each case he is able either to provide an intuitive feel for the economic processes involved, that is, for what people are supposed to be doing, or to show that no intuitive interpretation is possible. We aren't quite sure how much of this intuition to impute to *waiting* as a tool of analysis and how much to impute to the economist using this tool. But the two, taken together, yield results that the Austrian economists cannot afford to ignore.

Capter 8 is divided into twelve sections, each of which contains analyses and insights that would merit some comment. I have chosen, however, to limit my comments to three broad areas. I will attempt first to provide an Austrain perspective on the concept of waiting and to deal with the disadvantages of the term that Yeager himself itemizes. Second, I will deal with the eclectic view of interest rate determination and with Yeager's criticism of the subjectivist position. My remarks about technique reswitching and capital reversing will be saved for last.

An Austrian Perspective on the Concept of Waiting

If Austrian theorists are hesitant to embrace the concept of waiting or abstinence, their hesitancy can be attributed, in large part, to the debates between Clark and Böhm–Bawerk at the turn of the century and between Knight and Hayek during the 1930s. In these debates both Clark and Knight insisted that waiting, or something very much like it, is a simple magnitude or homogeneous fund of clearly determined size and that it has an existence quite independent of individual capital goods in which it is temporarily embodied.[1] Most objections to the concept of waiting found in the Austrian literature are well-founded objections to this Clark-Knight vision.[2] Professor Yeager is clearly on the Austrian side of these debates. He carefully differentiates his view of capital from the Clark-Knight view, and he rejects all mystical notions of capital with the statement that: "Persons supply waiting by refraining from current consumption out of their incomes and wealth and instead making loans, owning capital goods, and doing other quite unmysterious things."[3] This statement reflects the vision of Gustav Cassel rather than those of Clark and Knight. We might note, however, that Böhm-Bawerk in his third volume of *Capital and Interest* found no less mystery in Cassel's formulation. He rejects Cassel's concept of "waiting" primarily on the grounds that it has no independent existence.[4] It cannot exist, that is, apart from individual capital goods. But that this is true is made clear in Cassel's own *Nature and Necessity of Interest*,[5] and it is now reaffirmed by Yeager. The recognition of dependence in this sense does not require that the concept of waiting be rejected. Labor, after all, does not exist apart from the individual performing it. This does not preclude our viewing labor as a factor of production and wages as the price of labor.

Although Clark and Knight were responsible for turning the concept of waiting or abstinence into a red flag in the Austrians' view, the Austrian resistance to these notions predates the writings of Clark and Knight. Böhm-Bawerk in his *History and Critique of Interest Theories*[6] and Menger in his *Principles of Economics*[7] were critical of the abstinence theory of interest. The contexts of their critical remarks, however, suggest that it is not the notion of waiting or abstinence per se that is being called into question. Rather, the primary message we get from both Menger and Böhm-Bawerk is that these concepts cannot serve to shore up the cost-of-production theory of value. The message is well taken but it leaves most all of Professor Yeager's formulation intact.

Professor Yeager does not insist that the concept of waiting as a factor of production be adopted at the expense of all other alternative concepts.[8] In fact, he demonstrates that this view is fully compatible with the Austrian view of interest as the price differential between present goods and future goods.[9] He then goes on to single out a number of analytical contexts in which it is useful to think in terms of the supply and demand for waiting. Where the concept does fit, we are shown, it fits very well.

We ought to be able to make some generalization about when the concept of waiting is and is not appropriate. I am tempted to say that it is appropriate for the theory of interest but not for the theory of capital. This seems to be the gist of some of Hayek's scattered comments on the issue.[10] The distinction is unhelpful, though, without further clarification. Important propositions in Austrian capital theory hinge on the fact that some capital goods are specific or have limited uses and on the fact that there are complementary relationships between some of the elements of the capital structure. To the extent that these aspects of capital are central to our analysis, the concept of waiting obscures rather than captures the essence of the theory. This is only to say that if our theory is dependent on the heterogeneous nature of capital, then we do not want to use a term that is specifically designed to conceptually homogenize these factually heterogeneous elements. But to the extent that we want to call attention to the common and essential aspect of all capitalistic modes of production, then the concept of waiting seems preferable to any other.

We need only mention some of the alternative terms aimed at conceptually homogenizing capital to recognize their inferiority. We've all run afoul of Crusonia plants and shmoos and of capital jelly and putty–clay production processes. These are all purely physical conceptions totally detached from choosing and acting individuals. We can conceive of Crusonia plants growing wild and of shmoos running loose, but such conceptions have nothing to do with capital. It is impossible to conceive of waiting, however, apart from the individuals who decide to wait. And waiting can take as many different forms as there are different kinds of capital—and more. Professor Yeager shows how the concept of waiting helps us to break away from misleading physical conceptions, and to see the element of commonality between capital goods and such things as inventories of consumer goods, durable consumer goods, and the holding of land.[11]

To this point I have been treating the notion of waiting and abstinence as synonyms and contrasting them with purely physical notions of capital. This is consistent, I think, with Professor Yeager's own treatment of the terms. We might note, though, that Frank Knight viewed the shift from abstinence to waiting as a step backwards in the development of capital theory.[12] The reasons for this assessments are not immediately obvious. It is really necessary to understand Knight's vision of capital formation to follow his discussion of the relative merits of the terms abstinence and waiting. What he actually said can be capsulized as follows:

> The choice between investing and consuming is *absolute*.
>
> When savers "abstain" from consumption in order to create capital, they *abstain*.
>
> To call this "waiting" is misleading and false.[13]

These three statements don't quite pass muster as a syllogism, but if we know Knight, we know what he means. Capital in the Knightian vision is perpetual.[14] Knight couldn't conceive of an end to the waiting associated with it, and hence, he preferred the term abstinence. If we go along with Knight in associating a finite time period to the term waiting and an infinite time period with the term abstinence, then we must reject the latter term along with the notion of perpetual capital. Waiting is the more suitable term.

The disadvantages of the term waiting that Professor Yeager itemizes are more imaginary than real. He points out that the term is asymmetrical in that its meaning is not the same for both sides of the market. The supplier supplies waiting, but the demander demands to *avoid* it.[15] Actually, waiting in this respect is just like labor. The demander of labor does not demand to *do* labor; he demands to avoid it. Rather than being a disadvantage, this asymmetry plays up another parallel between waiting and labor as factors of production.

Professor Yeager frets a little over the fact that waiting (and abstinence) are not appraisal-free terms. They convey the idea of irksomeness.[16] I question whether this built-in connotation is a disadvantage at all. Labor, we can note, has the same connotation. This simply reflects people's attitudes towards waiting and laboring. The idea that waiting and laboring are irksome is on a par with the idea that the market rate of interest and the wage rate are greater than zero. To see the appropriateness in this respect of viewing interest as the return to waiting requires only that we contrast it with terms having different connotations. Could we conceive of interest, for instance, as the return to lounging, or as the return to loafing? Exploitation theorists could undoubtedly get some mileage out of these terms, but they serve only to distort what the term waiting describes.

There is one real problem with the term that Professor Yeager only hints about, and this has to do with the units in which waiting is measured. Clearly, waiting, both in his formulation and in Cassel's, stands for the product of value and time. It is measured in dollar-years. Yet, waiting in the ordinary sense of the term is measured in time units only. The term, then, can be misleading in this respect. In fact, this is the problem in several of the passages in *Capital and Interest* that were cited by Professor Yeager. Böhm-Bawerk was able to shift almost imperceptibly from dollar-years to years as his unit of measure. This is what gave rise to much of what Professor Yeager called the "sheer clowning around with questions about what it is that the supposed waiters are waiting for."[17]

The unit problem is our clue to another, more substantive question concerning the role of waiting in Austrian capital theory. At issue here is the relationship between the concepts of waiting and capital. Professor Yeager seems to be saying that although the two terms are not perfectly synonymous, waiting is a "sense" of capital and in many analytical contexts the latter term can be replaced with the former. It can be argued, though, that, in the context of Austrian capital theory, waiting and capital are complementary concepts. Professor Yeager's view of waiting as a substitute concept has its roots in the writings of Cassel, while the complementary view can be traced to William Stanley Jevons.[18]

In his formulation of what later came to be known as the Jevonian investment figures, Jevons made the critical distinction between the two complementary concepts:

> [We must distinguish] between the *amount of capital invested* and the *amount of investment of capital*. The first is a quantity of one dimension only—the quantity of capital; the second is a quantity of two dimensions, namely, the quantity of capital, and the length of time during which it remains invested.[19]

Jevons's terminology is unfortunate, but his meaning is clear. His first term corresponds to capital; his second corresponds to waiting. Both terms come into play in his discussion of the investment figures. Capital, which he expressed in pounds, is represented by the heights of the figures; waiting, which he expressed in pound-years, is represented by the total area.[20]

Hayek developed his structure-of-production triangles before he was aware of the Jevonian investment figures.[21] He found it necessary, though, to make a similar distinction. His exposition required that he make reference to the width of the triangle at various points along the time axis as well as the total area of the triangle.

In the formulations of Jevons and Hayek, the concept that waiting replaces is not the amount of capital, but the degree of roundaboutness. Professor Yeager seems to dismiss this view on the grounds that "[w]aiting . . . has the two dimensions of time and value units, whereas roundaboutness, conceived as some average period of production . . . has the single dimension of time units."[22] But roundaboutness, conceived as the *total* period of production, has precisely the same units as waiting, namely, dollar-years. The association of waiting with roundaboutness can also be found in Mises' and Rothbard's discussions of capital accumulation and the length of the structure of production. Mises writes of "processes in which the period of production and therefore waiting time are longer."[23] Rothbard makes reference to Bohm-Bawerk's use of the phrase "more roundabout processes," but prefers to use the alternative phrase "processes that require longer waiting periods."[24]

In sum, the amount of waiting can be associated with the degree of roundaboutness. It does not replace the concept of capital but is complementary to it. This view in no way discredits Professor Yeager's discussion of the concept. It simply provides a perspective that may be more palatable to Austrian theorists.

The Time Preference Theory of Interest vs. the Eclectic View

Dealing with capital and interest theory in terms of the supply and demand for waiting has one advantage that the Austrian theorists should not overlook. It puts the time preference theory of interest into its proper perspective. This theory, which is associated with Fetter, Mises, Rothbard, and Kirzner, is generally viewed as an extremely radical subjectivist position. By working in terms of the supply and demand for waiting, we are reminded that it is neither more nor less radical than subjectivist value theory in general. In a brief digression let me attempt to make clear just what subjectivist value theory is and what it is not. Austrian theorists have learned over the past several years that it is necessary for them to state that they are not solipsists, that the material world has an objective existence, and that there is such a thing as technology. What they deny is that value is inherent in any part of the material world. Value, rather, refers to a relationship between the valuing minds of individuals and the various elements of the material world. Economic value is determined by the interaction of numerous valuing minds. Stated in this way the subjectivist position doesn't seem very radical at all. What twentieth-century economist would deny it? What seems to be unique to Austrian economics is the consistent application of subjective value theory.

The Austrian theorists recognize that value, whether associated with the demand side of the market or with the supply side, must be reckoned in the utility dimension. This is to say that both blades of the Marshallian scissors are made out of the same stuff.[25] Professor Yeager goes a long way towards endorsing this view when he rejects the common practice of equating supply curves with objective factors, and demand curves with subjective factors.[26] But the notion that costs are objective seems to slip back into his reasoning. In one passage he explicitly includes "opportunity costs" among the "objective elements."[27] In another he suggests that for value theory to be subjective it must explain the relative prices of goods exclusively in terms of their marginal utilities.[28] This just isn't so. We can agree with Professor Yeager that the price relationship between pins and television sets (to use his example) cannot be determined from their marginal utilities alone. We must also consider the marginal utilities of the goods that were forgone in order that the pins and television sets could be produced. That is, we must consider the costs. The costs, though, are nothing but forgone utilities and are just as subjective as the marginal utilities of the pins and television sets.

The same contrast between the subjectivist view and the eclectic view can be made in terms of the intertemporal market.[29] Again, it would be wrong to claim that the subjectivists are concerned only with one side of the market. Their concern is that both sides are made out of the same stuff, namely, subjective evaluations.

By attempting to treat purely technical factors as a co-determinate of the interest rate, Professor Yeager is misled into believing that we can postulate a purely technical change and then deduce its effect on the market rate of interest. He postulates a general increase in physical productivity, and then deduces that the interest rate will rise.[30] We should note here that this is the conclusion yielded by standard Fisherian analysis. It doesn't follow at all from an analysis in terms of the supply and demand for waiting. If we adopt the analytical framework proposed by Professor Yeager, we would have to ask: Which direction and to what extent do the supply and demand curves shift? On the whole, do people prefer to wait more in order to magnify the effects of the technical change, or to wait less even though this will dampen the effects of the technical change? Nor can we say for sure which way the interest rate will go. Frank Fetter points this out in his discussion of the effects of a general increase in physical productivity. He begins by recognizing that:

> technical productivity has *some* influence upon the comparison of present and future gratifications, and hence upon the rate of interest. . . . Technical productivity is one of the facts, physical, moral, and intellectual, which go to make up the whole economic situation in which time preference is exercised.[31]

Fetter goes on to point out that an increase in productivity increases capital values and, hence, wealth. He suggests that to the extent that increased wealth is associated with a fall in time preference, a lower rate of discount and a lower rate of interest would result.[32] Thus, the subjectivists' conclusion is seen to be incompatible with the standard Fisherian or eclectic view, but fully compatible with the view that the interest rate is determined by the supply and demand for waiting.

Capital Reversing and Technique Reswitching

Professor Yeager uses the notion of waiting as a factor of production to dissolve the Cambridge paradoxes associated with capital reversing and technique reswitching.[33] He shows that, even within the analytical framework of the Cambridge school, the reswitching of techniques is not necessarily paradoxical. The amount of capital or waiting involved in the Cambridge examples depends not only on the technique used, but also on the interest rate itself. It is plausible that a continual falling of the interest rate could bring about a reswitching of techniques. That is, the economy could switch from technique A to technique B and then back to A. But because of the interest rate effect on capital values, the amount of waiting would increase as the interest rate falls with neither switch point constituting an exception.

The new vantage point provided by the concept of waiting should not be allowed to blind us to the root problem in all the reswitching literature. This whole literature owes its existence to the illegitimate use of the comparative-statics method in the analysis of a dynamic market process. The illegitimacy is frequently acknowledged by the reswitching theorists themselves. G. C. Harcourt, for instance, prefaces his extended analysis with the following caveat to the reader:

> Following Joan Robinson's strictures that it is important not to apply theorems obtained from the analysis of differences to situations of change . . . modern writers have been most careful to stress that their analysis is essentially the comparison of different equilibrium situations one with another and they are not analysing actual processes.[34]

In Robinson's 1975 article entitled "The Unimportance of Reswitching,"[35] I take her to be saying that the "unimportance" follows directly from these "strictures." But Robinson and Harcourt notwithstanding, reswitching theorists have not been careful in this respect at all. They repeatedly attempt to pass off comparative-statics analysis as if it were dynamic analysis. Typically, some mention is made of the static–dynamic problem in the introduction or in a footnote presumably to blunt criticism along these lines. They then plunge headlong into a discussion of a single economy that undergoes successive changes in production techniques in response to a continuous (and somewhat mysterious) fall in the rate of interest. The analysis is usually complete with detailed calculations of the economy's output during the transition periods. At the first switch point the output is relatively high; at the subsequent reswitch point the output is relatively low. Professor Yeager refers to these transitional outputs as spurts and slumps.[36] Samuelson called them splashes,[37] and, in a slightly different context, Professor Hicks used the terms crescendoes and diminuendoes.[38]

The point here is that if Harcourt's caveat is to be taken seriously, all this analysis of transitional outputs is completely spurious. If we are not to be misled by our own analysis, we must recast it in a comparative-statics mold. We must imagined that there are three economies economically isolated from one another. Drawing on Samuelson's arithmetic,[39] we can imagine that the interest rate is below 50 percent in the first economy, between 50 percent and 100 percent in the second, and above 100 percent in the third. What the reswitching literature demonstrates is that we can also imagine, without being inconsistent, that one technique is the more profitable for the economy with the intermediate rate of interest while a second technique is the more profitable in both of the other two economies. In this form the analysis is ridded of all its difficulties. The differences in interest rates can be attributed to differences in time preferences. There are no perverse changes in the capital structure because there are no changes at all. The question of transitional outputs simply doesn't arise. There are no spurts and no slumps. But if the difficulties are gone, so too are the appeal and the mystery; so too is the challenge to Austrian capital theory. Reswitching becomes a very sterile concept. In fact, the term itself, which connotes a temporal relationship, is clearly a misnomer. In the comparative-statics mold there is no switching at all. Possibly the only challenge left is the one of finding a new name for reswitching that captures the barrenness of the concept.

In his section on the consumption paradox, Professor Yeager clearly recognizes the misleading use of the comparative-statics method by reswitching theorists.[40] He first makes a heroic attempt to make some sense out of the mysterious movements of the interest rates. Is the fall in the interest rate caused by an increase in thrift? No, the subsequent pattern of consumption suggests that it isn't. Could the shifts constitute movements away from unstable equilibria? No, there seems to be evidence to the contrary. Aren't the reswitching theorists really only comparing alternative steady states rather than analyzing a process of change? Yes, this seems to be it. In his own words: "References to changes in the interest rate and switches in technique serve stylistic convenience only".[41] Recognizing that comparative-statics analysis has been dressed up in a dynamic garb, Professor Yeager blows the whistle on the Cambridge theorists:

> People who insist in crying paradox over examples of [reswitching] have an obligation, it seems to me, to spell out what they suppose to be happening in enough detail to disclose crucial assumptions and to permit comparison of their story with the real world. Standard theory need not be embarrassed by stories that do not even say how the interest rate is determined and changed, why one economy might be in a steady state employing one technique and another similar economy in a steady state employing another, or how an economy might make a transition between such states.[42]

My only complaint is that Professor Yeager didn't blow the whistle quite loud enough. We may be able to strengthen the impact of his conclusion and gain a better appreciation for it by imagining the use (or misuse) of a similar "stylistic convenience" in the hard sciences. We can refute Darwinian theory, for instance, by constructing a specie reswitching model. That is, a specie reswitching model will have the same implications for the theory of evolution as technique reswitching models have for the theory of capital. Let me suggest how we can construct the model. We all know that the polar bear is an animal well adapted for living near the North Pole or near the South Pole. The alligator, by contrast, is more suited for the tropical climate of equatorial regions. We openly recognize that, strictly speaking, we are discussing alternative life forms that exist in separate parts

of the world at a given point in time. But, for the sake of stylistic convenience, we want to ask what happens to an animal as we discend through
the degrees of latitude from $+90°$ down through $0°$ and then on down to
$-90°$. Well, the animal starts out as a polar bear. But before the latitude of
$0°$ is reached, it turns into an alligator. More significantly, by the time we
reach $-90°$, it turns back into a polar bear! (This is stylistic convenience
run amok.) If we had to, we could identify the switch and reswitch points
with the Tropic of Cancer and the Tropic of Capricorn respectively. It
should be apparent that this specie reswitching model casts grave doubts on
the theory of evolution and on the notion of the survival of the fittest. To
demonstrate this conclusively, we must first decide—using any criteria we
choose, so long as we don't make reference to climatic conditions—which
of the two life forms, the polar bear or the alligator, is the fitter. But we
can't have it both ways. If we decide that the alligator is fitter than the polar
bear, then the switch at the Tropic of Cancer is in full accordance with
Darwinian theory. This means, of course, that the reswitching that goes on
at the Tropic of Capricorn is a perversity. Thus, we have demonstrated the
possibility, if not the likelihood, that the less fit will survive. So much for
Charles Darwin. We can paraphrase Samuelson here and say that "If all
this causes headaches for those nostalgic for the old time parables of evolutionary theory, we must remind ourselves that scholars are not born to live
an easy existence. We must respect, and appraise, the facts of life."[43] As a
final payoff to this exercise, we now have a concretization of such things as
spurts and crescendoes. Spurts refer to all that white hair we have left over
when we switch from a polar bear into an alligator. A crescendo is a few
extra teeth and a long sweeping tail that's left over when we switch back. A
thorough investigation of this should keep neo–Darwinian specie reswitching theorists busy for years.

Concluding Remarks

Let me conclude my remarks by returning to the principal theme of the
paper. The concept of waiting as a factor of production is not at all new to
students of economics. Unfortunately, this tool of analysis has, more times
than not, been in the hands of those hostile to subjective value theory in
general and to Austrian capital theory in particular. Professor Yeager has
demonstrated that the hostility is not inherent in the tool itself. He has
thoroughly exorcised it of its mystical qualities; he has shown that the
concept of waiting complements rather than challenges Böhm–Bawerk's
treatment of capital and interest; and he has demonstrated how this alternative concept can be useful in several different analytical contexts. Both
Austrian theorists and Cambridge reswitchers can study Professor Yeager's
chapter with great profit.

Notes

1. Frank A. Knight, "Capital, Time, and the Interest Rate," *Economica* (new series), 1, no. 3 (August 1934): 257–286.

2. *See,* for example, Friedrich A. Hayek, "The Mythology of Capital," *Quarterly Journal of Economics* 50 (February 1936): 199–228.

3. Chapter 8, Leland B. Yeager, "Capital Paradoxes and the Concept of Waiting," pp. 197–198.

4. Eugen von Böhm-Bawerk, *Capital and Interest,* 3 vols., trans. George D. Huncke and Hans F. Sennholz (South Holland, Ill.: Libertarian Press), vol. 3 (1959): 196.

5. Gustav Cassel, *The Nature and Necessity of Interest* (New York: Macmillan, 1903).

6. Böhm–Bawerk, *Capital and Interest,* vol. 1, pp. 178–194.

7. Carl Menger, *Principles of Economics,* trans. and ed. J. Dingwall and Bert F. Hoselitz (Glencoe, Ill.: Free Press, 1950), pp. 156 and 172.

8. Chapter 8, p. 196.

9. Ibid.

10. Ibid. *See,* for instance, those passages in Hayek that Yeager cites in footnote 11.

11. Ibid., pp. 196f.

12. Knight, "Capital, Time, and the Interest Rate," p. 274.

13. Ibid.

14. Ibid., p. 273.

15. Chapter 8, p. 194.

16. Ibid.

17. Ibid., p. 210, n. 10.

18. William Stanley Jevons, *The Theory of Political Economy,* 2nd ed. (London: Macmillan and Co., 1879).

19. Ibid., p. 249.

20. Ibid., p. 251.

21. Friedrich A. Hayek, *Prices and Production* (New York: Augustus M. Kelley, 1967), p. 37ff.

22. Chapter 8, p. 210, n. 5.

23. Ludwig von Mises, *Human Action: A Treatise on Economics,* 3rd rev. ed. (Chicago: Henry Regnery Co., 1966), p. 495.

24. Murray N. Rothbard, *Man, Economy, and State: A Treatise on Economic Principles* (Los Angeles: Nash Publishing, 1962), p. 486f.

25. Joseph Schumpeter, *History of Economic Analysis* (New York: Oxford University Press, 1954), p. 922. I am indebted to Gerald P. O'Driscoll, Jr. for this citation.

26. Chapter 8, pp. 213–214, n. 34.

27. Ibid., p. 206.

28. Ibid.

29. Rothbard, *Man, Economy, and State*, pp. 323-32. Yeager would describe the intertemporal market in terms of the supply and demand for waiting; Rothbard's formulation is in terms of the supply and demand for present goods.

30. Chapter 8, p. 208.

31. Frank A. Fetter, "Interest Theories, Old and New," *American Economic Review,* no. 4 (March 1914); reprinted in Fetter, *Capital, Interest, and Rent* (Kansas City: Sheed Andrews and McMeel, 1977), p. 247.

32. Ibid.

33. Chapter 8, pp. 189-192.

34. G.C. Harcourt, *Some Cambridge Controversies in the Theory of Capital* (Cambridge: Cambridge University Press, 1972), p. 122f.

35. Joan Robinson, "The Unimportance of Reswitching," *Quarterly Journal of Economics* 89 (February 1975): 32-39.

36. Chapter 8, p. 192. The term "slump" is used in Yeager's earlier article, "Toward Understanding Some Paradoxes in Capital Theory," *Economic Inquiry* 14 (September 1976): 334.

37. Paul A. Samuelson, "A Summing Up," *Quarterly Journal of Economics* 80 (November, 1966), pp. 568-83; reprinted in *Capital and Growth*, ed. G.C. Harcourt and N.F. Laing (Middlesex: Penguin Books, 1971), p. 247.

38. J.R. Hicks, *Value and Capital: An Inquiry into Some Fundamental Principles of Econimic Theory,* 2nd ed. (London: Oxford University Press, 1946), pp. 187f., 223.

39. Samuelson, "A Summing Up," pp. 233ff.

40. Chapter 8, p. 193.

41. Ibid.

42. Ibid.

43. Samuelson, "A Summing Up," p. 250.

Selected Bibliography on Austrian Economics

Richard M. Ebeling

Equilibrium and Disequilibrium

Hayek, Friedrich A. "Economics and Knowledge." *Economica* (Feb. 1937). Reprinted in *Individualism and Economic Order,* pp. 33-56. Chicago: University of Chicago Press, 1948.

———"The Use of Knowledge in Society." *American Economic Review* (Sept. 1945). Reprinted in *Individualism and Economic Order,* ibid., pp. 77-91.

———"The Meaning of Competition." (1946). In *Individualism and Economic Order,* ibid., pp. 92-106.

———"Competition as a Discovery Procedure." (1969). Reprinted in *New Studies in Philosophy, Politics, Economics and the History of Ideas,* pp. 179-190. Chicago: University of Chicaco Press, 1978.

Kaldor, Nickolas. "The Determinateness of Static Equilibrium." *Review of Economic Studies* (Feb. 1934). Reprinted in *Essays on Value and Distribution.* Glencoe, Ill., Free Press, 1960.

Kirzner, Israel M. "Equilibrium versus Market Process." In *The Foundations of Modern Austrian Economics,* ed. by Edwin G. Dolan, pp. 115-125. Kansas City: Sheed and Ward, 1976.

Mayer, Hans. "Der Erkennitswert der funktionellen Preistheorien," ["The Cognitive Value of Functional Price Theory"]. In *Die Wirtschaftstheorie der Gegenwart,* vol. II, ed. by Hans Mayer, Frank A. Fetter, and Richard Reisch, pp. 147-239. Wien: Julius Springer, 1932.

von Mises, Ludwig. *Human Action, a Treatise on Economics.* 3rd rev. ed. Chicago: Henry Regnery, 1966.

Morgenstern, Oskar. "Perfect Foresight and Economic Equilibrium." *Zeitschrift fur Nationalokonomie* (Aug. 1935). Reprinted in *Selected Economic Writings of Oskar Morgenstern,* pp. 169-183. New York: New York University Press, 1976.

Robbins, Lionel. "On a Certain Ambiguity in the Conception of Stationary Equilibrium." *Economic Journal* (June 1930): 194-214.

Schams, Ewald. "Komparative Statik" ["Comparative Statics"]. *Zeitschrift für Nationalökonomie* (Aug. 1930): 27-61.

Applied Equilibrium Theorizing: Critique

Hayek, Friedrich A. "Socialist Calculation: the Competitive 'Solution'." *Economica* (May 1940). Reprinted in *Individualism and Economic Order,* pp. 181-208. Chicago: University of Chicago Press, 1948.

227

Kirzner, Israel M. "On the Premises of Growth Economics." *New Individualist Review* (Summer 1963): 20–28.

Lachmann, Ludwig M. "Model Constructions and the Market Economy." *Ordo* (1966). Reprinted in *Capital, Expectations and the Market Process,* ed. by Walter E. Grinder, pp. 112–129. Kansas City: Sheed Andrews and McMeel, 1977.

———"Ludwig von Mises and the Market Process." In *Toward Liberty.* Menlo Park: Institute for Humane Studies, 1971. Reprinted in *Capital, Expectations and the Market Process,* ibid., pp. 181–193.

———*Macro-economic Thinking and the Market Economy.* London: Institute of Economic Affairs, 1973.

Littlechild, S.C. *The Fallacy of the Mixed Economy.* London: Institute of Economic Affairs, 1978.

Robbins, Lionel. *The Nature and Significance of Economic Science.* 2nd rev. ed. London: Macmillan and Co., 1935.

Rothbard, Murray N. "Toward a Reconstruction of Utility and Welfare Economics." In *On Freedom and Free Enterprise,* ed. by Mary Sennholz. Princeton: D. Van Nostrand Co., 1956. Reprinted as *Occasional Paper* #3. New York: Center for Libertarian Studies, 1977.

Thirlby, G.F. "Economists' Cost Rules and Equilibrium Theory." *Economica* (May 1960). Reprinted in *L.S.E. Essays on Cost,* ed. by J.M. Buchanan and G.F. Thirlby, pp. 275–287. Birkenhead: Willmer Brothers, 1973.

Wiseman, Jack. "Uncertainty, Costs and Collectivist Economic Planning." *Economica* (May 1953). Reprinted in *L.S.E. Essays on Cost,* ed. by J.M. Buchanan and G.F. Thirlby, pp. 229–243. Birkenhead: Willmer Brothers, 1973.

———"The Theory of Public Utility Price—an Empty Box." *Oxford Economic Papers* (1957). Reprinted in *L.S.E. Essays on Cost,* ed. by J.M. Buchanan and G.F. Thirlby, pp. 247–271. Birkenhead: Willmer Brothers, 1973.

Profits and Entrepreneurship

Kirzner, Israel M. *Competition and Entrepreneurship.* Chicago: University of Chicago Press, 1973.

———"Entrepreneurship and the Market Approach to Development." In *Toward Liberty,* pp. 194–208. Menlo Park: Institute for Humane Studies, 1971.

von Mises, Ludwig. *Human Action, a Treatise on Economics.* 3rd rev. ed. Chicago: Henry Regnery Co., 1966.

———"Profit and Loss." In *Planning for Freedom.* South Holland, Ill.: Libertarian Press, 1974.

Rothbard, Murray N. *Man, Economy and State, a Treatise on Economic Principles.* Vol. 2. Los Angeles: Nash Publishing, 1970.

Schumpeter, Joseph A. *The Theory of Economic Development.* New York: Oxford University Press, 1934.

Expectations

Buchanan, James M. *Cost and Choice.* Chicago: Markham Publishing Co., 1969.

Hayek, Friedrich A. "Price Expectations, Monetary Disturbances and Malinvestments." (1933). Reprinted in *Profits, Interest and Investment,* pp. 135–156. New York: Augustus M. Kelley, 1969.

Lachmann, Ludwig M. "Uncertainty and Liquity–Preference." *Economica* (Aug. 1937): 295–308.

———"The Role of Expectations in Economics as a Social Science." *Economica* (Feb. 1943). Reprinted in *Capital, Expectations and the Market Process,* ed. by Walter E. Grinder, pp. 65–79. Kansas City: Sheed Andrews and McMeel, 1977.

von Mises, Ludwig. "'Elastic Expectations' and the Austrian Theory of the Trade Cycle." *Economica* (Aug. 1943): 251–252.

Schutz, Alfred. "Tiresias, or Our Knowledge of Future Events." *Collected Papers.* Vol. 2. The Hague: Martinus Nijhoff, 1976.

Thirlby, G.F. "The Subjective Theory of Value and Accounting 'Cost'." *Economica* (Feb. 1946). Reprinted in *L.S.E. Essays on Cost,* ed. by J.M. Buchanan and G.F. Thirlby, pp. 135–161. Birkenhead: Willmer Brothers, 1973.

Wicksteed, Philip H. *The Common Sense of Political Economy.* Vol. 1. London: Routledge and Kegan Paul, 1933. *passim.*

Intertemporal Exchange

von Böhm-Bawerk, Eugen. *Capital and Interest.* Vol. 2. *The Positive Theory of Capital.* South Holland, Ill.: Libertarian Press, 1959.

———"The Function of Saving." *Annals of the American Academy of Political and Social Science* (May 1901): 58–70.

Fetter, Frank A. "Interest Theory and Price Movements." *American Economic Review* (March 1927). Reprinted in *Capital, Interest and Rent,* edited by Murray N. Rothbard, pp. 260–316. Kansas City: Sheed Andrews and McMeel, 1977.

Hayek, Friedrich A. "Das intertemporale Gleichgewichtssystem der Preise und die Bewegungen des 'Geldwertes'" ["The Intertemporal Equilibrium System of Prices and Changes in the Value of Money"]. *Weltwirtschaftliches Archiv.* (1928): 33–76.

————*Monetary Theory and the Trade Cycle*. New York: Augustus M. Kelley, 1966.

————*Prices and Production*. 2nd rev. ed. New York: Augustus M. Kelley, 1967.

————*Profits, Interest and Investment and other essays on the theory of industrial fluctuations*. New York: Augustus M. Kelley, 1969.

Kirzner, Israel M. *Market Theory and the Price System*. Princeton: D. Van Nostrand Co., 1963.

Lachmann, Ludwig M. "Preiserwartungen und intertemorales Gleichgewicht" ["Price Expectations and Intertemporal Equilibrium"]. *Zeitschrift für Nationalökonomie* (Feb. 1937): 33–46.

von Mises, Ludwig. *Human Action, a Treatise on Economics*. 3rd rev. ed. Chicago: Henry Regnery Co., 1966.

Morgenstern, Oskar. "The Time Moment in Value Theory." *Zeitschrift für Nationalökonomie* (Sept. 1935). Reprinted in *Selected Economic Writings of Oskar Morgenstern,* pp. 151–167. New York: New York University Press, 1976.

Rosenstein–Rodan, Paul N. "The Role of Time in Economic Theory." *Economica* (Feb. 1934): 77–97.

Rothbard, Murray N. *Man, Economy and State, a Treatise on Economic Principles*. Vol. 1. Los Angeles: Nash Publishing, 1970.

Index

Index

abstinence theory, 215–219
allocation, as choice, 147–148
altruism, 111–112

Block, W., 98–100, 119
business cycle theory, and equilibrium, 153, 163–168, 177. *See also* political business cycle theory; rational expectations theory

capital, factor of production, 58–60; intensity, 191–192, 209–210; international movements, 194, 200–201; paradoxes, 187, 189–193; reversal, 187–193, 221–224; as waiting, 188, 189, 191, 193–198, 200
Cassel, G., 216, 218, 219
causality in law, economists' approach to, 74–78, 94–95
choice, and purposeful human action, 146–148; Shackle's theory of, 19–31, 33–34, 39, 147
Coase, R., 77, 79, 98
common law efficiency, 71–78, 80, 84–86, 109
competition, efficiency, and ethics, 113–114; process, entrepreneurship in, 128, 138
constraint concern, in X-efficiency paradigm, 129–130
consumption paradox, 192–193, 223
cost-benefit analysis, judicial, 71–87
cost containment, entrepreneurship in, 134–136
cost-pressure reaction relation, 132–133
costs, expected, and price, 78–81
crude approximation thesis, 84–86

demand, derived, and the interest rate, 194, 201–203; supremacy, doctrine of, 51, 65
Demsetz, H., 7
discoordination, economic, 1, 8, 178, 182–185

disequilibrium, 1–2, 6; entrepreneurship and, 140–144; market prices, 79–81, 86, 93

economizing theory, 37–39, 147
efficiency, Austrian view of, 118–122; in common law, 71–78, 80, 84–86; ethics and, 95, 98–110, 114–118, 120–124; property rights and, 102–110, 114–116, 118–122; Rothbard on, 90–95
entrepreneurship, 127–129, 138, 141–144; alertness in, 2, 9–10, 42–43, 46, 149–150; competition and, 128, 138; disequilibrium and, 140–144; equilibrium and, 138–144; errors and, 148–150; imagination and, 37–47; information and, in rational expectations and business cycle theory, 166–168; in X-efficiency market, 133–137
equilibrium, 4, 6, 81–82, 143–144; business cycle theory and, 153, 163–168, 171; choice and, 24; definition of, 4; entrepreneurship and, 138–144; Hicks on, 2–6, 53–57, 66–68; information processing and, 158; Kirzner on, 43–44; monetary disturbances and, 163–168; price and, 78–80, 85, 93; Rothbard on, 93; theorizing, 2–8
error, entrepreneurship and, 148–150; in rational expectations theory, 157, 166
ethics, Austrian economics and, 118–122; efficiency and, 95, 98–110, 114–118, 120–124; natural rights theory and, 122–124; property right assignments and, 98–102, 114–116, 118–122
expectations, development of, 2, 10–13; Hicks on, 52–53, 65–66; rational, 11–12; Shackle's concept of imagination and, 35–36, 46. *See also* rational expectations theory

About the Contributors

Harold Demsetz is a professor of economics at the University of California, Los Angeles, and a senior research fellow at the Hoover Institution.

John B. Egger is assistant professor of economics at Towson State University.

Roger Garrison is assistant professor of economics at Auburn University.

Sir John R. Hicks, Nobel laureate, is professor at All Souls College, Oxford.

Israel M. Kirzner is professor of economics at New York University.

Ludwig M. Lachmann is visiting professor of economics at New York University.

Harvey Leibenstein is Andelot Professor of Economics and Population at Harvard University.

Steven C. Littlechild is professor of industrial economics and business studies at the University of Birmingham (England).

Gerald P. O'Driscoll, Jr. is assistant professor of economics at New York University.

Murray N. Rothbard is professor of economics at New York Polytechnic Institute and a fellow of the Cato Institute (San Francisco, California).

G.L.S. Shackle is Professor Emeritus of economics at the University of Liverpool (England).

Richard E. Wagner is professor of economics at Virginia Polytechnic Institute and State University.

Leland B. Yeager is professor of economics at the University of Virginia.

About the Editor

Mario J. Rizzo received the Ph.D. degree in economics from the University of Chicago in 1977. He was a postdoctoral fellow in law and economics as well as in Austrian economics at New York University from 1976 to 1978. Since September 1978, he has been assistant professor of economics at New York University. Professor Rizzo has published articles in the *American Economist* and the *Journal of Legal Studies,* and in *Assessing the Criminal: Restitution, Retribution and the Legal Process,* edited by R.E. Barnett and J. Hagel III (Cambridge: Ballinger Publishing Company, 1977) and *New Directions in Austrian Economics,* edited by L.M. Spadaro (Kansas City: Sheed, Andrews and McMeel, 1978). Professor Rizzo's current interests involve economic theory, industrial organization, and the economic analysis of law.